The Sociology of Sports Coaching

Sports coaching is a social activity. At its heart lies a complex interaction between coach and athlete played out within a socio-culturally defined set of (sporting) practices. In this ground-breaking book, leading international scholars and coaches argue that an understanding of sociology and social theory can help us better grasp the interactive nature of coaching and consequently assist in demystifying the mythical 'art' of the activity.

The Sociology of Sports Coaching establishes an alternative conceptual framework from which to explore sports coaching. It firstly introduces the work of key social theorists, such as Foucault, Goffman and Bourdieu, before highlighting the principal themes that link sociology and sports coaching, such as power, interaction, and knowledge and learning. The book also develops connections between theory and practice by offering a constructive critique of each social theorist's work by current practicing coaches.

This is the first book to present a critical sociology of sports coaching and, as such, represents an important step forward in the professionalisation of the discipline. It is essential reading for any serious student of sports coaching or the sociology of sport, and for any reflective practitioner looking to become a better coach.

Dr. Robyn L. Jones is a Professor of Sport and Social Theory at the University of Wales Institute Cardiff, and a Professor II at the Norwegian School of Sport Sciences.

Dr. Paul Potrac is the Director of Undergraduate Studies (Coaching) within the Department of Sport, Health and Exercise Science at the University of Hull.

Dr. Chris Cushion is a Senior Lecturer in the School of Sport, Exercise and Health Sciences at Loughborough University, where he leads the MSc in Coaching.

Dr. Lars Tore Ronglan is an Associate Professor and former Head of the Department of Coaching and Psychology at the Norwegian School of Sport Sciences, Oslo.

The Sociology of Sports Coaching

**Edited by Robyn L. Jones,
Paul Potrac, Chris Cushion and
Lars Tore Ronglan**

Routledge
Taylor & Francis Group

LONDON AND NEW YORK

First published 2011
by Routledge
2 Park Square, Milton Park, Abingdon, Oxon, OX14 4RN

Simultaneously published in the USA and Canada
by Routledge
711 Third Avenue, New York, NY 10017

Routledge is an imprint of the Taylor & Francis Group, an informa business

Transferred to Digital Printing 2011

Typeset in Times New Roman
by Keystroke, Station Road, Codsall, Wolverhampton

British Library Cataloguing in Publication Data
A catalogue record for this book is available from the British Library

Library of Congress Cataloging-in-Publication Data
The sociology of sports coaching / edited by Robyn L. Jones . . . [et al].
    p. cm.
    Includes bibliographical references.
    1. Coaching (Athletics) 2. Sports–Sociological aspects. I. Jones, Robyn L.
    GV711.S67 2011
    796.07'7–dc22
    2010021652

ISBN 13: 978–0–415–56084–9 hbk
ISBN 13: 978–0–415–56085–6 pbk
ISBN 13: 978–0–203–86554–5 ebk

Contents

Editors and contributors

Editors

Chris Cushion is a Senior Lecturer in the School of Sport, Exercise and Health Sciences at Loughborough University, where he leads the MSc in Coaching. His research and teaching interests revolve around understanding the coaching process, coach education, learning and professional development, coach behaviour and learning environments, talent identification and performance analysis. He has published extensively, and continues to supervise a number of postgraduate projects in and around these areas. Chris works as an editorial board member and reviewer for a range of peer-reviewed journals. He is also a highly qualified football coach and has worked for a number of professional football youth academies, including those at Queens Park Rangers, Fulham and Derby County.

Robyn L. Jones is a Professor of Sport and Social Theory at the University of Wales Institute, Cardiff, and a Professor II at the Norwegian School of Sport Sciences, Oslo. He has authored numerous books and peer-reviewed journal articles on coaching and pedagogy. He serves on the editorial boards of *Sport, Education and Society, Physical Education and Sport Pedagogy* and the *International Journal of Sport Science and Coaching*. He is also a former Queens Park Rangers Football Club academy coach and a Director of Football for one of New Zealand's seven federations.

Paul Potrac is a Senior Lecturer and Director of Undergraduate Studies (Coaching) within the Department of Sport, Health and Exercise Science at the University of Hull. He is principally engaged in research projects that focus on how coaches experience the working environment and cope with the multitude of variations that exist within it. In addition to publishing his work in journals such as *Sport, Education and Society*, the *Sociology of Sport Journal, Quest* and the *Sport Psychologist*, he has co-authored *Sports Coaching Cultures: From Practice to Theory* and *Understanding Sports Coaching: The Social, Cultural, and Pedagogical Foundations of Coaching Practice* (both Routledge) with colleagues from the UK and New Zealand.

Lars Tore Ronglan is an Associate Professor and former Head of the Department of Coaching and Psychology at the Norwegian School of Sport Sciences, Oslo. Prior to his academic career, he was an elite player before becoming the Norwegian national handball coach. In 2000, he completed his Ph.D. thesis: 'Gjennom sesongen: en sosiologisk studie av det norske kvinnelandslaget i håndball på og utenfor banen' (During the season: a sociological analysis of the female Norwegian national handball team on and off the court). Recently, he has published several books and book chapters in both Norwegian and English with a sociological perspective on learning, leadership and team development in sport.

Contributors

Jim Denison is an Associate Professor in the Faculty of Physical Education and Recreation, University of Alberta, Canada, and Director of the Canadian Athletics Coaching Centre. A sport sociologist and coach educator, his research examines coach effectiveness in track and field and the social construction and historical formation of coaching 'knowledges', and coaching and athletic identities. He edited *Coaching Knowledges: Understanding the Dynamics of Performance Sport* (A & C Black) and co-edited, with Pirkko Markula, *Moving Writing: Crafting Movement in Sport Research* (Peter Lang).

Laura Purdy is a Lecturer at the University of Limerick, Ireland. Her research involves using sociological theories to understand better the relationship that exists between coach, athlete and environment. She has published articles which examine social power in the coach–athlete relationship. In addition to working in the academic area of coaching, Laura is an active rowing coach and coxswain. Although Canadian, she has represented Ireland internationally and uses her experience as a coxswain and coach to fuel her research.

Part I
Background and context

1   Introduction

Robyn L. Jones

Introduction and aim

The origins of this book lay in our respective sports coaching experiences, watching others coach and reflecting upon how we coached ourselves. Between us, we've coached along the spectrum, from children's primary school teams, through professional age-group sport, to national squads at international competitions. Although the context tended to dictate action, what remained constant was our common struggle with the complexity of trying to influence, teach and inspire others to improved performances. Through serendipitous encounters we eventually came to share academic ideas and careers. Initially, our talk was of mutual dissatisfaction with the reductionist treatment of sports coaching by other scholars. It just didn't ring true; a sentiment constantly thrown at us by other coaches. We had no reply, except to agree timidly. Acknowledging that it was easy to criticise from the sidelines, we began to try to do something about it, which led to a sociological investigation of sports coaching. Why the social emphasis? No doubt, this was influenced by our largely social scientific backgrounds. Of greater importance, however, was our burgeoning belief that sports coaching is, above all, an interactive, communal endeavour; a social practice. Of course, coaches must plan sensitively, continually developing and communicating their sport-specific expertise, and manage the physical environment carefully and decisively. Overriding such concerns, however (a point we reached through experience), was how to generate the appropriate relationships with athletes so that they would trust our requests and demands as coaches. Questions of significance related not so much to which exercises to use, but what to say to whom, when and how? What would be the consequences of such actions? And is the social cost worth it? Within our coaching, every utterance seemed to count; every gesture had an effect in terms of securing, maintaining or losing the respect of those we wanted to influence. We came to realise what we perhaps already knew: that coaching happens in our 'comings and goings, our givings and gettings' with athletes (Lemert, 1997). What mattered then, and what our coaching relied on, was what Lemert (1997: x) described as our 'social competencies'; our basic social logic of how to get things done; the 'tugging, hinting, proposing, judging, punishing, comforting, depriving and frightening' of our charges, both pro- and re-actively, so that they would learn and absorb what we deemed was important. We also came to recognise that coaching was less about us as heroes or villains, and more about how we managed the pressures, constraints and possibilities of context (Stones, 1998b).

A decade ago, then, with the goal of generating a sociological investigation of coaching in mind, we began to ask publicly: 'Why does sports coaching need sociology?' (Jones, 2000). Here, the case was made for sociology's relevance to coaching, building on initial work arguing that social thought was the under-appreciated, yet crucial 'invisible ingredient' in coaches' knowledge (Potrac & Jones, 1999; Jarvie, 1990). It was an attempt to interrogate and lift our practical understandings of coaching, particularly how coaches deal with athletes, into 'the light of clear thinking' (Lemert, 1997: xi).

More recently, as coaching has come to be increasingly acknowledged as a social activity, the argument has been further refined through empirical and theoretical study (e.g., Jones *et al.*, 2005; Jones *et al.*, 2002). This has included recourse to the thinking of such sociologists as Michel Foucault (Denison, 2007; Johns & Johns, 2000), Pierre Bourdieu (Cushion & Jones, 2006), Erving Goffman (Jones, 2006a) and Anthony Giddens (Purdy *et al.*, 2008), among others. Despite this development, a wider application of social theories to sports coaching has not been forthcoming. This leads us to question the perceived relevance (or irrelevance) of social thought to coaching scholars and coach educators as a theoretical framework from which to explore and subsequently understand the activity. For example, at a recent international coaching conference organised by Sports Coach UK entitled 'Expert Coaches – Expert Systems: Benchmarking Best Practice' no sociologist was invited as a keynote speaker. Clearly, then, our message, at least within the coach education fraternity, is not being heard.

The purpose of this book is to present the case further, and more fully, for sociology as an appropriate theoretical location from which to view sports coaching. It aims to do so through illustrating the work of nine key social thinkers, and how their writings can be used to inform coaching. Why did we choose these theorists? Sympathising with Guilianotti (2004: 3), who embarked on a similar project in relation to social thought and sport in general, we also found 'team selection difficult'. Some global theorists, it could be argued, pick themselves. For example, Pierre Bourdieu, Erving Goffman, Anthony Giddens and Michel Foucault come instantly to mind. These theorists would also be more initially recognisable to scholars and students of coaching as they have, to varying degrees, begun to be used to analyse the activity. Giving a more in-depth account of their thinking, then, would prove to be less of a step for others' engagement. We were also influenced by personal interest in including less prominent theorists who, on discussion and reflection, we thought would be fascinating and relevant (for example, Niklas Luhmann, Arlie Hochschild and Peter Blau). Indeed, we believe each key thinker discussed in the book gives a distinctive, valuable perspective on the social world of coaching, 'shining a torch' on parts of it, while leaving further corners to be discovered by other theorists holding torches 'at slightly different angles' (Stones, 1998b: 5). We openly acknowledge that there are many other thinkers we could (and perhaps should) have used, and their omission should not in any way be read as intellectual dismissal (Guilianotti, 2004). However, for the reasons given above, we hope to be allowed this latitude and penchant.

Context, significance and the value of theory

In questioning top-level international coaches about the nature and essence of what they do, their responses were almost unequivocal:

> Unless you understand [athletes] as people, the best coaching book in the world isn't going to help. It all comes down to how well they really want to do for you . . . to the relationship you have with your players.
> The art of coaching is about recognising the situation, recognising the people and responding to the people you are working with.
> A big thing is the manner you put things across . . . Really, it's the ability to handle men, that's the big thing, to handle people.
> Coaching to me is about reading the individual. People, people, people. That's what it boils down to in the end.
>
> (Jones *et al.*, 2004: 28, 18, 19–20, 92–93)

The affirmed social skills required appeared to outweigh other sport-specific and scientific constructs. Despite such conviction, an initial reaction to such a finding, as recently witnessed by one of us when attempting to dissect and deconstruct such notions with a group of coach educators, has often been: 'but that's just common sense'. When the audience was challenged to conceptualise and articulate the meaning and nature of such skills, however, they found the task very problematic: an interesting if rather unsatisfactory response from coach educators in terms of the stated fabric of coaching. Such common sense, then, as Wenger (1998: 47) reminds us, 'is only common sensical because it is sense held in common'. The educators' response in this instance is not altogether surprising, for, as Lemert (1997: xiii) reminds us, most of the time people exist and survive with very little instruction or consideration about 'how to practice their lives with others'. What gets us by is a seemingly implicit, unconscious, highly practical ability; we somehow know what's going on and how to handle it. Far from some innate, in-born aptitude, however, our guide here is the hidden hand of our social competencies or sociologies (Lemert, 1997).

Such competencies relate to behaving appropriately in context, in socially valued ways, in order to maintain and improve relationships. Without them, we would be forced to learn anew what to think and how to behave in every social situation we encounter (Lemert, 1997). But where and how did we initially learn such behaviours, and how can we better interpret them? That is, if coaching is about social things and how we get on with and exert influence over others, where do we look to generate a better understanding of how we go about them? The answer lies in sociology, and perhaps more specifically in developing what

C. Wright Mills (1959) famously dubbed a *sociological imagination*. Here Wright Mills was referring to the capacity of individuals to recognise the influence of larger structural forces on their everyday lives and concerns; understanding that their personal troubles were often public issues. This ability to link the micro-level minutiae of behaviour to broad macro-structural factors such as gender and ethnicity is one of the principal attractions of sociology to such leading theorists as Loïc Wacquant (2005). By having the potential to do precisely this, Mills believed that sociology held the power not only to inform academic debate but to enrich and enable the lives of ordinary people (Lemert, 1997); to help them understand why they behave as they do and, hence, what alternatives are possible. In Lemert's (1997: 46) words, to 'break out of the silences by looking at the practical realities' as related to the assumptions, biases and stances of everyday life. Such a practical sociology was viewed as liberating individuals to take the decisions they can; to give confidence and possibilities in personal worlds and provide a more nuanced understanding of contextual 'social geography' (Marsh *et al.*, 1996). Hence, it has been argued that sociology has an 'immediate relevance which other subjects cannot boast' (Marsh *et al.*, 1996: 5). Sociology, then, can and should be deemed a functional and doable skill, holding particular relevance for coaches whose job it is to influence others directly towards a perceived greater good. In this respect, sociology can be considered 'the inquisitive child of modernity' (Guilianotti, 2005: xiii), being concerned with questioning, challenging and generally injecting a degree of reality to the traditional rationalistic or modernistic view of social development.

Some of the earlier work undertaken by myself and others, being founded on the theorising of Erving Goffman, gives further credence to the value of sociology to coaching. This is in terms of the performances coaches give to manipulate, tease, coax, flatter and bully best effort and achievements from athletes (e.g., Jones *et al.*, 2004). Although they may seem unique, such performances closely conform to accepted social rules; thus representing a dance of agency within a bounded social choreography. As Goffman (1974: xiii) put it, 'interaction is governed by unstated rules more or less implicitly set by some larger entity'. This is not to view such wider structures in a totally restrictive sense, as they can also be considered 'fragile and precious achievements' that keep social chaos at bay (Goffman, 1974: xviii). Like other sociological work, our previous efforts marked an attempt to put into words the secrets everybody seemed to know but never discussed; to deconstruct and dispel the fog of taken-for-granted knowledge, thus developing a critical coaching consciousness (Jones, 2009a, 2007). It was an effort to 'decode' a culture (Hatchen, 2001) through realising the sociologist's alchemy of uncovering the 'constitutive rules of everyday behaviour' (Goffman, 1974: 5). What helped frame the analysis here was Gardiner's (2000) social project into mundane daily action. Following Hegel's maxim that 'the familiar is not necessarily the known', Gardiner's (2000: 5) central thesis was to explore the 'fine grain' and 'connective tissue' of human activities by critically focusing on the 'practical accomplishments of skilled social actors in the course of their day-to-day lives'. As with Gardiner's (2000: 6) book, the purpose of our project is to problematise coaches' everyday practice better, 'to expose its contradictions and hidden potentialities', thus raising 'our understanding of the prosaic to the level of critical knowledge'. In essence, to help us understand 'what is going on' in coaching. At the heart of such micro-action lies the omnipresent phenomenon of power. Indeed, this book is largely a response to existing work on coaching which has failed to engage adequately with the power differentials that exist within it. It is not surprising, then, that power is the first topic to be tackled in Part III of the text (Chapter 11). But more of that later.

The principal value of this book lies in building on the foundational work done by undertaking a rigorous sociological analysis of coaching. This is not in respect of what Gouldner (1970) criticised as 'cow sociology' (a reference to domicile, tame enquiry) or merely to duplicate what has gone before, but critically to deconstruct and credibly to reconstruct some of coaching's central concepts and notions. This is particularly so in terms of the power balances ingrained within coaching and the 'non-logical logics' to which they are subject (Gardiner, 2000). Lest we overstate the case here, however, we openly admit to borrowing unavoidably from existing sources and the insightful thoughts of others (i.e., our chosen social theorists), only really claiming to bring them together within a sports coaching context.

The significance of the text also lies in further addressing the theory–practice gap in coaching, which, unfortunately, still remains. Thompson (2003) has suggested that this may be the consequence of academics viewing theory development as more important than improvements in practice, with practitioners being equally culpable of 'anti-intellectualism' or the rejection of theoretical matters on the grounds that they are irrelevant to coaches' everyday actions. Certainly, the entrenchment of both camps in their respective positions has done little to advance the relationship between academics and coaches, or reduce the divide between theory and practice. Consequently, Thompson (2003: 99) argues that both parties have 'a shared responsibility to break down such barriers' if we are to maximise the effectiveness of practice. In order to address this issue, the work of the selected social theorists is placed alongside current practising coaches' views of such theory. The practitioners' commentaries were elicited to ascertain and demonstrate the relevance of social thought to coaches and students of coaching; to see if their earlier words about the interactive relational nature of coaching continue to hold true, albeit from a different cohort at a different time. It also reflected an appreciation that (despite being former coaches ourselves) the featured coaches held the potential to experience things in ways we do (or could) not; a position which gives added authority to the personal nature of the activity. Honouring their voices in this way also allowed us 'to see past the edges of our own vision' (Ely *et al.*, 1997: 315), while bestowing credence and recognition on the 'social and contextual dimensions' of practitioners' knowledge, aspects that should be considered when creating theory related to hard-to-define field situations (Ely *et al.*, 1997: 317).

Both the coaches' reflections and the chapters themselves, then, were contested and negotiated between the coaches and ourselves as primary authors. In engaging in such an exercise, we deliberately tried not to romanticise our theoretical positions or the coaches' thoughts about them. It made us question our writings, as we were forced to move away from the typical and ideological to the tensions and contradictions of coaches' work. What informed our thinking here was both Apple's (1999: 14) call that 'theory needs to be connected' to issues and people, and Anderson and Herr's (1999) belief in the 'importance of getting our hands dirty through forming alliances with practitioners' (Macdonald *et al.*, 2002: 148). By including practitioners' comments we also sought to alleviate any potential 'theory anxiety' that readers could have, thus firmly embedding abstract concepts in practical experiences and perceptions (LeCompte & Preissle, 1993). In this way, the text marks an attempt to take theory 'off the table and into the field' (Macdonald *et al.*, 2002: 149), allowing for the development of more realistic preparation programmes for coaches which better mirror the complex reality of their work (Jones, 2006b).

No doubt, some will take issue with the seeming academicisation of sports coaching, where many familiar concepts are rendered awkward, strange and troublesome (Perkins, 1999). This is because the theories presented here hold the potential to undermine previous beliefs 'in so far as they uncover the limits of rationality and truth claims' (Meyer & Land, 2003: 3). They will also push some out of well-established cognitive comfort zones to confront the contested and problematic reality of coaching, making a degree of resistance inevitable (Jones, 2007). Taking our lead from earlier writings (e.g., Jones, 2006b, 2007), we make no apology for this. Coaching is full of problems, dilemmas and tensions, so it should be portrayed as such. To do otherwise would be a disservice to both coaches and students of coaching. A retreat into common-sense superficiality may make us feel better in the short term, but 'it is false comfort' (Stones, 1998b: 5). The challenge, then, is to engage and embrace the social complexity of coaching; a goal towards which we hope this book will make a progressive contribution. Like Ball (1991), who also questioned the 'if . . . then' predictable-relations approach to understanding social life, our end points are complexity and interrelatedness rather than simplicity. It is a position which 'rebels against and distrusts easy conclusions in academic knowledge' (Ely *et al.*, 1997: 11). It is also a stance which has led us into conflict with (more than a few) colleagues who continue to cling desperately to the security of clear-cut distinctions; of seemingly painless ways to do hard things (Ely *et al.*, 1997). Nevertheless, the hope is that, like DiPardo's (1993) teachers who initially feared the abstract discourse of graduate school, readers, once they get past the 'language barrier', will experience powerful new ways of conceptualising and expanding on the familiar.

This book, then, is premised on the view that we have much to learn from the presented range of sociological thinkers who 'have taken the time and made the effort to think long and hard about a whole variety of social aspects most of us would have barely sensed' (Stones, 1998b: 1). They give us more than concepts, though: rather, a new grammar and everyday language with which to communicate and think; a fresh vocabulary through which to reflect on new ideas that are often compatible with hitherto unarticulated beliefs (Ely *et al.*, 1997). Although the information presented here might be novel to many, the purpose is as much to do with 'ordering the stuff we know' as with giving 'new stuff' to coaching students, educators and coaches (Stones, 1998b). This is another reason why we need to engage with theory and thinkers, because doing so helps us make sense of what we know so we can make better use of it. In the words of Elliot Eisner (1993: viii), theory can 'make coherent what otherwise appear as disparate individual events', while being 'the means through which we learn lessons that can apply to situations we have yet to encounter'. It was a point made by O'Sullivan (2005: 6) in her British Educational Research Association inaugural lecture when she stated that we need to link our thinking 'to some conceptual frame [otherwise] we can't advance the field. If we can't understand what is happening and explain why it may be so, we are not in a position to inform our stakeholders (and practitioners) as to how to forward their agendas.' It is important to note here, however, that we are not calling for some 'Grand Theorising' of coaching, a singular 'truth' or a holy grail of practice to resolve all debate. We certainly want to avoid any 'tyranny of ideology'. Rather, we hope that the theoretical positions outlined might be used as scaffolds and frameworks with which to think, as they have the potential to inform about different social dynamics at work (Powers, 2004). They can be viewed as a set of eye-glasses to 'bring into focus, sharpen and angle our understanding of what might otherwise be a blurred stream of perception' (Ely *et al.*, 1997: 228). Good theory, then, echoing the point made earlier, can liberate one's sociological imagination to explore why things are as they are and how they can possibly be done better. In this respect, we agree with Madison's (1999: 109) sentiment that, although 'I would surely lose myself without performance, I cannot live well without theory'.

Structure

The book is divided into three principal parts. Following this Introduction, in which the scene is set, the second part (Chapters 2–10) outlines the principal theories of nine established social thinkers, and how such work can be related to sports coaching. Each of these chapters follows a broadly similar four-section or thematic format. This involves: (i) a short biography prefacing a brief introduction to the theorist in question; (ii) a description of the principal tenets and works of that theorist; (iii) an outline and some examples of how such work can be used better to inform sports coaching; and (iv) a commentary by a practising coach related to how he or she might benefit or has benefited from the knowledge presented. More specifically, Chapter 2 explores Erving Goffman's theories on interaction, the dramaturgical perspective, impression management and front. Chapter 3, on Michel Foucault, discusses his work on discipline, discourse, knowledge and power; while Pierre Bourdieu's notions of habitus, field, capital and the complicity of the dominated are examined in Chapter 4. Arlie Hochschild's writings on emotion management, feeling rules, deep and surface acting, and the inauthenticity of self are considered in Chapter 5, followed by Anthony Giddens's work on structuration theory and its modalities – namely interpretative schemes, facilities or resources, and norms – in Chapter 6. The German sociologist Niklas Luhmann's ideas on communication, complexity, systems and environment are discussed in Chapter 7, while an examination of Etienne Wenger's thinking on knowing, meaning and identity generated through communities of practice is examined in Chapter 8. Peter Blau's (1964: 91) notion of social exchange as a relationship between specific actors 'contingent on rewarding reactions from [each] other', inclusive of the concepts of dependency and alternatives, is considered in Chapter 9. Finally, the work of Jürgen Habermas (Chapter 10) on moral conscious-ness, the discourse of ethics, and communicative action concludes Part II. As stated, in keeping praxis high on the agenda, each chapter ends with a commentary from a practising coach in relation to the relevance of the concepts discussed to their everyday practice.

Part III (Chapters 11–14), drawing primarily on the theories presented, focuses on certain themes deemed particularly relevant for a social analysis of sports coaching. Here, we take our lead from Guttman (1992: 158), who, in asserting that 'no key turns all locks', depicted the craft of sociology as requiring imaginative engagement with different theoretical constructs to explain social phenomena (Guilianotti, 2005). We acknowledge that an inescapable element of overlap exists between the chapters here. This, however, is not taken to be altogether a bad thing, as the resultant conceptual blending makes it possible clearly to identify and grasp the most illuminating and consistent of sociology's ideas as related to coaching. These include power (Chapter 11), social interaction (Chapter 12) and learning (Chapter 13). Each of these chapters is also organised along similar lines, exploring the presented themes from the viewpoints of coach, athlete and context. Specifically, this is done by examining the micro-everyday actions of both coaches and athletes, before placing such actions within their wider macro-context. For example, within Chapter 11, and building on French and Raven's (1959) work, the analysis of coaches' power is principally based upon Goffman and others' work (e.g., Kelchtermans, 2005) on the micro-political presentation of the self, and Foucault's ideas relating to the authoritative gaze. These notions are discussed in light of recent coaching literature. The chapter then switches to explore, from a power-full perspective, why athletes behave as they do within the coaching context. The discussion here is framed by Bourdieu's work on false consciousness and the compliance of the dominated, Giddens's writings on ontological security and the dialectical nature of power, and Nyberg's (1981) ideas on consent and resistance. This final notion is to do with power over power, where the seemingly subservient still hold considerable sway because they assent to power being exercised over them. Following this, an exploration of how power operates at a contextual level in coaching is undertaken. Here, Foucault's work on discourse and institutions, Bourdieu's notions of fields and the 'space of the possible', and Blau's social exchange, among others, are utilised as theoretical pegs to guide thinking.

In Chapter 12, Goffman's conceptualisation of roles, performances and impression management, in addition to Giddens's notions of social norms and social positioning, are used to illustrate how and why coaches and athletes interact as they do. In addition, exchange theory, through the work of Blau, is applied to exemplify how an exchange of symbolic goods between coach and athletes might find expression in coaching situations. A particular aspect engaged with here is the use of humour within coaching interaction, again exploring how and why it is used as it is. The latter part of the chapter tends towards macro-sociological concepts to examine how face-to-face interaction is embedded in societal contexts that impress the coaching situation in different ways. Here, Bourdieu's work on field and habitus is used to guide understanding of similarities and differences in recreative as opposed to professional, competitive sport. Similarly, Luhmann's concepts of communication and complexity are employed to describe how social systems represent constraining and enabling forces of importance to actors in the coaching process. Finally, it is suggested that a deeper understanding of face-to-face interaction, as well as the contextual factors that influence these interactions, can provide coaches, athletes, administrators, and coach educators with valuable tools for guiding critical reflection on coaching practice.

Chapter 13 argues that a sociological analysis of learning and knowledge has much to offer a broader understanding of coaching. In keeping with previous chapters, coaching is regarded as a contested space where social thought and theory can serve to problematise taken-for-granted assumptions about knowledge and learning, for both athlete and coach. The case is made that engagement with the given theories not only holds the potential for raising awareness and understanding, but provides opportunities for reflection and a subsequent fertile ground for meaningful change. The chapter centres on the relationship between coaching as a social practice, identity construction, learning and knowledge. This is principally examined through Wenger's notion of communities of practice, supported by Lave and Wenger's ideas on situated learning, Luhmann's selective observations, Bourdieu's habitus and Blau's concept of exchange, among others. The chapter draws to a close with a discussion of the value of this analysis to developing a more critical tradition in coaching through challenging current modes of thought and practice, and suggests that the development of coaching as a profession, particularly in regard to coach education, is dependent upon a theoretically driven body of knowledge.

Finally, a concluding chapter (Chapter 14) summarises the main points made throughout the book, in particular the structure–agency debate which lies at the heart of much sociological enquiry, before providing recommendations for future research directions.

Part II
Sociological thinkers

2 Erving Goffman: Interaction and impression management

Playing the coaching role

*Robyn L. Jones, Paul Potrac, Chris Cushion
and Lars Tore Ronglan with Chris Davey*

Erving Goffman: a short biography

Erving Goffman was born on 11 June 1922 in Alberta, Canada. He received his bachelor's degree from the University of Toronto in 1949 and his Ph.D. in 1953 from the University of Chicago, where he studied sociology and social anthropology. During an academic career which took in positions at the University of Chicago, the University of California, Berkeley and the University of Pennsylvania, he pioneered the study of face-to-face interaction, or micro-sociology. Many consider his greatest contribution to be his formulation of symbolic interaction in his 1959 book *The presentation of self in everyday life*, although other influential and insightful texts include *Stigma: Notes on the management of spoiled identity* (1963), *Strategic interaction* (1969a) and *Frame analysis: An essay on the organization of experience* (1974). Through these and other works he developed an understanding of the way we convey social information through symbols and images, and how those images are incorporated into social expectations. He subsequently elaborated upon a 'dramaturgical' approach to human interaction in a detailed analysis of what he termed 'the interaction order'. Indeed, interaction underpinned all of his work as, for Goffman, interactions were important rituals that worked to maintain moral as well as social order (Birrell & Donnelly, 2004). Consequently, his substantive contribution to social analysis (and, we would argue, sports coaching) lies in uncovering the everyday routine of social encounters, and how that impacts on personal identity (Smith, 2006). Erving Goffman died of cancer on 19 November 1982, aged sixty.

Introduction

The aim of this chapter is to provide an insight into the work of Erving Goffman and how it can be related to sports coaching. The chapter begins with an introduction to Goffman's writings and an accompanying outline of his principal theoretical notions. These include stigma, interaction, the dramaturgical perspective, impression management and front. Such concepts are then located within coaching research, with the concluding part given over to a critical commentary by Chris

Davey, a top-level rugby union coach, in relation to the value of such work for coaches.

Using Goffman to examine coaching may appear strange, as his writings have traditionally suffered from the criticism of under-theorising power and its workings; an identified core concept in coaching (Jones *et al.*, 2004). Recent work by Dennis and Martin (2005), however, has taken an opposing stance, arguing that the micro-focus adopted by Goffman does show a fundamental concern with power phenomena. This is particularly so with regard to the social processes through which power is enacted. Viewed as such, Goffman's work is to do with examining the political process by which rules of social engagement are established, enforced, challenged and broken (Dennis & Martin, 2005). Becker's (1963: 17) seminal interactionist study on deviance further emphasised the point that the questions of 'who can force others to accept their rules and how they do it' are matters of political power. Consequently, far from neglecting power relationships, Goffman was inherently concerned with understanding precisely the ways in which power is enacted in real contexts.

Supporting the argument that Goffman was concerned with power, his theorising has been positioned as having a good deal in common with that of Foucault (see Chapter 3) – a much more prominent thinker in this regard (Hacking, 2004). Although acknowledgement is made of their differing perspectives – in terms of Foucault being an abstract theorist of discourse while Goffman was concerned with the micro-concrete of social exchange – the subject matter of institutions and the social processes through which power is enacted were common to both. It can therefore be said that while Foucault explored ways to understand what is said and what can be said, Goffman examined how, in 'everyday life, one comes to incorporate those possibilities and impossibilities as part of oneself' (Hacking, 2004: 300). Although different in one sense, then, both perspectives investigated how classified people, as individuals and groups (e.g., athletes and coaches) interact with each other and why they do so in the ways they do. Indeed, Goffman's own conceptualisation of his work was as an 'analysis of the social arrangements enjoyed by those with institutional authority' (1983: 17), or perhaps more famously as how 'persons in authority have been so overwhelmingly successful in conning those beneath them into keeping the hell out of their offices' (1971: 288). Although this latter quote was in reference to the 1968 student rebellions at Columbia University, the broader question was clearly posed in terms of social power relations and how dominant groups or those in power try to maintain their positions by means that often amount to impression management and 'deceitful' presentations (Lemert, 1997).

We therefore evoke Goffman as a theorist of everyday power relations. This is because his central concerns with order, (re)action and performance hold great promise for an insightful analysis of sports coaching. Being grounded in the symbolic interactionist Chicago tradition, which itself derived from the work of Blumer and Mead into the subjective meaning of human behaviour and social processes, he demonstrated clearly not only that reality was constructed but precisely why and how. Through such analysis, and his literary interpretations, perhaps more than any other theorist, he left us with vivid accounts of how we organise and sustain ourselves within society. His field-work at St Elizabeth's Hospital in Washington, D.C., under the guise of 'assistant to the athletics director' (which gave him some Goffmanesque legitimacy!), also brought into sharp focus that 'everyone is a gatekeeper in regard to something' (Goffman, 1983: 8); a position which resonates strongly with sports coaching in terms of coaches' relative power to decide on issues of who, where, when and how.

Presentation of the self and stigma

Goffman (1969a) described the self as a 'performed character'; as a product of social circumstances, the management of which was conceptualised as 'self-work'. Hence, he considered that an,

> individual does not . . . merely go about his business. He goes about constrained to sustain a viable image of himself in the eyes of others. Some local circumstances always reflect upon him, and since these circumstances will vary unexpectedly and constantly, footwork or rather self-work, will be continuously necessary.
>
> (Goffman, 1971: 185)

For self to work, the cooperation or at least the forbearance of others was deemed to be required. Consequently, the self was seen as a collaborative achievement, accomplished through face-to-face interaction. According to Goffman, then, in our social encounters we present an impression of selves that we wish others to receive in an attempt to control how those others see us; action which requires the selection of the appropriate role for the situation in which we find ourselves from the large repertoire we have available (Smith, 2006). Acting out one's appropriate role, however, is not just about getting through the interaction without stumbling, but about honouring the role itself (Birrell & Donnelly, 2004). This is an important point, as only properly observed rituals of deference (respect for others) and demeanour (respect for the role) are able to maintain interactional order (Goffman, 1967). On the other hand, failure to maintain smooth interaction holds the potential to expose individuals' problematic areas or stigmas.

In *Stigma: Notes on the management of spoiled identity* (1963) Goffman explored the grounds upon which individuals find participation in interaction difficult (Smith, 2006): that is, where persons find themselves in situations where they are stigmatised or 'disqualified from full social acceptance' (Goffman, 1963: Preface). The concept of stigma involved three related notions: 'social identity', the everyday way that people are identified and characterised; 'personal identity', which marks out a person as distinct from all others; and 'ego' or 'felt identity', the feelings a person has about their identity (Smith, 2006). Social identity is further developed by a distinction between virtual and actual identity. Virtual identity refers to the assumptions and anticipations made on the basis of first appearances (Smith, 2006), while actual identity relates to the attributes that experience proves a person to possess (Goffman, 1963). Interaction proceeds smoothly when virtual identity and actual identity match. However, when there is incongruence between the two, there is potential for disruption. In particular, when this discrepancy works to discredit and downgrade initial anticipations, stigma will occur (Smith, 2006).

As stigma may be concealed, two classes of possessor become possible: the discredited, those who can assume that their stigma is evident in any encounter; and the discreditable, whose stigma is not always observable (Smith, 2006). With regard to the discredited, although obvious discomfort or tensions arise in their interactions, 'sympathetic others' may help with the management of these tensions. Meanwhile, for the discreditable, the flow of information about their stigma becomes their basic interactional problem, which is entirely contextual: 'To display or not to display, to tell or not to tell, to let on or not let on, to lie or not to lie, and in each case, to whom, how, and where' (Goffman, 1963: 42). According to Goffman, to disclose information about a stigma is to reveal a potentially damaging aspect of personal identity. The discreditable may guard their personal identity by strategic management of information about the self (Smith, 2006). Indeed, Goffman's in-depth discussion of the strategies and contingencies around the control of information about stigma form the basis for his notion of 'impression management'. Here, Goffman also reflects upon the concept of 'passing' – that is, attempting to conceal the stigma in everyday life – and describes practices such as 'covering', where attempts are made to minimise the stigma's obtrusiveness.

Goffman's notion of ego or felt identity concerns the subjective sense of one's own situation, and relates to what an individual feels about their stigma and its management. Here, the stigmatised can be torn between contrasting loyalties and identification with those sharing the stigma and 'normals'. This can lead to ego conflict as a result of the varying pulls of the 'in-group' and the 'out-group' (Smith, 2006). Indeed, Goffman argued that the outward 'good-adjustment' of the stigmatised may conceal a phantom acceptance of actual experience. For Goffman, there is no good adjustment, but a play of contrasting identifications leading to a politics of identity with the stigmatised caught in a crossfire of arguments about what their ego identity ought to be (Goffman, 1963).

Throughout his discussion of stigma and its effects, Goffman (1963) is at pains to emphasise the influence of interactional roles. His concept of stigma, then, is not grounded in the 'type of person' but in the intricacies of difference and, crucially, the control of information of self in interactional encounters. Stigma management, therefore, is a social process of differentiation related to individuals' widely varying degrees of power over the enactment of their self-presentation, according to these individuals' disparate locations in society (Birrell & Donnelly, 2004).

The interaction order: rules to live by

By describing and analysing many day-to-day routines, Goffman uncovered invisible, underlying codes governing our behaviour and interaction. In his *Interaction ritual* (Goffman, 1967: 12) social rules are compared with traffic rules: 'To study face-saving is to study the traffic rules of social interaction, one learns about the code the [other] person adheres to.' At the same time, in allowing space for agency, Goffman recognised our reflexive ability to manipulate the procedures of social interaction. Consequently, in contrast to rules in games like chess which are fixed and determinate, he considered rules in social life as indeterminate guides to the practical problems of daily interaction; rules which were founded on a strange mix of cynicism, ritual and trust (Manning, 1992).

The analysis of interaction viewed as drama (Goffman, 1959), as game (Goffman, 1961a) and as ritual (Goffman, 1967) draws attention to the interplay between rule-following behaviour and strategic action. Indeed, Goffman's (1961a) role analysis was an attempt to understand the relationship between individuals and the behaviour expected of them. To Goffman (1967), social rules appeared as general guidelines about the things that happen during face-to-face interaction. He assumed such rules to be an underlying code to human behaviour, in that they simultaneously regulate and constitute the structure of social interaction. Rules, then, were often seen to surface as reciprocal obligations and expectations, usually functioning as background constraints on action without which the social world would be chaotic (Manning, 1992). Goffman also demonstrated that social rules were not all of the same type. Some were viewed as instructions, some as expectations, and some as obligations. Furthermore, he pointed out that rules are subject to interpretation, to exceptions and to decisions not to abide by them.

This Goffmanian view of the social world based on rituals and rule-following enables a nuanced reading of actors' possibilities to manipulate social situations strategically to reach their goals (Goffman, 1959, 1961a). The focus is on actors' personal interests in the interaction, and how social situations allow individuals to use suitable techniques to give the impression that they intend. The perspective is shifted from rules' function as constraints on action to how social rules and situations offer the role-player resources to influence the course of interaction. The game and theatre analogies point to the calculative element in everyday dealings, and present us as information managers and strategists.

In his development of the concept of role, Goffman (1961a) also made distinctions between role commitment, role attachment, role embracement and role distance. Role commitment refers to roles which are imposed on the individual; role attachment to those we wish to play; role embracement to those roles whose 'virtual self' we freely adopt; and role distance to roles from which we wish to remain separate (Manning, 1992). These four concepts are useful tools. They facilitate a more flexible analysis of the constraining and enabling aspects of social roles, and more detailed investigations of the interplay between personality, individuality and roles. Hence, roles are not 'just played', as they may be adjusted, utilised or personally formed for different purposes and by different individuals.

The dramaturgical perspective

One of Goffman's major strategies early in his academic career was to develop extended metaphors, specifically those of social life as a theatre and as a game. In *The presentation of self in everyday life*, Goffman (1959) unfolded the dramaturgical metaphor, comprising the notions of performance, impression management, team and region (front and back). Performance was defined as 'all the activity of an individual which occurs during a period marked by his [*sic*] continuous presence before a particular set of observers and which has some influence on the observers' (Goffman, 1959: 32). The intention of a performance is to give a certain impression to the people present which, in turn, dictates future interaction. In his analyses of this social performance, Goffman introduced the concepts of front, dramatic realisation and idealisation. The personal front refers to the expressive equipment of the individual, which more or less consciously is used as part of the performance. Dramatic realisation relates to the performer's use of dramatic signs to ensure that the audience will understand the points that are difficult to see. Similarly, performances are not only dramatically realised but idealised: that is, they are put in the best possible light and shown to be compatible with a culture's general norms and values.

When describing the dramaturgical perspective, Goffman emphasised that performances not only deal with the single individual's presentation of self but are usually staged by groups or teams. A team is understood as 'any set of individuals who cooperate in staging a single routine' (Goffman, 1959: 85). The team develops and tries to sustain a certain consensus on the definition of the social situation, which makes it possible for the participants to act suitably. Simultaneously, the team works to sustain the definition of the situation to outsiders. According to Goffman, most of us participate in several teams; thus, we all contribute to such dramas.

Goffman also introduced two regions where the behavioural performances are guided by different principles: a 'front region' (front stage) and a 'back region' (back stage). The front region refers to the place where the performance is given. Here, some aspects of the actor's or the team's activity are expressively accentuated while other aspects, which might discredit the fostered impression, are concealed. On the other hand, the back region is a place 'where the suppressed facts make an appearance' (Goffman, 1959: 114). Here, the personal front may be adjusted and scrutinised, the team can run through its performance and poor members of the team can be schooled; it is where the performer can relax, drop his or her front and 'step out of character'. Despite this distinction, Goffman did not consider the back region as a place of authenticity where the 'real self' could emerge (Branaman, 1997), as people give performances even here.

In the decade following the publication of *The presentation of self*, Goffman abandoned the extended use of the theatrical metaphor as a description of social life (Manning, 1992). His self-criticism in this regard was evident in his later *Frame analysis* (1974), where the theatrical analogy was moderated: 'All the world is not a stage' (Goffman, 1974: 1). The key to the reformulation of the dramaturgical model was a shift away from the actual interaction to the frame in which the interaction occurs (Manning, 1992). As Goffman said, 'the first issue is not interaction but frame' (1974: 127). The term 'frame analysis' refers to an examination of how we perceive and organise experience. This included the view that people see the same events somewhat differently: for example, what is play for the golfer is work for the caddy (Goffman, 1974). Goffman (1974: 247) believed that, given their 'understandings of what is going on, individuals fit their actions to this understanding', which marked a greater appreciation of how contexts structure our perceptions of the social world.

How can Goffman's concepts inform sports coaching?

The purpose of this section is twofold. First, to provide a review of the existing literature that has used Goffman's work to examine coaching behaviour and coach–athlete interaction. And, second, to suggest potentially valuable areas of future enquiry where Goffman's work could be utilised to enhance our current understanding of coaching. Indeed, within the context of coaching research, we echo the sentiments of Schegloff (1988: 89), who has suggested that scholars have 'undoubtedly not finished learning from the work which he [Goffman] has left us'.

In recent years, Goffman's work has begun to be utilised to explore coach–athlete interaction, predominantly in the context of top-level sport (e.g., Jones *et al.*, 2003, 2004; Potrac *et al.*, 2002). This research has focused on issues relating to how coaches present their activities to athletes, the ways in which coaches guide and control the impressions that athletes form of them, and the things that coaches may or may not do to sustain their performances. Many of the coaches referred to here deemed that maintaining athletes' regard and reverence, often through presenting a particular image of themselves as knowledgable, caring yet decisive experts, was central to their practice (e.g., Potrac *et al.*, 2002). In doing so, they often engaged in scheming actions, such as the telling of 'white lies' which they believed to be in the athletes' greater interests: actions which call to mind Goffman's concern with both manipulation and morality (Jones *et al.*, 2004).

This line of enquiry has highlighted how coaches attach considerable importance to presenting the 'right front' to athletes in order that the latter, seemingly voluntarily, act in accordance with or 'buy into' the coaches' respective agendas and programmes (Goffman, 1969a). Such fronts include exuding an aura of authority, deliberately showing a human side, and expressing themselves in a supremely confident manner so that athletes believe the coaches know what they are talking about (Jones *et al.*, 2004; Potrac *et al.*, 2002). The findings here provide coaching-specific examples of Goffman's (1969a: 6) contention that, when in a leadership role, it may be in an individual's best interest to act 'in a thoroughly calculating manner, expressing himself in a given way solely in order to give the kind of impression to others that is likely to evoke from them the specific response he is concerned to obtain'.

A further examination of the process of impression management in coaching noted that coaches are not entirely free to choose the image they portray in a particular context (Jones *et al.*, 2004). Instead, in order to present a compelling front, they are obliged to behave consistently 'like a coach' in the eyes of athletes. Indeed, the expectations of athletes may be a crucial factor in determining the style or performance that a coach utilises. It is a notion in keeping with Goffman's (1969a) belief that an individual may put on an act or show for the benefit of his or her audience, sometimes regardless of its sincerity, to achieve desired goals. Such actions should not be unproblematically termed cynical, however, as like the mechanics who 'resignedly check and re-check tyre pressures for anxious women motorists, these are performers whose audiences will not allow them to be sincere' (Goffman, 1959: 18). Nevertheless, great care has to be taken not to present a 'transparent' or 'phoney' coaching front which would undoubtedly result in a loss of credibility (Jones *et al.*, 2003; Jones *et al.*, 2004; Potrac *et al.*, 2002).

On deeper inspection, what the coaches in this body of work alluded to was a fear that the audience would question not their coaching performance but their right to perform as they did. To buttress their legitimate authority (although taking care not to do so overly), the coaches would often refer to past successful achievements and dealings (Potrac *et al.*, 2002). Additionally, in order to 'exclude from the performances expressions that might discredit the impression being fostered' (Goffman, 1959: 66), the coaches tended to utilise a number of protective or defensive strategies. These included the maintenance of social distance between themselves and athletes, demonstrating dramaturgical discipline, and circumspection (Jones *et al.*, 2004; Purdy *et al.*, 2008).

With regard to the concept of distance, Jones *et al.* (2004) found that coaches were aware that restricting their contact with athletes to particular settings and durations allowed them to generate some space or leeway to build up an impression. The coaches perceived this to be a valuable strategy for two key reasons: initially, it helped create an environment where they were viewed as acting in the best interests of the athletes; then, the maintenance of such a space was considered to help reduce the chances of the presented image being discredited by protecting it from too close an inspection, thus allowing a state of 'mystification' about the performance (Goffman, 1959).

According to Goffman (1959), dramaturgical discipline refers to the ability of a social actor to remain conscious of the role he or she is performing even while being immersed or engrossed in it. Such a presence of mind was evidenced in the coaches studied by Jones *et al.* (2004), d'Arripe-Longueville *et al.* (1998) and Potrac *et al.* (2002), who utilised a number of ploys or stratagems, such as selective feedback, pretence, deception and withholding information. For example, the judo coaches researched by d'Arripe-Longueville *et al.* (1998: 323) deliberately displayed indifference to the players as a means of stimulating them and to assert their own authority further. The coaches here also focused considerable attention on meticulous planning as a part of their professional practice. Such planning not only concentrated on which exercises to utilise in training sessions but involved an in-depth analysis of how they were to behave when in the presence of the athletes. This strategy echoes Goffman's (1959: 227) emphasis on detailed advanced preparation for 'all possible expressive contingencies'. While such planning was perceived to help maintain an idealised image in the eyes of the athletes, the coaches also highlighted the need to maintain a degree of flexibility and interpretation when working. In this respect, they considered it essential for a coach to respond to the perceived needs of athletes at a particular moment in time. Again, this resonates with Goffman's (1959: 228) belief that rigid adherence to a script can lead to performers getting 'themselves in a worse position than is possible for those who perform a less organised show'.

While the work of Jones and colleagues has provided some useful initial inroads into demonstrating how Goffman's work can help understand coaches' practice, such analysis could be developed in greater depth and breadth. For example, while athletes are obviously at the heart of the coaching process, coaches have to interact with a number of other stakeholders and groups within their respective working environments (e.g., assistants, administrators and parents). Such relationships could also be examined in relation to Goffman's (1959) notion of performance teams. In order to produce a successful performance, Goffman (1959) suggested that all members of the team must, in addition to dramaturgical discipline, demonstrate 'dramaturgical loyalty', which refers to the moral obligation of protecting the secrets of the team. Such a concept could be usefully employed as an analytical framework for enquiry that addresses such questions as: what is the role of the head coach in relation to the assistants and support staff? And what is the nature of the interaction that takes place between them, both horizontally and vertically? Furthermore, Goffman's (1959) work could be used to explore the 'face-to-face' strategies that coaches utilise to encourage and persuade different groups to 'buy into' their coaching programmes, as well as how they deal with issues of dissent and resistance.

As previously highlighted, Goffman's (1963: 3) *Stigma* focused upon how an individual manages 'deeply discrediting attributes' that could lead to them 'being disqualified from full social acceptance'. In the context of coaching, there has been a paucity of enquiry which has drawn upon this particular sensitising framework. To date, it has been utilised only in Jones's (2006a) auto-ethnography of a dysfluent coach, which provides an insight into the emotional nature of coaching. This study highlights how Goffman's concepts of the discredited and the discreditable can help us understand coaching in relation to both the management of information about the self and the 'tension generated during social contact' (Goffman, 1963: 62). By revealing this tension and defect within his story, Jones (2006a) highlights coaching's fundamental link to audience perception and the negotiated nature of the self within the complexities of the interaction order (Goffman, 1983).

Future research, then, could develop the work of Jones (2006a) by further exploring the notion of stigma within the coaching environment. For example, researchers could address how coaches manage their working relationships following a perceived failure (i.e., being a 'losing' coach) in a previous position. Such enquiry could also focus on the self-doubts and worries harboured by coaches in relation to their coaching knowledge and practice, further illustrating how coaches act to control information about themselves in order to 'pass' as the person they wish to be. As such, Goffman's (1963) work could be productively utilised to explore how coaches utilise a number of behaviours, such as feigning ignorance, self-depreciating humour, and total avoidance, to protect the 'evidentness' (1963: 48) of their personas. Indeed, exploring how coaches attempt to cope with and 'cover-up' their 'shortcomings' could lead to a better understanding of interaction within coaching 'that might otherwise be too much taken for granted to be noted' (Goffman, 1963: 104).

A coach's commentary by Chris Davey

I am currently the Director of Rugby at UWIC (University of Wales Institute, Cardiff), a position I've held for a number of years. Until relatively recently, I was also coach of the Welsh Under-21 side. During my time in charge of this latter group we were successful in winning two Grand Slams against the other Six Nations teams, which I suppose is my most visible accomplishment. I am also heavily involved in developing the UKCC Level 4 qualification for rugby union while continuing to make a teaching contribution on the MSc in Sports Coaching here at UWIC.

As coaches, I genuinely think we are always, to an extent, playing roles. The coaching role, then, is just that, a performance you give, no doubt. For example, this week we had an issue to deal with where I had to act the disciplinarian over an incident that had happened at the club. I know that my image has now changed among the players; it's more authoritarian, that's for sure. I'm also aware that I'll have to behave in a certain way to get our generally approachable relationship back on track. Reading the chapter made me think about this a lot more in concrete terms. As I said, I was aware that I'd have to change my actions and persona a bit after that incident, but now it's much more ordered and clear to me why and how I can do it.

The difficulty for me no longer lies in accepting the fact that I have to engage with certain roles as a coach, but in which role to play when, and in ensuring a degree of evenness and regularity between these roles. Even though I know I have to be different in my interactions, I can't be seen to behave too differently, otherwise I'll be open to accusations of inconsistency. For me, then, you need to be consistent in role; always to be supportive of the players. I can't be seen to drift away from that too much. I like the players to think of me in that way; so I suppose, according to Goffman, that is the performance I give, although I'm not particularly conscious of it (not before reading this chapter anyway).

I also use humour quite a lot in my coaching. For example, we've got a player at the moment who's doing really well; he's working hard at his game, looks after himself and has come on leaps and bounds. A slight issue with him, though, is that he knows it, so he's acting the 'cock of the walk'. Anyway, at a practice the other night (after he had been somewhat surprisingly beaten in a race to the ball by an opposing player in the last match), I paired him with a much slower forward, on the basis of making an even match. Everyone saw the funny side of it, not least the player in question. On reflection, I suppose it was a power play, just to make him aware that I see and remember 'everything' that happens; and to keep his feet on the ground; that he still has things to learn. It was also sending a similar message to the others.

What I have become increasingly aware of, having read this chapter, is how I sometimes 'step out' of role. As I said, I tend to use humour a lot in my coaching; it's not much fun coaching on a dark, rainy winter's night in Cardiff. Sometimes, I like to show the players that I'm the same as they are (well, *almost* the same); that, basically, we are all trying to do the same things and suffering in the same ways. Goffman's notion of role distance, especially after further discussion with Robyn [Jones], really resonated with me here, and helped me make better sense of what I seemed to do naturally. I can also say that I step out of role a bit by not always giving the players what they want. Very often, when they show up for training, they want to be told what to do, to be led by the nose. Of course, the game isn't like that, so I'll put on some 'spoof' sessions, designed to go wrong. I'll then have a quick chat with the players about what went wrong, why, and how it can be fixed. It's not always what the players want – to think and verbalise their understanding – because they just want to play, so I'm definitely not reacting to their expectations. In this respect, I suppose I'm making my own coaching role. Sometimes it doesn't work, but more often it does. I'm not sure how my practice relates to hiding weaknesses or stigmas. Not because I don't have any, but because I believe in being as honest as I can with players. So, I'm not afraid of saying 'I don't know' to a question, because I think that humility and being realistic are important when coaching. I suppose, in Goffman-speak, this is a part of the mask I wear; one related to honesty and openness.

I do like to involve the players quite a bit, to try to give them some responsibility over things. We have a 'leadership group' within the club, made up mostly of senior players, although it is still led by me. (I'm not sure what that says about me.) I like the idea of a player-driven environment with me overseeing it. It's an effort at getting some social consistency and honesty in the group, where the players are allowed to say things and critique each other constructively. This is how I want the players to see me and each other, so I try to 'walk the walk' and let them have their say. To make this happen, I need to give them the example, though. So I'm never late, always prepared and ready to listen. If I don't agree with what's said I'll also say so and, importantly, provide the rationale for why. I think the players respect me to a certain degree for that. It shows them that I'm not asking anything that I don't 'deliver' myself. Reading the chapter certainly made me think a bit more about that: the image I want to present to the players and why; what my ideal coaching self really is; and how far I deviate from it.

As far as my dealings with others (that is, not players) are concerned, I can definitely relate to giving something of a performance here; or, more accurately, I can see the performances of others. I understand that there has to be some give and take in meetings with assistants, managers and such like, so this is the stance

I basically take, and subsequently how I act. There has to be some negotiation, so that's what I become – a flexible negotiator – unless, of course, there's something that I believe is fundamental at stake. On the other hand, even though I can be accommodating, I naturally want things in my favour when I leave the meeting, so I am trying to engineer desired ends through the persona adopted.

In conclusion, after thirty years of coaching, I was already definitely aware that I occupy different roles or wear different 'faces' as a coach. Reading this chapter has helped me to reflect a little more on how I should act in certain situations in order to get what I want. It's also made me very reflective of the consequences of my actions. So now I tread even more carefully than before while still carrying the proverbial stick!

Conclusion

The purpose of this chapter was to outline the value of the work of Erving Goffman to coaches and coaching. Within it, in addition to outlining many of Goffman's most insightful treatises, we've tried to bring the theory to life by relating it directly to sports coaching. Highlighting this link was important but not difficult, as much of Goffman's work seems to fit coaching quite well. However, we don't claim to have totally explored or explained Goffman's thinking; thus readers are encouraged to dig deeper and develop their own understanding of his interpretations. We also appreciate that many criticisms of Goffman's work exist: for example, that his writings failed to consider the political, thus trivialising the sociological project (Gouldner, 1970). However, in highlighting that most people in some form are tethered to each other, and are therefore engaged in strategic manipulations to maintain or improve their respective positions, Goffman's *Presentation of the self in everyday life* (1959) was nothing if not an exposé that social relations are more about the 'appearance than the content of things' (Lemert, 1997: xxxii); that social reality has little to do with essential values. Similarly, *Stigma* (1963) and his earlier *Asylums* (1961b) are patently political analyses of institutions and how they do their work from the viewpoint of marginal groups. In this respect, through deconstructing assumptive reality, he was among the 'first to tell us what we hated to hear' (Lemert, 1997: xxxiii).

Whatever position one takes on Goffman's work, even his critics agree that he developed an extremely sensitive lens through which to observe and interpret human interaction (Birrell & Donnelly, 2004). Hence, his work helps us to organise what we know: that is, our vastly under-explored tacit understanding. In this way, it helps us to see through much of the mystification and the common-sense superficiality that currently plagues coaching as an academic subject of enquiry. With coaching being an obligation-ridden social activity, as opposed to an uncluttered world of 'free-floating heroes and villains' (Jones, 2006a; Stones, 1998b), applying theory which takes account of such interactive complexity appears very appropriate. Through it, a greater appreciation of the social nature of coaching and how it can be deconstructed and reconstructed can be developed.

3 Michel Foucault: Power and discourse

The 'loaded' language of coaching

Jim Denison with Dave Scott-Thomas

Michel Foucault: a short biography

Michel Foucault remains one of the most influential scholars of his time. Over the course of his academic career he published numerous books, interviews, papers and lectures. Foucault did not explicitly write about sport, but his focus on the body as a site for domination and control makes his work relevant to the study of coaching and athlete development. Foucault was primarily a historian, but his interest and commitment to understanding people's experiences led him to examine the role of the individual within force relations. To do this he tried, through his numerous projects, 'to sketch out a history of the different ways in our culture that humans develop knowledge about themselves' (Foucault, 1988: 17). Analyses completed included those related to madness, rationality, language, economics, sexuality, punishment and ethics. Through these studies he developed a number of concepts concerning the constitution of individuals' subjectivities that have been used by contemporary scholars across the social sciences.

Foucault, born in France in 1926, completed his academic studies in 1948 at the École Normale Supérieure, the principal elite centre for higher education in France. His main focus was philosophy, but this did not satisfy Foucault's desire to understand the complexities of contemporary life, so in 1950 he completed a degree in psychology. It was during his time as an intern and a technician in an asylum that Foucault began to formulate his ideas concerning the development of the human sciences, such as psychiatry, and how they were formed through changes in the social world – politics, economics, discovery – rather than objective or rational processes. At the same time, Friedrich Nietzsche became a huge influence on Foucault. Through Nietzsche, Foucault gained an appreciation of history as contingent, and the self as a social construction. In this respect, he rejected the dominant social theory of his age, Marxism, and the idea that society was on a progressive path towards a socialist utopia. Rather, he was interested in 'seeing historically how effects of truth are produced within discourses which themselves are neither true or false' (Foucault, 1980: 118).

After numerous academic posts across Europe, in 1960 Foucault returned to France, where he completed most of his major works, including *The birth of the clinic: An archaeology of medical perception, The order of things, The archaeology of knowledge, Discipline and punish: The birth of the prison* and *The history of sexuality, Volume 1: An introduction*, among others. The central theme Foucault explored here was how power, exercised through various practices of domination, works to discipline individuals and control social life. It is this theme that present-day scholars, including those who study sport, continue to examine, using a number of concepts that Foucault developed to analyse the social world.

Foucault died in 1984.

Introduction

The way that individuals today understand themselves and their relations with others has largely been shaped by the rise of modern psychology – the cult of the individual self, the modern science of the subject. However, as a number of critical psychologists have begun to ask (e.g., Burr, 2003; Kvale, 1992; Widdershoven, 1994), what if the self is a position in language, something created from the dominant meanings that exist in society and culture? Accordingly, how identities are constituted and formed, and who we believe we are, may be a result of contingency and chance and historical circumstance instead of our unique characters or inevitable anthropological constraints (May, 2005).

It was precisely this concern with the constraints and limits of individual experience that sparked Michel Foucault to consider how subjects were made not through their own will or inner essence, but through an intricate web of power relations, contingency and chance. Foucault examined how identity and action were not necessarily products of an autonomous self, but social productions lived into existence through the productive influence of culture (May, 2005). He was consequently sceptical of the humanist assumption of one true self who holds some specific knowledge about him- or herself within his or her being. Instead, he claimed that 'subjects are constituted through a number of rules, styles and inventions to be found in the cultural environment' (Foucault 1972: 24).

Foucault's anti-humanist perspective has been adopted by a number of sport researchers to understand such practices as dieting (Chapman, 1997; Johns & Johns, 2000) and competition (Heikkala, 1993). Few studies, however, have applied Foucault's ideas directly to coaching and how coaches' practices can be understood and enhanced. This is surprising, considering that Foucault saw great value in examining how those with responsibility (e.g., coaches) used their power ethically to form productive relationships with those around them (Markula & Martin, 2007). Therefore, in this chapter, the aim is to outline some of Foucault's key concepts, such as discourse, power and knowledge, and to suggest how coaches can develop new and innovative understandings of what coaching might mean by a consideration of how their knowledge of coaching and themselves has been shaped and formed by rules and conventions. Following this, a commentary from a practising coach is provided regarding the use and application of Foucault's concepts to 'real' coaching problems and issues.

Discourse and knowledge

A key concept that underpinned much of Foucault's work and his analytical approach was 'discourse'. This term has a similar meaning, in some respects, to the Marxist-derived term 'ideology'. According to Pringle (2007: 387), 'discourse can be simply understood as referring to a relatively consistent set of ideas that people use to navigate social life and make sense of their experiences'. More specifically, discourse refers to the unwritten rules that guide social practices, produce and regulate the production of statements, and shape what can be perceived and understood (Johns & Johns, 2000). Discourses such as 'sport builds character' or 'sport participation is good for health', Pringle further explained, often go unchallenged, despite many examples to the contrary, as they are conceptualised as discursive 'truths'. In a reciprocal manner, discourses also act to obscure what can be understood. For example, 'the discourse that produces the "truth" that rugby union is a man's sport . . . acts to prevent recognition that females might enjoy and benefit from rugby participation' (Pringle, 2007: 387).

Through the analysis of discourses, Foucault believed it was possible to understand what shapes 'actions and thoughts and how the making of choices is permitted within its own rules' (Johns & Johns, 2000: 220). In contrast to ideology, Foucault did not assume that dominating discourses act to reproduce and reinforce ways of thinking and that social practices primarily act to favour the ruling classes. Nevertheless, he tied the circulation of discourses to the workings of power and was interested in critically examining how certain discourses produce advantages or disadvantages for different individuals and groups.

With respect to coaching, one can begin to think about the 'coaching act' as a discursive formation based on a number of theories, concepts and descriptions derived from several disciplines such as biology, psychology, nutrition, pedagogy, sociology, education, management, medicine and even law. In this way, coaching is not a unitary scientific discipline. According to Markula and Pringle (2006), Foucault believed that groups of elements like coaching, which are 'formed in a regular manner by a discursive practice and which are indispensable to the constitution of a science, although not necessarily destined to give rise to one, can be called *knowledge*' (Foucault, 1972: 182; italics in original). Knowledge and discursive practices, therefore, Markula and Pringle continue, are inexplicably linked: knowledge is discursive and discursive practices form knowledge. In this way, 'knowledge is defined by the possibilities of use and appropriation offered by discourse . . . there is no knowledge without discursive practice; and any discursive practice may be defined by the knowledge that it forms' (Foucault, 1972: 182–183). Accordingly, to trace the discursive formation of a practice such as coaching, and to examine how it has been understood in culture, it is important to identify how we have come to know how to practise coaching and how this knowledge works to assert the truth about coaching. In other words, discourses for Foucault were never real: they were socially constructed ways in which we 'know' about ourselves, our bodies and our practices.

In research done with middle-distance running coaches, the formation of these coaches' understanding of periodisation and planning, and similarly its constraint by a number of discourses related to the body and performance, was examined (Denison, 2007, in press). It was argued that periodisation is not the result of some objective scientific process but a human-made creation to help coaches break down a training year into phases and cycles. This allows different kinds of work to be prioritised at specific periods to prepare an athlete for a designated competition (Bompa, 1994). Many coaches expect their athletes' performances to progress systematically – inputs produce specific outputs. In this way, the discourse that produces the truth that planning athletes' training is a rational and technical practice survives quite effectively, even though many athletes turn in outstanding performances despite deviating from their coaches' so-called scientifically derived training plans. Likewise, many athletes perform disastrously despite following their coaches' plans to the letter. This ambiguity illustrates how discourses, as Foucault (1980) would say, are by no means true but how, through a range of complicated relations and taken-for-granted practices, they come across as if they were natural laws or facts. Similarly, the same discourse that produces the 'truth' that planning athletes' training is a technical practice, marginalises athletes' own knowledge or experiences about their bodies or how to achieve peak performance. So it is that effective planning becomes understood in a very exact way with specific recommendations and practices developed that, thickened through the circulation of specific stories that support this way of thinking, perpetuate a limited view of planning. And it was precisely this – how ideas and practices became limiting and constraining – that concerned Foucault.

Through his analysis of discourses, Foucault wanted to understand what shapes our actions and thoughts, and how the making of choices is permitted within its own rules. In other words, he appreciated that even though how we decide to live our lives is not necessarily of our own choosing, because no discourse is totalising in its effects, the possibilities for change are multiple. Importantly, naming and then attempting to determine a discourse that one believes shapes a practice was not what Foucault advocated. As argued above, this would be to disentangle knowledge and discourse, and assume that answers to our problems and questions could be found by locating the discourse from which they derived. Alternatively, and in another contrast to ideology and the assumption that there are true and false ways of viewing reality, Foucault (1980: 118) was interested in 'seeing historically how effects of truth are produced within discourse, which themselves are neither true or false', as well as how 'knowledge and discourse are intertwined into societal practices as we know them in a particular historical moment and in a particular societal context' (Markula & Pringle, 2006: 54). So it was that discourses, for Foucault, were not stand-alone ideas but took on their importance through the workings of power. We now turn to a discussion of how Foucault understood power.

Power as relational

Unlike many prominent social theorists of his age who were greatly influenced by Marxism and viewed power as being organised in a hierarchical manner, Foucault

(1983: 221) defined power as a relationship whereby the actions of some help to guide or direct 'the possible field of action of others'. He regarded power not as operating in some top-down manner but as a series of relations within which an individual interacts with others. Markula and Pringle (2006: 138) explained this idea further: 'It [power] is an interplay of nonegalitarian and mobile relations that are in constant transformation due to the acts of individuals who can be located anywhere within these relations.' In this way, an individual's action within a relationship of power does not determine or physically force the action of others. To illustrate how Foucault understood power as relational, Prado (1995) provided the following example. Imagine a number of small magnets spread out on a surface not quite close enough to one another to clump together. Among the magnets there will be various force-vectors that exert some kind of influence or pull. However, imagine shifting around the magnets. In doing so, the force-vectors change and new relationships – influences, pulls, tensions – are created between the magnets. In this analogy, Prado (1995: 76) explained, 'power is the force-vectors and agents are the magnets. Each move of a magnet, or each act on the part of an agent, changes the "strategical situation" in its vicinity and so affects the whole.' In other words, the totality of power is not any one agent's or any one group's any more than the totality of force-vectors is any one magnet's magnetic field. Rather, all movements within a field contribute to the relational totality of power. Or, as Foucault (1977) would say, power is a set of actions upon other actions.

Markula and Pringle (2006) applied Foucault's understanding of power to coaching through the following example that illustrates the non-unidirectional workings of the coach–athlete relationship:

> A coach and an athlete exist within a specific power relation, in that the coach typically attempts to guide the athlete's conduct or performance. Although the coach can develop strategies to direct the actions of the athlete, such as by keeping the athlete on the bench, the athlete is still relatively 'free' to decide his or her response and ultimately whether he or she will continue to be coached. The actions of the athlete can also reciprocally influence the actions of the coach. If the athlete, for example, tells the coach that he or she is thinking of quitting, this might induce a change in the coach's future actions. Thus, although the coach and athlete's relationship of power may be unbalanced, they can still be viewed as existing within a specific power relation.
>
> (Markula and Pringle, 2006: 35)

To gain an insightful understanding of sport's complexities, and how, for example, coaches develop and use their knowledge of coaching, it might be fruitful to examine how the practice of coaching has been produced through the workings of discourse and power. Rather than suggesting that coaches' personal experiences indicate some truth about coaching, or that coaches as individuals are wholly responsible for their own decisions, as well as being the sole influence over certain others' decisions, or that select groups hold all the power and exercise it as they wish and upon whom they wish, it might be worth analysing the discursive construction of sport and power as positive, multiple and omnipresent, yet constantly changing, to understand relations between individuals. For example, the discourse that proclaims the 'coach as leader' is perhaps better understood as an effect of productive power, not an absolute power, that influences athletes to abandon their own sporting autonomy and follow someone supposedly wiser and smarter. In other words, individuals themselves are not powerful leaders; it is the position they occupy, formed through discourse, that comes with power. This sporting discourse (i.e., the coach as leader), therefore, is not true but indirectly works to guide the conduct of others and is accordingly linked to the workings of power.

Foucault (1972), in recognising the difficulty of identifying who might be responsible for promoting or controlling particular discourses, suggested that discourses worked somewhat anonymously as they circulated through a variety of human interactions via a capillary-like network with no one seemingly in control. However, this did not mean that discourses or power relations could not be modified, especially when they were unjust or ineffective. Quite the contrary: it meant that the focus of our interventions should have less to do with changing people than with changing dominant conceptions of how social relations are organised (Denison & Winslade, 2006). For example, as a number of scholars have shown, bodies in sport are as a matter of course disciplined and, as a result, can become docile through various power relations enacted via the track, the field and the gymnasium, as well as through timetables, schedules, drills and exercises (e.g., Heikkala, 1993; Shogan, 1999). All of these practices have the potential to transform athletes into what Foucault termed 'objects of knowledge' that can be efficiently controlled and shaped. In this broad manner, it is possible to consider coaches as 'agents of normalization' (Halas & Hanson, 2001: 123). However, this does not necessarily need to be the case, for no practice is inherently disciplining.

The prime disciplinary techniques Foucault analysed correspond very closely with the systems and tactics used to train and produce contemporary athletes. Accordingly, the sport sciences have become an integral aspect of the workings of disciplinary power in sport. For example, Shogan (1999) discussed how Foucault's descriptions of the techniques of disciplinary power read like a 'how to' manual for coaches, and explained quite clearly how coaching can work as a practice to discipline modern-day athletes. This form of power, which focused primarily on the control and discipline of bodies, was exercised, according to Foucault (1979: 104), fundamentally 'by means of surveillance'. Markula and Pringle (2006) added that Foucault's (1972) descriptions of disciplinary power almost perfectly parallel the way that many coaches control and regulate their athletes through the use of various graduated training activities, rigid training schedules and practices of observation and judgement. Sport in this sense, as practised by many coaches, can be thought of as a modern discipline that is 'both an exercise of control and a subject matter' (Shogan, 1999: 11).

To explain the connection between discipline and control in more detail, Markula and Pringle (2006) referred to the work of Heikkala (1993) to illustrate how athletic bodies are normalised by the disciplinary techniques of modern sport and the logic of competition. According to Heikkala (1993: 398), the organisation of modern sport is such that coaches are strongly influenced to think of their athletes as 'productive bodies' who exist to generate winning results. The effect of such thinking can easily lead to coaching practices that produce within athletes an identity that is narrow, machine-like and fixated on performance outcomes above any emotional sensitivity or awareness as an embodied sportsman or -woman (Denison, 2007). As an example, one way that disciplinary techniques become enacted by coaches over their athletes is through the idea that overseeing and monitoring an athlete's training is a vital aspect of effective coaching. However, control also comes through the coach's gaze and various technologies of surveillance; control that can be maintained by the all-knowing coach which positions the athlete as a subject to the coach's 'expertise' and knowledge.

Foucault (1991) explained how this controlling gaze of surveillance, discipline and power operated through the example of the panopticon. This was Jeremy Bentham's design for a building to maximise the efficient workings of power. It consisted of a tower at its centre with windows looking down on a peripheric building that was divided into separate rooms or cells. Within each cell an individual is located in a position to be observed by the supervisor in the tower. Importantly, for Foucault's analogy to work, the position of the tower in relationship to the cells made it impossible for individuals in their cells to know whether they were being observed. The prime effect of the panopticon, therefore, was to induce in each individual 'a state of consciousness and permanent visibility that assures the automatic functioning of power' (Foucault 1991: 200). The omnipresent gaze of authority subsequently disciplines subjects to survey their own behaviour in a manner that renders them docile, whereby they discipline themselves to be obedient, conforming and non-complaining.

Critically, this self-policing that Foucault described did not occur through force or physical coercion but through individuals' internalisation of certain rules, regulations and procedures of what leading a responsible life meant. In this way, self-surveillance was tied to a possible field of appropriate actions that were not necessarily true but had been effectively shaped and constrained by various technologies of dominance. A complex challenge for contemporary scholars stemming from Foucault's concerns with disciplinary control and self-surveillance is to identify the mechanisms of disciplinary power and the related modes of domination present in society today. Within the sociology of sport, a number of scholars have undertaken this challenge by examining how sport and fitness practices act as technologies of domination that encourage individuals to comply with a number of normalising practices such as dieting and playing through pain. In this way, sport becomes an integral part of the workings of disciplinary power in contemporary societies. However, as already explained, for Foucault, these workings were not fixed or permanent; they were just dominant and, therefore, could be challenged if deemed to be unjust or ineffective. Accordingly, Foucault believed that each of us has a responsibility to act ethically within our various power relations in order to minimise harmful modes of domination. It is here, therefore, that one can see that Foucault was not a strict determinist. He believed individuals had the opportunity to negotiate and to work within power relations in productive and positive ways.

The job of coaching scholars working from a Foucauldian perspective should be to promote possibilities for innovation and change by questioning coaching's numerous taken-for-granted practices and possible unintended consequences. For, as Foucault (1988) said, a powerful way to begin to develop more ethical procedures and actions in life is to become critical of how we make sense of the limitations set for ourselves within the truth games in which we are involved. In other words, until we understand that the tensions that operate within competitive sport, and between coaches and athletes, are socially constructed and not fixed or permanent, we will never be in a position to make sport a healthier and more ethical practice for everyone involved. What concerned Foucault (1972) was the pervasive and cumulative effect of disciplinary techniques and how this could induce insidious social consequences. His 'seminal idea was that a disciplinary power is exercised over all citizens in contemporary societies, and although individuals find it difficult to discern the workings of this form of power it, nevertheless, contributes to a general discomfort that pervades life' (Foucault, 1972: 16). More specifically, he theorised that the pervasive use of systems of surveillance, examining and ranking, in conjunction with the control of time and space, produce normalised individuals who have internalised mechanisms of constraint, and who subject themselves to self-surveillance in the search for signs of abnormality. Foucault's prime aim, then, was to raise critical awareness concerning the widespread use of disciplinary technologies to help individuals negotiate how they govern themselves in relation to technologies of domination.

According to Foucault, it is possible for an athlete or a coach to question whether he or she has to be locked into a specific pre-defined or dominant sporting identity. In other words, athletes and coaches should be able to search for ways of constructing their sporting identities that are less limiting and disciplining. For example, an athlete could problematise conforming to his or her coach's instructions or to tolerating pain and injuries as 'natural' effects of training and competition. Likewise, a coach could problematise the pressure he or she experiences to be the all-knowing expert, and how this encourages secrecy among the coaching ranks and leads coaches to feel isolated and lonely. Or a coach could question how he or she has come to believe that it is unacceptable to experiment with tactics and training theory, and challenge the so-called authority of the sport sciences. In other words, it could be anything because every aspect of the coaching 'act' has a social component that can be problematised. Coaches who understand this will be in a stronger position to make real changes for the better and attain, as Foucault (1988: 18) said, 'a certain state of happiness, purity, wisdom, perfection, or immortality'.

Although many of the ideas and strategies for change mentioned above might appear vague, over the past three years a number of positive comments from practising coaches regarding what they see as the practical value of Foucauldian thinking have been received. These have typically followed presentations given to a group of coaches, or from a coach studying for his or her master's degree after reading related work. In some cases, one of us has even sent research examining coaching and Foucault to coaches who might be willing to consider how Foucault could inform their coaching. So what would a practising coach make of Foucault?

A coach's commentary by Dave Scott-Thomas

I am currently the head coach of cross-country and track and field at the University of Guelph in Ontario, Canada. I am also the coach of the National Endurance Centre at Guelph, working with one of the strongest groups of national team athletes in Canada. Two of the athletes I work with ran in the 2008 Beijing Olympics. Over the past twelve years, I've contributed to establishing the varsity programme at Guelph as the premier distance-running programme for men and women in Canada. I have also been a team coach for Canada at a number of global events, including the World Student Games, the World Cross-Country Championships and the World Track and Field Championships.

Reading this chapter on Foucault and coaching really helped me to understand some of my own coaching practices – what I do and why. For example, when a coach has to analyse a poor performance by an athlete, this is usually done in a pretty linear way by trying to determine the causes with a focus on the physical factors. Of course, many times psychological factors are considered in this diagnosis but hardly ever sociological factors. In our group, I would say that both tend to be really important, and for that reason this chapter resonated quite strongly with me – it offered some theoretical rationale for how I tend to coach.

As an example, I recently had a conversation with one of the top post-collegiate runners I work with who was struggling to decide whether to continue with running since he felt immense pressure to get a job and enter the 'real' world. My sense was that this was based on his perception of other people's expectations of what a 'normal' life was. I gently tried to lead him to the understanding that he could shift that perception and create his own sense of purpose, his own narrative of what he wanted to do in life. While I genuinely believed there was some good modelling going on around him in our group to do just that, I wasn't sure if it was strong enough to help him overcome twenty years of social inertia in a different direction. In the end, he did decide to stick with running and, in fact, had his best year ever. He made the 2009 World Championship team, won the national championships and ran the sixth fastest time for a Canadian in his event. In addition, he called his choice to stay with running one of the most pivotal decisions in his life. Not just because he had a good year on the track, but in terms of his growth as a person and his confidence to follow his own path in life.

As a coach, I need to understand how influential cultural expectations about what constitutes a proper life often shape an athlete's commitment. What I learned from this chapter was to see how this process of identity formation occurs within and through power relations and not just an individual's own self-desire. As a result, when I am trying to help an athlete construct a new narrative for himself, I can see that I need to be careful not to make it seem like something he has to become more motivated to do. Rather, it requires recognition that his identity has been formed through a number of historical contingencies, and that to change this he needs to think differently not just about himself but about this construction and how he has been positioned by history.

Accordingly, I can see why, for Foucault, critical thinking was so important to bring about any type of real change. From what I understood from this chapter, change without critical thinking is simply changing the order of things, not their logic. Again, when it comes to trying to explain why a runner might have inexplicably under-performed, perhaps she felt unable to determine or to shape her running destiny and as a result her motivation waned? I think, as coaches, we really need to help our athletes understand why they want to compete. If they have a nebulous concept of what drives them and are unsure of all the complex relations that are pushing and pulling them here and there (as was earlier explained through the example of the magnets), it will be difficult for them to focus and to work through the physical discomfort required of middle- and long-distance running.

Likewise, when I read about discipline and docility, I think there are lots of subtle ways of avoiding the potential problems associated with this by giving athletes more responsibility. For example, when determining workouts I often allow the athletes to define routes and training zones, encouraging input from them so they can shape the session with me. Sometimes, I show up to practice and the guys will have already guessed the workout. I like that; it shows they're thinking, and sometimes I get new ideas from them that I put into use.

We also do a ton of training that I would classify as open-ended; hence, I try to discourage the athletes from using heart-rate monitors and other machines. We do a relatively large amount of work that in my view is not time or distance dependent. I agree that it is so important to question the dominance of ideas like the 'body as machine' or 'training as a technical practice' that tend to permeate coaches' thinking – in many cases, without them even knowing it. That's one big idea I took from this chapter: the importance of recognising the socially constructed nature of training theory, and how understandings of what makes an athlete fit are often based on tradition and what supposedly counts as real knowledge as opposed to anything objective. I can see when it comes to encouraging coaches to change their practices it's important to show them how their ideas have been formed historically by people, chance and even accidents – because if something isn't hard or fixed, it can be revised if it is not working as you intended. In this way, it's clear how Foucault's ideas, although quite philosophical, can be put into use within practical situations. Also, over the course of the training year we do lots of running off the track. In Foucault's terms, I suppose I am trying to be careful not to enclose the spaces around which my athletes train by giving them lots of variety; I can really see now how not doing that can have some pretty unproductive consequences.

The part about surveillance also made me think about what I am doing at practice: what I am watching, what I am recording, what I am monitoring. While

I believe it can be effective to watch athletes run and note how they move, when they move and how they react to the environment and the various bodies around them, there are also times when I need to step out of this surveillance mode. I was glad to read that Foucault supported this idea, and how it was especially important to be careful that surveillance did not lead to docility. Like him, I do not see docility as a positive. I believe that educated, aware and questioning athletes will be more effective performers than docile, obedient athletes. Certainly, coach control is important at some level, but not always, as it is the athlete who ultimately needs to take (at least some) responsibility. I can also see how Foucault believed that while there might be some power relations that are unbalanced, in all relations all sides do have some power. The long quote from Markula and Pringle (2006) helped me understand this. What I took from that example was that leaders need to use their power responsibly in order to manage various complex relations; also, everyone on the team needs to understand how they too have some responsibility for the team to grow and to succeed. It's not just about the coach leading and controlling.

I can see now through a number of deliberate strategies regarding how I construct my athletes' training that I am in some ways undermining my control by encouraging them to construct their own identities as runners. This is a good application of Foucault for me. Sure, I might have been doing this 'instinctively', but seeing the theory behind it makes it more salient. At the same time, I need to be careful that my athletes do not see the construction of their identity as some humanistic process of self-discovery where they try to determine their true selves, but rather as an active process of formation, transformation and problematisation based on the power relations they operate within. In this way, the identity they end up making can be built on an active problematisation of what's presently real to them, and not on some romantic idea that has somehow come to dominate their thinking. And, as Foucault advocated, this should lead to a more informed understanding of our interests, desires, goals and opportunities: something that's located within the contexts in which we live and operate as opposed to some old ideas from the past which can be inappropriate or even irrelevant. You see this a lot in distance running, where in many Western countries performances are below what they were thirty years ago. Many people can't understand this, and critique contemporary athletes for being weak or lazy. But society is so different than it was thirty years ago. So, to help today's runners develop their dedication and work ethic to become great distance runners, I don't believe it is productive to call them weak or lazy. Rather, we have to think of new motivational strategies and training approaches that are relevant to our current cultural context, and that can work to inspire today's generation to find meaning for training hard.

Finally, I also think it's worthwhile mentioning coach, in addition to athlete, docility. This is a big problem, and I believe it is why so many coaches coach the way they were coached – they do not know how to think differently. Ironically, formal coaching training courses, like the ones organised by national federations, that are meant to encourage thinking can easily become a disciplining practice. That is not to say I am against formal education. Rather, invoking Foucault, as a coach who often ends up being part of various coach education schemes, I think coach educators need to be more aware of their power and how they define what knowledge counts and what doesn't, and how this can affect coaches. In this case, educators and administrators have to know how to use their power responsibly. I definitely think it would be useful for the next generation of coaches to be taught more about Foucault so they could learn to critique and problematise their knowledge of coaching and themselves. This should be something coach education really concentrates on if we want to develop innovative, ethical and effective coaches.

Conclusion

It goes without saying that coaches are in general concerned with performance. And when an athlete under-performs it is likely to get a coach's attention, as he or she is often the one charged with figuring out what went wrong. In most cases, the search for a solution typically turns to the traditional sport sciences as the coach pursues a likely diagnosis of causes and effects. In some cases, this line of reasoning may prove fruitful. For example, a decline in a runner's anaerobic threshold could explain why he or she faded midway through a race. Or a poor follow-through could explain why a golfer's driving distance has dropped significantly. Or an increase in body fat might explain why a swimmer performed far below his or her personal best. However, what if no clear relationship to explain what went wrong, and why, can be found? In such cases, what should the coach do next? It was this question that initially sparked an interest in Foucault and particularly his ideas about docility. While docility may not manifest in an obvious under-performance, the same way an injury or an illness might, its effects on an athlete's sense of control and commitment can easily contribute to an athlete performing well below his or her potential (Denison, 2007). However, this is a very subtle process, and a coach who is unaware of Foucauldian theorising is unlikely to consider docility as a problem; instead, they might ascribe his or her athlete's under-performance to some character fault or individual weakness – for example, he or she 'psyched out'.

Docility – that is, the development of athletes who are steadfast and non-complaining – should not be seen as a desirable condition of high-performance sport, let alone an unavoidable one. Rather, it should be seen as a state-of-being where an athlete's performance has possibly reached a plateau. And like any plateau reached by an athlete, a change to the training environment – usually made by the coach – needs to occur in order for the athlete to move forward. In the case of a plateau produced by docility, this change might involve the coach considering the mechanistic coaching discourses that have informed his or her practices and the consequences these might be having (Denison, 2007, in press).

Developing such an intervention is not easy, of course. It requires more than using different words: the coach reflecting on what he or she has said. It requires a change to one's philosophy of coaching and the application of knowledge. Drawing on Foucault, sport does not have to be seen as an inherently disciplining process that, by default, will produce 'docile bodies that monitor, guard and discipline themselves' (Eskes *et al.*, 1998: 319). On the contrary, coaches can be educated to talk to their athletes about their training, their performances and their bodies in ways that can reduce the onset of docility and lead to a more productive sporting culture. In this way, Foucault's ideas related to discourse, power and knowledge can provide coaches with some useful strategies to enhance their effectiveness by changing the way they think about their athletes' bodies, power relations and the advent and application of various training practices and knowledges.

Of course, new practices have the potential to become just as disciplining and constraining as the ones they replaced. This is a point Foucault was careful to make, and why he believed that critical thinking and active problematisation can never end. In this regard, Foucault has been criticised for focusing his analytical efforts too much on power's relational qualities and ignoring the structural realities of society that lead some people to be dominated by others. Accordingly, a number of scholars have claimed that Foucault's work does not allow space for individuals to create change through resistance (e.g., Hekman, 1996). Therefore, Foucault, it has been said, ignored the role of the individual in his theory. Markula and Pringle (2006) countered thiese critiques quite comprehensively in the concluding chapter of their book. There is not enough space here to present their full argument. But suffice to say that any critique – including those offered by Foucault – must be judged as coming from a particular view of reality, knowledge, the self and power. And Foucault was clear in expressing his disdain of a hierarchical or dualistic understanding of human relations through, for example, the structure–agency divide that, in his view, ignored how 'the self was discursively constructed within constantly changing power relations' (Markula & Pringle, 2006: 218). Accordingly, before arguing for any social theorist's perspective to address a specific problem, it is crucial to understand first the premise behind that individual's work.

Coming from a subjective and social constructionist perspective of reality and knowledge, we strongly believe that educating coaches to understand that athletic bodies are not independent entities but are formed through a range of social interactions could lead to many sport problems being understood as products of discursive conditions, not sport's oppressive nature or individuals' own lack of specific coping resources. As a result, coaches might begin to examine themselves, their programmes, or the language they use as part of developing innovative practices, interventions and problem-solving strategies. Coaches might also begin to assume more responsibility regarding how they talk to their athletes and establish unwritten subjective standards for their athletes to adopt. Clearly, such tactics are not about revolution, but they are about change. And this is what Foucault can offer coaches: a set of ideas for thinking more ethically about how sport can become a positive force for the development of healthy athletes.

4   Pierre Bourdieu: A theory of (coaching) practice

Chris Cushion with Will Kitchen

Pierre Bourdieu: a short biography

Pierre Bourdieu is widely acknowledged as one of 'the most influential social theorists of his generation, both in his home country of France and throughout the sociological community' (Tomlinson, 2004: 161). During his career, Bourdieu researched a wide range of sociological and anthropological issues. He is perhaps best known for his extensive work concerning the maintenance of a system of power by means of the transmission of a dominant culture. One of his central themes was that culture and education are central in the affirmation of differences between social classes, and in the reproduction of those differences. Importantly, Bourdieu's writing is an argument for an integrated analytical approach, where history, anthropology and sociology all overlap in the cultural analysis of practice (Tomlinson, 2004). For Bourdieu (1986: xiv), then, it is possible to 'observe and understand everything that human practices reveal only when they are seen in their mutual relationship . . . as a totality'.

Pierre Bourdieu was Assistant Professor of Sociology at the Faculté des Lettres, Paris, in 1960, before serving as Professor of Sociology at the Faculté des Lettres in Lille. From 1964, he worked as Professor of Sociology at the prestigious École des Hautes Études and later, from 1981, at the Collège de France, both in Paris. By the late 1980s, Bourdieu had become one of the most frequently cited social scientists and, subsequently, had a considerable influence on sociology (Tomlinson, 2004). In the mid-1990s, he participated in a number of activities outside academic circles, including supporting striking rail workers and speaking for the homeless, while in 1996 he founded the publishing company Liber/Raisons d'agir. Bourdieu's last publications dealt with such topics as masculine domination, neoliberal newspeak, Edouard Manet's art and Beethoven. Pierre Bourdieu died of cancer at the Saint-Antoine Hospital, Paris, on 24 January 2002.

Introduction

> Of all the oppositions that artificially divide social science, the most fundamental, and the most ruinous, is the one that is set up between subjectivism and objectivism
>
> (Bourdieu, 1990a: 27).

Two things are immediately appealing about Bourdieu's work in terms of its application to coaching. First, the focus upon the visible social world of practice. Second, the attempt to transcend epistemological couples – that is, agency–structure, micro–macro and subjectivism–objectivism – with his relational or interrelated emphasis (Bourdieu, 1998; Bottero, 2009; Jenkins, 1992; Jarvie & Maguire, 1994). Bourdieu, rather, proposed a dialectical or two-way relationship between objective structures and subjective phenomena in social practice (Jarvie & Maguire, 1994). Coaching clearly denotes 'doing' – that is, it is practical – but not just doing in and of itself; it is doing in a historical and cultural context and, in this sense, coaching practice is always social practice (Wenger, 1998; Cushion *et al.*, 2006).

Using Bourdieu's concepts as analytical tools enables the examination of a social actor's behaviour and how resultant relationships are played out in communal arenas, such as coaching (Brown, 2005). This then facilitates a common language through which complexity and interaction can be described and understood, which is arguably a key necessity in the conceptual understanding of coaching. Bourdieu's work also allows an appreciation of coaching and the coaching process as contextualised, contested and embodied through its ability to illuminate multiple, interrelated dimensions (Hunter, 2004). In this respect, it is able to take account of coaching's inherent personal nature.

Bourdieu's attempts to address the issue of agency and structure in terms of articulating the relations of production between the individual (e.g., as a player or a coach), their body and society (e.g., a club or a sport) are also particularly useful in this case (Brown, 2005). Here, Bourdieu's constructs of habitus, field, capital and practice (which are discussed later in this chapter) hold relevance. Together, they enable a consideration of coaching as 'cultural economy' (Nash, 1990), as opposed to being a benign or simply beneficial activity dropped into a given context. Furthermore, using Bourdieu's integrated conceptual framework, it is possible to consider cultural transmission within coaching as a form of social reproduction, an essential process for the survival of groups within society (Nash, 1990). Hence, it can be postulated that certain social groups come together to produce the coaching process, through regulating and managing the generation and transmission of real and symbolic capital.

Despite the individual nature of each coaching position and context, coaches form a sub-society of interlocking groups, 'a community rooted in sport and what it symbolizes', identifying themselves 'collectively as a meaningful social segment' (Sage, 1989: 88). This creates a social network that enables the expression of shared attitudes and value orientations through which cultural traditions flow (Cushion & Jones, 2006; Coakley 1986; Sage, 1989). Such a system represents a 'social structure' that influences how coaches act. The interaction of structure (e.g., a club or a sport) and agent (e.g., a coach or an athlete) within the field of coaching creates a discursive space for constituting the development of coaches and athletes within a context – what Hunter (2004: 176) describes as the 'embodied subjectivities of those within [that] space'. Indeed, any consideration of interaction and discourse devoid of context is flawed and limited (Cushion, 2007;

Cushion & Lyle, 2010). This is because 'it denies the relational positioning of the individual within social fields' (Hunter, 2004: 176). But how do social structures and individual coaches come together and interact to define and create coaching practice? A Bourdieuian framework enables an insightful analysis of 'structure', allowing a dialectic perspective of the coaching process as one that is both structur*ed* and structur*ing*.

Because coaching can be readily represented as individual 'episodes', it is too easy to overlook how the interrelatedness and interconnectedness of such 'episodes' create and sustain a social process (Cushion, 2007). As a result, it becomes (and has become) easy to take an asocial linear view of coaching (Cushion, 2007; Cushion & Lyle, 2010). Indeed, conceiving a social structure such as coaching as the 'mere aggregate of individual strategies makes it impossible to account for their resilience as well as for the apparent objective arrangements that these strategies perpetuate or challenge' (Bourdieu & Wacquant, 1992: 9–10). For the practitioner, such 'frozen' formulae, dressed in 'theoretical tinsel' (Everett, 2002: 58) seem disconnected from the (coaching) context, and thus remain unable to capture the richness of lived experience (Cushion, 2007; Cushion & Lyle, 2010). Such portrayals merely serve to obscure both the social and historical roots of coaching and those involved in it (Bourdieu & Wacquant, 1992; Cushion, 2007).

The purpose of this chapter is to offer a conceptual view of coaching from the theories and thinking of Pierre Bourdieu. Everett (2002: 56) argues that Bourdieu offers a 'fine critical yet reflexive vista' which encourages people to make sense of their own situations. The analysis allows coaching to be considered from two 'perspectives'. First, through laying 'the foundations of a self-analysis' (Bourdieu, 1988: xv); and, second, through a less detached perspective of coaching that positions the activity closer to its social, dynamic and complex nature.

Bourdieu's work here is not presented as a panacea to coaching's conceptual problems but, like other sociological theories throughout the book, as a 'set of thinking tools visible through the results they yield' (Bourdieu, 1989: 15). This link to practical results (i.e., theory as a means to inform practice) is crucial, particularly in such an applied field as coaching. The significance of the chapter, again echoing one of the prime purposes of the book, lies in suggesting a discernible link between practice and credible theory, thus underlining the belief that although 'theory without research is empty . . . research without theory is blind' (Bourdieu & Wacquant, 1992: 160). The chapter first outlines the key concepts that characterise Bourdieu's theoretical approach, namely field, capital, habitus and reproduction. In drawing on a range of existing empirical work, these concepts are then applied to coaching as explanatory tools. The aim is to strive for a double process of interpretation and application. Finally, a commentary in terms of his understanding of the work is presented by Will Kitchen, a cricket coach.

Bourdieu's key concepts

Bourdieu asserted that social life is simultaneously the result of social rules and 'individual flourishes' (Lemert, 1997: 44) – 'a mutually constituting interaction of structures, dispositions and actions' (Calhoun *et al.*, 1995: 4). It is a position which acknowledges that structures shape and are shaped by individuals' practice. Practice is subsequently seen as resulting from a process of improvisation structured by cultural orientations, personal goals and the ability to play the game of social interaction (Calhoun *et al.*, 1995). Lemert (1997) describes this as being what is original to oneself and at the same time common to those of a similar social kind. This notion of structured improvisation forms Bourdieu's key concept of 'habitus' (Calhoun *et al.*, 1995).

Habitus

Habitus is a concept that is challenging to define in strict terms (Brubaker, 1995). Wacquant (1998) describes habitus as a system of durable dispositions through which we see, judge and act in the world. Put another way, people are endowed with a series of internalised schemes, and through these schemes they produce, perceive and evaluate their practices (Ritzer, 1996). In Bourdieu's words, it is 'the social inscribed in the body . . . a feel or sense of the "social game" . . . the source of most practices' (Bourdieu, 1962: 111). These unconscious schemata are acquired through lasting exposure to particular social conditions and conditionings, via the internalisation of constraints and possibilities (Wacquant, 1995). Bourdieu described this phenomenon as 'the product of the internalisation of the structures' of the social world (Bourdieu, 1989: 18). Because habitus is acquired as a result of occupation of a position within this world, not everyone has the same habitus; however, those who occupy the same positions will tend to have similar habitus (Ritzer, 1996). The existence of a multitude of habitus means that the social world and its structures do not impose themselves uniformly on all actors. Therefore, habitus captures the practical mastery people have of their situation while grounding that mastery socially (Calhoun *et al.*, 1995). In this respect, 'each person has a unique individual variant of the common matrix' (Wacquant, 1998: 221).

As the mediator or arbiter between past influences and present stimuli, habitus is both structured by the patterned social forces that produced it and structuring in that it gives form and coherence to the various activities of an individual across the spheres of life (Wacquant, 1998). On the one hand, then, habitus is a *structuring structure* (that is, a structure that structures the social world), while, on the other, it is a *structured structure* (that is, a structure that is structured by the social world). Bourdieu defined habitus with typical verbal flair as 'the product of structure, producer of practice, and reproducer of structure', the 'unchosen principle of all choices' and the 'conductorless orchestration of conduct' (Wacquant, 1998: 221). Habitus is also both durable and transposable; it is transferable from one field to another. However, Bourdieu considered that it is also possible for people to have an inappropriate habitus and to suffer from what he describes as 'hysteresis', the inability to cope in a new social environment.

Unsurprisingly, habitus is considered to function 'below the level of conscious-ness and language, beyond the reach of introspective scrutiny and control by the will' (Bourdieu, 1984: 466). Even though we are not conscious of habitus and its operation, it manifests itself in our most practical activities, such as how we eat, talk and walk (and coach). The body, then, acts as an important social memory where the basics of culture are imprinted and encoded in both a formal and an informal manner. Similarly, the occupation of a social position influences the development of schema or patterns of behaviour, with the knowledge needed to occupy that position requiring the development of a habitus. Lessons are absorbed about manners, customs, style and deportment that become so ingrained they are forgotten in any conscious sense (Jarvie & Maguire, 1994). This results in 'the accumulative practice of same, ensuring that the motor schema is drawn on intuitively' (Wacquant, 1992: 221).

Habitus is neither static nor eternal, because it is the combination of a social actor's deeply ingrained identity and his or her less fixed, occupational identity (Meisenhelder, 1997; Everett, 2002). A person's habitus is also continually changing. This is because the experiences to which it is constantly subjected are many and varied, with most of them both reinforcing and modifying (Bourdieu & Wacquant, 1992). However, the notion of 'unconscious' means that Bourdieu's (1977) social actor is far from 'rational' (Everett, 2002). Indeed, as Everett (2002: 72, 87) argues, Bourdieu's approach is to challenge individualism and the notion of the free and independent subject: 'meaning and consequences of action are not transparent to the actors themselves . . . habitus is that part of practices which remain obscure in the eyes of their own producers'. On the other hand, however, Bourdieu believed that agents are not helpless or at the mercy of social forces, or indeed objects guided simply by rules or codes (Cushion & Jones, 2006; Everett, 2002). Rather, they pursue strategies and weigh their interests, acting with planned calculation (albeit within established habitus).

In summary, according to Bourdieu it would be a mistake to see social actors (e.g., coaches and/or athletes) located in a structure external to them. Such actors are part of the structure, and the structure is part of them. The habitus is the expression of social structure through the person, the battery of dispositions that orientates actions (Hodkinson & Hodkinson, 2004b). These dispositions are tacit in that we are largely unaware of them but they are rooted in both our past and our present position.

Capital

The system of dispositions or habitus that people acquire depends on the position they occupy in society: that is, on their particular endowment and accumulation of capital (Bourdieu, 1986). Capital is described by Bourdieu as being the capacity to exercise control over one's own future and the future of others, and is, in effect, a form of power (Ritzer, 1996). Capital can occur in a number of forms: economic (that which can be immediately and directly converted to money), cultural (such as educational credentials), social (such as social position and connections), symbolic (from honour and prestige; Calhoun, 1995; Ritzer, 1996) and physical (the development of bodies in ways recognised as having value; Shilling, 1997).

Bourdieu asserts that society is structured along differences in the distribution of capital, with individuals constantly striving to maximise their own capital (Calhoun, 1995). As within any field, social groups in coaching possess different forms of capital and actively pursue strategies to improve and transmit this capital. The position of any individual, group or institution can be charted by two coordinates: the overall volume and composition of the capital they possess. A third coordinate is variation over time, which records the trajectory of both volume and composition through the social space. In doing so, it provides valuable clues as to individuals' habitus by revealing the manner and path through which they reached the position they presently occupy (Wacquant, 1998).

Within coaching practice, capital is unequally distributed. The different positions occupied within the field have differing amounts of various types of capital attached to them. Those with superior positions (i.e., those with more capital) have advantages, and more influence on the rules that determine success (i.e., what counts as capital; Hodkinson & Hodkinson, 2004). Coaching, therefore, needs to be understood not as a nonaligned or dispassionate social space, but as one that creates and recreates difference (Nash, 1990); a space where the bases of identity and hierarchy are endlessly disputed and contested. For example, both coaches and athletes when initially entering a sport or sporting environment have limited social gravitas. They thus immediately strive to accumulate symbolic and cultural capital to guarantee status. As Potrac (2004) contends, the task is to ask not whether power is exercised within coaching, but how it is exercised. Indeed, in terms of understanding the complexity of the coaching process, unravelling power and how it constrains and/or enables practice is a crucial step. By utilising the concept of capital (among others) it is somewhat possible to explain the origins, uses and consequences of power, and the interaction it engenders within coaching.

Due to the unequal distribution of capital, coaching exists within a hierarchical structure. In sports such as football, social, cultural, symbolic and physical capital all contribute to a formal and informal hierarchy that encompasses both coaches and players (Cushion & Jones, 2006). For example, in a study of youth professional football, Cushion and Jones (2006) found that individuals' possession of social capital derived from the position they occupied on the coaching or playing staff (i.e., head coach or assistant, professional or youth player), cultural capital from the qualifications and experience of each coach or player (knowing the cultural codes, language, signs and stories of the game) and symbolic capital from the prestige or renown derived from personal accomplishment. Taken together, they determined the social hierarchy and structured practice within the club. Symbolic capital is described by Bourdieu and Passeron (1996 [1977]) as that which is valued in the field as resolved by the dominant power group. For example, for an athlete, a 'good attitude' or perceived effort level can have symbolic value and subsequently define the athletic experience (Wilson *et al.*, 2006; Cushion & Jones, 2006). Similarly, Purdy *et al.* (2008) found that social, physical and symbolic capital ('credibility') was crucial in framing the contention and struggle within a high-performance sporting programme. The presence and influence of capital within coaching contexts are, therefore, being increasingly discussed.

Field

The social arena in which individuals manoeuvre and scuffle, often for access to capital, is described by Bourdieu as a field (Jenkins, 1992). Each field has its own logic and taken-for-granted structure of necessity and relevance. Such logic is both the product and the producer of habitus specific and appropriate to the field (Jenkins, 1992). A field is a structured system of social positions, with each position interacting with the habitus to produce actions (Jarvie & Maguire, 1994; Jenkins, 1992). Additionally, each position within a field is not static but determined, as discussed above, by the allocation of capital. Consequently, the system is characterised by a series of power relations where positions are viewed as more or less dominant or subordinate, reflecting their access to valued capital (Jarvie & Maguire, 1994; Jenkins, 1992).

Each field is also a crucial mediating context wherein external factors or changing circumstances are brought to bear upon individual practice (Jenkins, 1992). The structure of the field, then, both 'undergirds and guides individuals' strategies whereby they seek, individually and collectively, to safeguard or improve their position' (Bourdieu cited in Wacquant 1989: 40). In this respect 'the field is very much a field of struggles' (Bourdieu & Wacquant, 1992: 101). Coaching can similarly be characterised as a series of power relations where positions are viewed as more or less dominant or subordinate, reflecting an individual's access to capital (Jarvie & Maguire, 1994; Jenkins, 1992). Coaching, then, may be investigated as a field of its own or as a social process going on within a field (i.e., a particular sport – the sports field). As fields 'all follow specific logics' (Bourdieu & Wacquant, 1992: 97), the sports field can be considered to have its own rules and regularities. Like other fields, sport can be divided into several sub-fields (e.g., specific sport disciplines) characterised by different adjustments or variations related to the overall logic. This connects the local (team or coach) with the global (international sport structure or national coach education body). By localising the specific process under study (e.g., coaching practice) within the overall (sport) field, it is possible to specify the degree and in which ways 'the global sport structure influences the local through the imposition of rules, regulations and standards' (Galipeau & Trudel, 2006: 82). For example, a study of the institutionalisation of elite sport in Norway (Augestad *et al.*, 2006) demonstrated how field struggles over time are responsible for certain national discourses. In turn, these ways of talking structure understandings of roles (e.g., those of athletes and coaches), relations (e.g., within and between institutions and agents) and power (e.g., legitimate knowledge) within the sporting context. Consequently, through employing a Bourdieuian perspective to study local coaching practices as embedded within certain field discourses, it is possible to gain an understanding of dynamic processes, such as adaption and resistance. Similarly, we can see how, when likened to Bourdieu's field, coaching contexts shape and control the process and acts of coaching.

The structure of the field of coaching through the selection of those with 'desired qualities' (e.g., athletes with a 'good attitude') contributes to the production and reproduction of the power relations within it. Thus, coaching's basic social structure (like any other for Bourdieu) can be seen as one centred on power. For example, in professional football, the clubs control access to professional careers (Cushion, 2010a, 2010b). This locates coaching as a de-limiting field of production that exists to perpetuate the supply-and-demand cycle for valued cultural goods (i.e., embodied perceived competencies). It is also a screening process for such competencies, and gives a practical logic to the supply-and-demand cycle (Brown, 2005). Indeed, those who set criteria for evaluation of performance and progression (that is, coaches) reflect the balance of power relations in the field. Such a position supports existing work (e.g., Cushion & Jones, 2006; Purdy *et al.*, 2009; Wilson, *et al.*, 2006) in affirming that coaches have a positive bias towards those who are 'conforming, co-operative [and] orderly' (Martinek, 1983: 65).

The coaching process thus knits together a converging social legitimacy, class culture and technical knowledge. The habitus and accrued capital of performers (both coaches and athletes) means that those who are equipped and able to work within the field's discursive space become more closely aligned to those in power (e.g., often head coaches). Consequently, players and athletes come to embody subjectivities such as competence, behavioural compliance and demonstrative effort. Here, the 'good athlete' is positioned closer to the coach and, as a result, both discourse and proximity serve to maintain and reproduce certain aspects of the field. In this way, coaching 'responds' to those who are 'ready' for coaching and privileges them in that sense, while allowing the rest to 'withdraw', having failed to interrupt the process (Brown, 2005). This 'unevenness' was evident among the athletes in Cushion and Jones's (2006) study, with the 'favourites' having a much more positive experience than the 'rejects'.

Fields and capital in coaching

The links between field and capital imply that the value of a particular capital 'hinges on the existence of a game, of a field in which this competency can be employed' (Bourdieu & Wacquant, 1992: 98). Thus, the performers within sports coaching can be seen as striving, more or less successfully, to gain the sufficient volume and appropriate composition of capital to become and remain valued members within the field. This, however, takes time and results in a dynamic between those who hold the capital (often the coach) and those who aspire to it (often the athletes).

According to Hunter (2004), this distinction between individuals is necessary so as to maintain the game. Indeed, evidence would suggest that those engaged in the coaching process within their respective groupings do not face an undifferentiated social space (Cushion, 2010b; Cushion & Jones, 2006; Purdy, *et al.*, 2009). For example, in Purdy *et al.*'s (2009) study of elite rowing, differential treatment was experienced by the athletes who possessed different amounts of physical capital. The treatment of the athletes was also subject to coach-assigned symbolic capital based on the athletes' acceptance of perceived contextual norms: 'They were given symbolic capital by the coaches in return for their willingness to be "connected" to the field. Hence, they were accordingly defined as "good" athletes' (Purdy *et al.*, 2009: 331). Similarly, in work by Cushion and Jones (2006) and Cushion (2010a), the coaches featured were central figures in assigning capital valued by the field; here, the space of 'good player' depended on acceptance and compliance with 'professional ideals' legitimated by the coaches. Relatedly, individuals try 'to safeguard or improve their position [within the field] and to impose the principle of hierarchisation most favourable to their own products' (Bourdieu cited in Wacquant 1989: 40). Such actions were clearly visible in Cushion and Jones's (2006) study, where constant jostling for favoured positions was evident both within and between groups of players and coaches.

In considering coaching as part of a wider field of power, Taylor and Garret (2010) believe the UK government's drive to develop coaching as a 'profession' to be a political act. They argue that this apparently positive development for coaching hides a deliberate attack on the value of symbolic capital linked with the concept of volunteerism, which has been part of British sport for at least 150 years. Taylor and Garret further contend that the governmental interjection can also be regarded as a coordinated attempt to redefine the field of coaching by privileging certain forms of knowledge and regulated practice over more 'organic' and locally inspired others. Therefore, in coaching, new forms of occupational structure and professional knowledge, endorsed and legitimated by the state, are currently challenging existing forms of capital, thereby relegating the latter's currency and status. This illustrates Bourdieu's notion that, within particular fields, types of capital are constantly in a state of struggle to improve their positions in given hierarchies.

Notwithstanding the above examples, there remains a paucity of research examining the nature and structure of the coaching field, and the strategies of actors within it. As such, future ethnographic enquiry which utilises concepts such as capital, field and practice in a variety of settings (e.g., elite, amateur and youth sport) could further our understanding of the complex power-dominated nature of coaching. Indeed, the ethnographic approach advocated by Bourdieu represents a potentially valuable means for exploring how different groups within coaching utilise varying strategies and tactics to obtain and advance their symbolic and cultural capital. Such a method is in keeping with Bourdieu's suggestion that 'it is the field which is primary and must be the focus of the research operations' (Bourdieu & Wacquant, 1992: 107), and that the 'boundaries of the field can only be determined by empirical investigation' (Bourdieu & Wacquant, 1992: 100). We similarly believe that such an enquiry could illuminate how dilemmas in actual coaching situations reflect the actions of competing discourses, creating a 'differentiated sports field'. These dilemmas could revolve around goals (i.e., team versus individual; long term versus short term), hierarchy (i.e., degree of involvement; given roles versus individual creativity), and task structures (i.e., formal versus informal), among others (Jones & Wallace, 2006). In this way, it would be possible to begin to understand how the day-to-day actions and 'solutions' of coaching practice are influenced by the characteristics of the contextual sub-field.

Power difference and reproduction: the coaching process

Bourdieu developed the view that social practice is a central dynamic of social production (Brown, 2005). This means that activities such as coaching are likely to reproduce and legitimise certain orientations of coaches and athletes that gradually stabilise into schemes of disposition or habitus. The coaching process has the power to shape consciousness. Hence, it cannot or should not be considered passive but active in the legitimation of acquired habitus. Thus, coaching, like education, is a product of a particular habitus, which gives rise to 'patterns of thought which organise reality' (Bourdieu, 1977: 194).

In these terms, coaching practice is significant because it contributes to the construction of reality at the most fundamental level of perception. This is what Bourdieu (1998) described as the vision/division of experience, where frames of reference and schemes of expression are conditioned through social reinforcement, between the individual and his or her body (Bourdieu, 1990a). In this context, the development of coaches' practice through repetition becomes deeply embedded within the habitus. Resulting actions are often seen as tacit, with coaches appearing to act intuitively (i.e., the so-called 'art' of coaching). According to Bourdieu, however, practice is learned through such processes.

In coaching, habitus can be traced back to early (or earlier experienced) practices. Embedded within these practices is a series of material and symbolic 'legitimations' around rituals, language and notions of difference. Over time and with constant practice, these turn into intransient dispositions. Thus, from the perspective of practice and habitus, coaches are positioned as key agents in the production of practice as they represent the embodied human link between successfully experienced and internalised past and present practice (Brown, 2005).

Habitus thus disposes actors to behave in certain ways that have legitimacy within the field: the 'correct ways' at the expense of limitless others (Schubert, 2002; Cushion & Jones, 2006). This legitimacy can often obscure power relations, making them unrecognisable to, and misrecognised by, agents (Kim, 2004). Actors' acceptance of these arbitrary dominant values and behavioural schema leads to the development of an imposed system of meaning and symbols that, in turn, is 'perceived as legitimate' (Jenkins, 1992: 104). Bourdieu describes this process as symbolic violence where order and restraint are maintained through indirect cultural mechanisms as opposed to direct, coercive control (Jenkins, 1992). It is a form of intimidation that is not aware of its nature (Bourdieu & Passeron, 1996 [1977]).

In Cushion and Jones's (2006) study, the coaches viewed their authoritarian and sometimes abusive actions as legitimate. They justified their dominating discourse as being in the players' best interests, a specific motivational strategy to improve on-field performances. Similarly, the players did not perceive the coaches' actions as overly discouraging, but instead saw them as part of professional football. A form of symbolic violence was therefore evident. This kept the players 'in their place' 'as they misrecognised their role as unquestioning of authority' (Hunter, 2004: 180). This misrecognition was fed by the players' desire to improve their position in the field, to become professionals. It was also influenced by their perception of the coaches as the 'gate-keepers' to such a future, which overrode any dissatisfaction with the working climate that was established (Cushion & Jones, 2006). In this respect, as Cushion and Jones argue, the complicity of the dominated becomes obvious as an essential element within symbolic violence, which can be exerted only on a person predisposed through the habitus to feel it.

Habitus and coach education

An underlying utility or value of the concept of habitus to coaching, and coach education in particular, is its recognition that coaches have a series of strongly formed competencies and dispositions that serves as a foundation for subsequent practice. Coaches, then, continually reinforce and confirm ways of organising, coaching and assessing, which formalise the vision and division of experience. Without explicitly addressing this habitus, coaching practice will incline towards reproducing the relations that satisfy the logic of practice within the field; that is, without addressing these deep-seated social issues, despite rhetoric to the contrary, current practice is merely reinforced and reproduced.

Because coaches learn predominantly from experience (Gilbert & Trudel, 2001; Cushion *et al.*, 2003, 2010), coaching provides an almost perfect practical apprenticeship for the transference of habitus. It is a model for reproducing dispositions rather than one for change. The interaction that coaches experience with both each other and the cultural context takes place within the confines of power relationships where often the only option is compliance or failure. 'Traditional' coaching is the implicit model that is drawn upon. Hence, coaches are encouraged to watch, listen and copy more experienced coaches, and incorporate dispositional practices into their own coaching (Cushion *et al.*, 2003, 2010). Having capital to draw upon means that a coach has a valued habitus to supply the field. Where the habitus 'correctly' supplies the field it becomes reinforced and further ingrained. The whole coaching process, then, can be viewed as one in which the habitus is systematically refined and reinforced until it fits with the demands of the field.

This is a particularly important issue for coach educators to consider. Especially so when educational interventions focus on coaching philosophies, techniques and methods that are 'new' or 'alien' to coaches, and/or are in conflict with entrenched beliefs regarding how a 'good' coach behaves and what 'good' coaching looks like (Light, 2004; Cushion *et al.*, 2010). Indeed, educators may experience considerable resistance when their initiatives are not only in conflict with individual coaches' embedded long-held beliefs but challenge the values of entire coaching cultures and structures (Cushion *et al.*, 2003; Light, 2004). Efforts to introduce significant changes to existing social practices and power relations may result in coaches experiencing what Bourdieu termed hysteresis: a form of culture shock caused by the disintegration of the ontological security between habitus and habitat (Iellatchitch *et al.*, 2003). As such, research addressing the experiences of coaches and coach educators on this topic could provide valuable insights into the impact and meaning of coach education. This line of enquiry may be particularly relevant in many Western nations where new and 'player-centred' national coach education initiatives, which often contrast with the dominant cultures of coaching in many sports, are in the process of being developed and implemented (e.g., Nelson & Cushion, 2006).

A coach's commentary by Will Kitchen

I am currently employed by the England and Wales Cricket Board as a Coach Development Manager. I also fulfil a number of coaching roles with Warwickshire County Cricket Club on their talent development programme. Bourdieu's exploration of socio-political influences sheds light upon issues that characterise the daily life of coaches, coach educators and coach developers alike. As a coaching practitioner, I have found that there can at times appear to be a 'reality gap' between what I read in coaching research and actual practice. However, Bourdieu's work provides a means of analysing one's coaching practice, the embedded processes, behaviour, underpinning philosophy – everything really. To do this it is crucial for me (and others) to breach the 'discursive gap' between coaching research or writing and what I do by developing a meaningful way of thinking about my own practice. Drawing on my coaching experience, it is a relatively easy task to relate the issues highlighted by Bourdieu and to describe the influence each one has had on my coaching and development. However, what is perhaps more useful and interesting is how, by unpicking some of the key issues raised, it is possible to determine a route for utilising and reflecting upon them as tools to develop and learn.

For me, the concept of habitus, 'the source of most practices', provides a logical beginning for self-examination. In light of my own coaching, if I reflect upon significant others and situations, my upbringing, education and current role, I find it impossible to determine how and where these influences have impacted upon how I behave as a coach and how I frame my coaching; importantly, what I do know is that they all have. While habitus is largely tacit, comprising the very nature of conduct and practice, it becomes undeniably topical when I consider the impact of the environment and culture created for athletes. Operating within a talent development system, it is easy to highlight what is at stake for the players, a potential route to a professional cricket career. My challenge is to identify, through my coaching, what I believe best prepares the players for that environment, and what culture exists as a result.

Beyond that, an appreciation of habitus is also useful when considering how to approach the different issues presented by players' dispositions. Cricket attracts an ethnically diverse range of players. The sport's popularity on the Asian sub-continent in particular means its playing population will often contradict the assumption that those in a similar role, in this instance players, share similar habitus. For a coach, understanding this becomes a useful way of thinking about how best to react to individual players. Assuming habitus is subconsciously embedded, then it may be relevant to consider how it can influence a player and his or her actions. In my experience it is all too easy to dismiss player behaviour as 'inappropriate' or 'unwanted', when perhaps the actions are coming from an unconscious habitus. Coaches should consider very carefully the social structure and processes that have contributed to their players' habitus. This, in turn, should involve critical thought about the nature of the environment and practice they create for their players, based on the understanding that it too will contribute to their players' behaviour and practice.

Logical extensions of this are the questions raised about coaching through the issues of 'field' and 'capital'. There can be no question for anybody involved in coaching that it is a messy, complex practice. The phrase 'best-laid plans' is heard frequently in coaching, as my Under-15 squad will testify, having recently scaled an eight-foot gate in order to train at a major international sports venue! Accepting the complexity is one thing; catering for it and being able to develop players in spite of it can be quite another. So where does that leave a practitioner?

I have considered the 'field' as the context within which I work. This includes the club, institution or body within which practice is situated. This also includes the nature or domain of coaching: for example, participation with young children, talent development with aspiring professionals or working with a national team. Identifying my field(s) is useful, but even more so is understanding the impact of the field and how this frames my practice and influences what I do. The approach a club or organisation adopts with regard to player development, and what comprises the 'norm' for that club, frames and influences the way in which a coach is able to practise. This is often demonstrated by the means by which a club recruits its coaching staff (and players). I have often found that a coach's capital or the capital 'lent' to others by those with 'power' in a club tends to be biased towards those who simply replicate or mirror their own beliefs, traditions or values.

This raises a number of issues. What is valued as capital? How is this attributed to coaches? What is this based on? How is capital valued? How is this determined, and attributed to coaches and players? What cycle does this create with those individuals involved in pursuing that capital? And, finally, how does it impact on coaching? No doubt coaches and coaching as a whole should question the status and necessity of capital within coaching contexts. In my experience, values and traditions are held and upheld by those with the most power. However, the credibility and usefulness of those values and traditions should be subject to intense (self-)reflective discourse for those involved in coaching. This would help to mediate and determine the context that is most productive for players and coaches alike.

By contextualising Bourdieu's thinking, I can critically evaluate the meaning it holds for my work. I believe it calls for groups of coaches, clubs and bodies to engage in reflective discourse. I believe this examination is an absolute necessity in order for coaches to determine how they can be most useful for their players. Needless to say, this does not mean a 'tear it up and start again' approach; more a means of determining how best to evolve based on a clear examination and appreciation of the socio-political issues which undoubtedly influence coaching practice for everybody involved.

Conclusion

The field of coaching often doubles as a workplace. Hence, it is racked with competing egos, hierarchies, constraints and opportunities, making it, in its own right, a complex social system (Cushion & Jones, 2006; Potrac *et al.*, 2006). It is important to recognise that the sporting environment is more than a place for learning sport skills or somewhere that can be captured to any degree through a series of linear blocks and arrows (Cushion *et al.*, 2006; Jones & Wallace, 2005). This suggests a need to investigate the multifaceted relationship between coach, athlete and environment in order to grasp more fully the complexity of the process(es) involved (Cushion, 2007; Potrac *et al.*, 2000; Jones *et al.*, 2002). It is here we think that Bourdieu can really help.

The aim of this chapter was to introduce the work of Bourdieu, to trigger discussion and debate about power and reproductive practice in coaching. Explanatory and seemingly objective representations are as subjective and politically motivated as any, as they obscure the idea that the symbolic systems of coaching and coaching practice are social products that constitute social relations. Essentially, by transforming representation (i.e., how coaching is portrayed and conceptualised) we start to ask different questions around issues of socio-political importance rather than about simple empirical objects (Everett, 2002). Importantly, coaching and coach education cannot be viewed as neutral, nor are they devoid of political content. On the contrary, they are, as has been illustrated here, often the very expression of it (Swartz, 1997).

5 Arlie Russell Hochschild: The managed heart, feeling rules, and emotional labour

Coaching as an emotional endeavour

Paul Potrac with Phil Marshall

Arlie Russell Hochschild: a short biography

Arlie Russell Hochschild was born in Boston, Massachusetts in 1940. After finishing her undergraduate degree in international relations at Swarthmore College, she went on to undertake postgraduate work in sociology at the University of California, Berkeley. Having successfully completed her doctoral studies, Hochschild was appointed as a member of the faculty. She was to spend her entire academic career at Berkeley until she retired in 2006.

Hochschild was a prolific researcher and is most known for her accounts addressing the binds, intimacy and emotions that are features of social life (Dillon, 2010; Williams, 2008). This is perhaps best illustrated in her *The managed heart: Commercialization of human feeling* (2000 [1983]), *The second shift: Working parents and the revolution at home* (with A. Machung; 2003 [1989]), *The time bind: When work becomes home and home becomes work* (1997) and *The commercialization of intimate life: Notes from home and work* (2003). She has received honorary doctorates from Swarthmore College, the University of Oslo and Aalborg University, and a lifetime achievement award from the American Sociological Association, among other honours.

Her interest in the emotional nature of social life stemmed from her fascination with the work of her parents, who were employed as diplomats in the US Foreign Service. In particular, she was intrigued by how, after entertaining foreign dignitaries, her mother and father would interpret 'the tight smile of the Bulgarian emissary, the averted glance of the Chinese consul, and the prolonged handshake of the French economic officer' (Hochschild, 2003: ix). Such experiences led her to engage in an academic career where she focused on the relationship between the emotions that an individual really felt and those that are acted out for the benefit of other people (Theodosius, 2008; Williams, 2008). She is perhaps best known for her detailed study of the everyday realities of flight attendants in the commercial airline industry (Hochschild, 2000 [1983]), from which she developed the concept of 'emotional labour'. Her work not only provided a significant foundation for the rise of the sociology of emotions as a 'bona fide' area of enquiry, but continues to underpin and influence contemporary explorations of the emotional nature of practice in health (e.g., Theodosius, 2008), management (e.g., Brook, 2009) and education (e.g., Isenbarger & Zembylas, 2006).

Introduction

The purpose of this chapter is to explore how Hochschild's work on 'emotional labour' could be used to develop our critical understanding of sports coaching. Like many of the other theorists in this book, Hochschild's writing did not directly address coaches, athletes or indeed sport in general. However, her focus on the relationship between the emotions a person feels, the emotions he or she displays for the benefit of others, and the social context within which such emotions are manifest can provide a fertile sensitising framework for scholars of coaching, coach educators and practising coaches alike (Theodosius, 2008). Indeed, we believe that her work on emotional labour and management can help us to chart the complexities, nuances and realities of coaching more adequately than has been achieved to date.

In terms of structure, the chapter initially focuses on introducing Hochschild's work as presented through her text *The managed heart* (2000 [1983]). In particular, following some brief information related to her motivations and influences for engaging in such enquiry, we provide some background definitions and examples related to her notions of emotion management, feeling rules, surface and deep acting, emotional labour and the inauthenticity of the self. Our attention then shifts to offering suggestions as to how these concepts could be productively related to our understandings of sports coaching. Finally, a commentary is provided by a practising coach, Phil Marshall, regarding the value of Hochschild's thinking for his coaching practice.

The managed heart: commercialization of human feeling

Perhaps Hochschild's most insightful work addressing the interrelationship between social interaction and emotion is provided in *The managed heart* (2000 [1983]). Here, Hochschild described how her understandings of social life were influenced by, and sought to build upon, the classic work of C. Wright Mills and Erving Goffman. With regard to the former, she alluded to how she became excited by his work on 'The great salesroom' (Wright Mills, 1956), in which he argued that those involved in the selling of goods and/or services are required to sell their personalities (Hochschild, 2000 [1983]: ix). Wright Mills suggested that this often self-estranging process is one that is increasingly common among workers in advanced capitalist societies. However, for Hochschild, this did not fully address the active emotional labour involved in the 'selling', arguing that in order to sell a personality, an individual needed to do more than just have one. She eloquently noted that, 'simply having personality does not make one a diplomat, any more than having muscles makes one an athlete' (Hochschild, 2000 [1983]: ix). The search to address this issue led her to consider the dramaturgical work of Erving Goffman, whom Hochschild admitted being 'indebted [to] for his keen sense of how we try to control our appearance even as we unconsciously observe rules about how we ought to appear to others' (Hochschild, 2000 [1983]: x). Stimulating as she found Goffman's treatise on social life, Hochschild considered that this work failed substantively to address how a person acts on, or stops acting on, feeling, as well as if and how a social actor may stop feeling (Hochschild, 2000 [1983]).

For Hochschild, then, *The managed heart* became her forum for addressing a number of pressing issues that remained largely unexplored in the sociological literature. Her work sought to address a number of burning questions related to how emotion may 'function as a messenger from the self, an agent that gives us an instant report on the connection between what we are seeing and what we had expected to see, and tells us what we feel ready to do about it' (Hochschild, 2000 [1983]: x). She also sought to investigate how, if at all, the emotional nature of work may be 'one part of a distinctly patterned yet invisible emotion system – a system composed of individual acts of "emotion work", social "feeling rules", and a great variety of exchanges between people in private and public life' (Hochschild, 2000 [1983]: x). Her quest was to 'understand the general emotional language of which diplomats speak only one dialect' (Hochschild, 2000 [1983]: ix–x).

She explored these issues in her work with flight attendants (and bill collectors) in the United States. As she engaged in exploring the realities of these individuals' daily working lives, she began to appreciate the challenges they faced when attempting to maintain a sense of self in their labour. Specifically, she described how they engaged in acts of 'circumventing the feeling rules of work, how they limit their emotional offerings to surface displays of the "right" feeling, but suffer from a sense of being "false" or mechanical' (Hochschild, 2000 [1983]). She subsequently concluded 'that the more deeply a commercial system carves into the private emotional "gift exchange", the more the receivers and givers alike take up the extra work of discounting what is impersonal in order to accept what is not' (Hochschild, 2000 [1983]: x). The insights gleaned from this project have left a lasting legacy not only theoretically but practically, at a personal level. As Hochschild noted, it has influenced how she interprets the smiles encountered in her daily life.

Hochschild's conceptual vocabulary

The purpose of this section is to introduce the key conceptual vocabulary included in Hochschild's (2000 [1983]) work. Specifically, it provides some definitions and everyday examples relating to her notions of emotion management, feeling rules, surface and deep acting, emotional labour and the inauthenticity of the self.

Emotion management

According to Hochschild (2000 [1983]: 7), emotion management refers to the 'management of feeling to create a publicly observable facial and bodily display'. In the context of everyday life, it could be suggested that social actors learn to do this as a consequence of the various socialisation experiences to which they are subjected (Theodosius, 2008). For example, when my [Potrac's] daughter receives an unwanted gift from a family friend, she may show pleasure and gratitude to him as the person presenting the gift rather than ingratitude, disappointment or anger. Such a response could, in part, have been influenced by my wife and myself, who had previously explained to her that it is necessary to control one's true feelings and, instead, express the emotions that are expected to be seen in this situation. The key point to note here is that such emotion management requires emotion work. That is, it is an action that necessitates effort and practice (Theodosius, 2008).

Hochschild's (2000 [1983]) work on emotion management also distinguishes between the private and public spheres of social life. Similar to Goffman's notions of 'front stage' and 'back stage' (e.g., Goffman, 1959), she argued that emotion work takes place in our private lives and homes. In contrast, 'emotional labour' takes place at work, where it is a commodity that is sold for a wage (Theodosius, 2008). However, the clear-cut distinction between our private and public lives has been the subject of increasing challenge in the literature (e.g., Wouters, 1989a, 1989b, 1991). Indeed, in the example of our daughter receiving an unwanted gift, it could be suggested that 'front stage' and 'back stage' often coexist in the private realm. According to Theodosius (2008: 15), the key point to recognise here is that 'the distinction is really one of difference of self, between what individuals consider belongs to them, representing their "real" selves, and what is socially acceptable for public consumption'.

Feeling rules

Hochschild (2000 [1983]) suggested feeling rules not only represent what emotions people should demonstrate, but the degree to which that expression is in keeping with their respective social role. Here, she described how:

> Acts of emotion management are not only simple private acts; they are used in exchanges under the guidance of feeling rules. Feeling rules are standards used in emotional conversation to determine what is rightly owed in the currency of feeling. Through them, we tell what is 'due' in each relation, each role. We pay tribute to each other in the currency of managing the act. In interaction, we pay, overpay, underpay, play with paying, acknowledge our due, pretend to pay, or acknowledge what is emotionally due to another person.
>
> (Hochschild, 2000 [1983]: 18)

An example of these feeling rules in action can again be understood in relation to the previous example of our child receiving the unwanted gift. Here, as parents, we tell our daughter that our friend has expended some time, money and emotional energy in obtaining the gift. In return, therefore, she is required to demonstrate pleasure and gratitude in receiving the gift (Theodosius, 2008). It is through feeling rules that individuals learn to show and hide particular feelings as they are connected to their relationships with other people. Theodosius (2008) suggested that feeling rules are not only the means by which an individual comes to make sense of the emotions that they actually feel but how they come to know which emotions they should express in a social encounter, and to what degree.

Surface acting and deep acting

Similar to the theorising of Goffman (1959), Hochschild (2000 [1983]) suggested that, as social beings, we engage in a certain amount of acting. In this regard, she identified two levels, or types, of acting that we employ during social interaction. First, she identified what she labelled 'surface acting'. This is acting in relation to our body language, 'the put on sneer, the posed shrug, the controlled sigh' (Hochschild, 2000 [1983]: 35). She argued that such acts are used to deceive others in terms of how we are really feeling without deceiving ourselves. That is, we know we are pretending (Theodosius, 2008): for example, when, in the company of friends, an individual laughs out loud at a joke that they do not really find particularly funny. In this situation, the individual uses facial and body gestures in a particular way, in order to be seen to be entering into the spirit of enjoyment and fun (Theodosius, 2008).

In contrast to 'surface acting', 'deep acting' is the result of an individual working on his or her feelings through 'conscious mental work' to the extent that he or she really believes in the emotions that are being expressed (Hochschild, 2000 [1983]: 36). In drawing upon the work of the method actor and theatre director Constantin Stanislavski, Hochschild argued that an individual's public display 'is a natural result of working on the feeling; the actor does not try to *seem* happy or sad but rather expresses spontaneously a real feeling that is self-induced' (Hochschild, 2000 [1983]: 35). Hochschild suggested that there are two ways in which an individual can engage in deep acting. The first is through exhortations, which can be understood as the efforts that people make to feel about having feelings. By way of an example, Hochschild asked students to describe an everyday event in which they experienced a deep emotion. Specifically, she recorded that:

> the responses were sprinkled with such phrases as 'I psyched myself up', 'I squashed my anger down', 'I tried hard not to feel disappointed', 'I forced myself to have a good time', 'I mustered up some gratitude', 'I put a damper on my love for her', 'I snapped my out of depression'.
>
> (Hochschild, 2000 [1983]: 39)

Hochschild noted here how such responses evidenced acts of will among the individuals involved, as they tried to suppress or allow a change in feeling in order to consider or sense what was expected in a particular situation or setting.

In addition to exhortations, Hochschild (2000 [1983]) suggested that deep acting can occur as the result of an individual training his or her memory and imagination. She argued that a person can use their memory and imagination so effectively that it becomes possible for them to believe the feelings that they are experiencing. In such situations, an individual may forget, or be unaware of, the extent to which they had worked on themselves to create those feelings (Theodosius, 2008). Once again, this form of deep acting could be understood in relation to the example of my daughter receiving an unwanted gift. Here, we, as parents, could say to her, 'Do you remember how excited you were when you made that lovely Easter card for us, and how much effort you put into making it as well as you possibly could? Can you remember how you felt when we were so pleased with it? I expect that's how our friend felt when he brought that gift for you.' Through such interaction, the child is asked to transfer memories of her emotions to the current situation. In this way, she comes to produce the proper emotional response (Theodosius, 2008).

Emotional labour

The central thesis of Hochschild's *The managed heart* is that the workplace exploits our private emotion work for commercial purposes. She defined such emotional engagement as:

> Labour that requires one to induce or suppress feeling in order to sustain the outward countenance that produces the proper state of mind in others [such as] the sense of being cared for in a convivial and safe place. This kind of labour calls for communication of mind and feeling, and it sometimes draws on a source of self that we honour as deep and integral to our individuality . . . Emotional labour is sold for a wage and, therefore, has exchange value.
>
> (Hochschild, 2000 [1983]: 7)

Her conceptualisation of emotional labour was the result of an ethnographic study based predominantly on the working practices of flight attendants employed by an American airline. The findings provided some fascinating insights into how employees were carefully recruited and trained to sell the company through a heavily managed and prescribed image of 'Southern charm' and 'hospitality'. Hochschild's work highlighted how, during the recruitment phase, the company set out to identify and select candidates who could 'convey a spirit of enthusiasm [and] project a warm personality' (Hochschild, 2000 [1983]: 97). Following the selection process, Hochschild charted how the attendants were instructed to act out the idea of Southern hospitality when welcoming passengers on to the plane, to present a warm smile when in the presence of passengers, and to recognise that the passenger is always right. For example, she described how:

> The trainees, it seemed to me, were also chosen for their ability to take stage directions about how to 'project' an image. They were selected for being able to act well – that is, without showing the effort involved. They had to be able to appear at home on the stage . . . they were constantly reminded that their own job security and the company's profit rode on a smiling face . . . There

were many direct appeals to smile: 'Really work on your smiles.' 'Your smile is the biggest asset – use it.'

(Hochschild, 2000 [1983]: 98)

Significantly, then, Hochschild's (2000 [1983]) work underscored how the flight attendants were required, and taught, to manage their emotions so that they could maintain a happy, smiling public exterior for the benefit of the passengers, something that was monitored throughout the training programme. Indeed, while 'the airline passenger may choose not to smile . . . the flight attendant is obliged to not only smile but also to try to work up some warmth behind it' (Hochschild, 2000 [1983]: 19). Through such practices, Hochschild argued that the flight attendants' private emotion work was transmuted into emotional labour. That is, the warm and friendly service provided or demonstrated by the flight attendants was used to get 'bums on seats', and to generate greater profits for the airline company (Theodosius, 2008). She subsequently affirmed that organisations and corporations train their workers to take an instrumental view towards their emotions, noting that:

> [Acting] in a commercial setting, unlike acting in a dramatic, private, or therapeutic context, makes one's face and feelings take on the properties of a resource. But it is not a resource to be used for the purposes of art, as in drama, or for the purposes of self-discovery, as in therapy, or for the pursuit of fulfilment, as in everyday life. It is a resource to be used to make money.
>
> (Hochschild, 2000 [1983]: 55)

Inauthenticity of self

For Hochschild (2000 [1983]), a number of issues and problems can occur when an organisation or company requires individuals to engage in emotional labour. She suggested that while the motivation for emotional labour is frequently one of profit, it also requires individuals to draw on their sense of self. Here, she asserted that, when employees are required to engage in emotional labour, they may experience a subversion of their true selves. For example, the flight attendants were taught that they were wrong to feel angry about a difficult passenger and should, instead, look at an issue from the passenger's perspective. In such scenarios, the flight attendants were instructed that their own feelings should be denied, as they were not considered to be appropriate or justifiable in these circumstances (Theodosius, 2008). Ultimately, the outcome of such practices can be a sense of alienation, as 'the worker may lose touch with her true feelings as in burnout, or she may have to struggle with the company interpretation of what they mean' (Hochschild, 2000 [1983]: 197).

This situation was exacerbated when the airline company expanded, resulting in longer flights, larger aircrafts and a significant increase in passenger numbers. As a consequence of such changes, the flight attendants found themselves with little time to engage with the passengers or carry out the requisite emotional labour. Hochschild (2000 [1983]) described how this change impacted upon the flight attendants in three different ways. First, because some of the attendants were so successful with their deep acting, they overidentified with their work. Their own selves had thus become inextricable from the image that the company portrayed. When expansion in flights and passenger numbers took place, these flight attendants were more vulnerable to stress and burnout. Second, while some flight attendants were successful in terms of separating their real selves from their working role, they subsequently blamed themselves for being able only to surface act. They felt deficient, insecure and alienated from their work. Third, another group of flight attendants not only distinguished themselves from the act of emotional labour, but became estranged from the acting itself. In this regard, they 'became cynical and alienated from their sense of self as well as from their work' (Theodosius, 2008: 23). It is hardly surprising that Hochschild's conclusion was that the commodification of emotional labour can ultimately alienate workers, and lead to the loss of an individual's sense of self and an inauthentic expression of emotion (Dillon, 2010; Theodosius, 2008; Williams, 2008).

Towards an emotional understanding of coaching

As indicated in the introduction to this chapter, Hochschild did not write directly about 'emotion management' and 'emotional labour' in sports coaching. However, she suggested that her work can apply to other jobs when they meet the following criteria:

> First, they require face-to-face or voice-to-voice contact with the public. Second, they require the worker to produce an emotional state in another person – gratitude or fear for example. Third, they allow the employer, through training and supervision, to exercise a degree of control over the emotional activities of employees.
>
> (Hochschild, 2000 [1983]: 29)

Interestingly, and somewhat surprisingly, given these criteria, her work has yet to be applied to coaching. Nevertheless, we believe that Hochschild's insights into the emotional nature of practice can provide some valuable analytical tools for supporting efforts to develop a more critical understanding of the social nature of coaching. In addition to providing us with a potentially refreshing viewpoint from which to theorise coaching practice, the application of her work could support the development of coach education provision that more adequately reflects the emotional realities of the job.

While the value of putting the person back into the study of coaching has been increasingly voiced (e.g., Cushion & Jones, 2006; Jones, 2009a; Potrac & Jones, 2009a; Purdy *et al.*, 2008), there remains a paucity of research addressing the emotional nature of practice for both coaches and athletes. Indeed, save for a few notable examples (e.g., Jones, 2006a, 2009a; Jones *et al.*, 2005; Purdy *et al.*, 2008; Roderick, 2006), it has been surprising that the emotional nature of a coach's and an athlete's work has been largely ignored. Our accounts of coaching have tended to be 'emotionally anorexic', with coaches and athletes presented as calculated, dispassionate and rational beings (Fineman, 1993; Hargreaves, 2005). However, in light of the recent contentions regarding the messy nature of coaching (e.g., Jones & Wallace, 2005; Jones 2006a; Jones *et al.*, 2004; Potrac *et al.*, 2002; Potrac & Jones, 2009a), coaches and athletes no doubt experience a variety of strong emotions as they strive to navigate the challenges and opportunities of their dynamic sporting worlds. Given the interactive and pedagogical nature of coaching (Jones *et al.*, 2004; Jones, 2006a), it could be argued that it is impossible for coaches and athletes to 'separate feeling from perception [and] affectivity from judgement', as coaching involves 'intensive personal interactions' (Nias, 1996: 294, 296) and an investment of the self in practice (Jones *et al.*, 2004). Similarly, it has also been contended that emotions are indispensable to rational decision-making in pedagogical activities in terms of narrowing the assortment of potential actions into a manageable range (Damasio, 1994; Hargreaves, 2005; Sacks, 1995). This was certainly evidenced in Jones's (2006a, 2009a) auto-ethnographies on coaching practice, which reinforced Hargreaves's (2005: 280) contention that 'you can't judge if you can't feel'. Unfortunately, however, emotions within coaching have, in the main, been treated as little more than another variable that coaches (and athletes) need to manage appropriately so that they can focus on the 'really important' technical and cognitive components of their role (Hargreaves, 1998).

From an empirical perspective, then, Hochschild's notions of emotion management, emotional labour, surface and deep acting and the inauthenticity of the self could be utilised to explore the emotional struggles of coaches and athletes. They could help us uncover and interpret the emotions that coaches and athletes experience, and how these actors fake, enhance, modify or suppress their emotional expressions and understandings in order to achieve organisational goals (Isenbarger & Zembylas, 2006). Such work could also highlight the consequences of such emotional labour in terms of how coaches and athletes come to understand their respective selves and their actions, and how this may impact upon their continued engagement in coaching and sport. In this way, it becomes possible to examine issues such as cynicism, self-esteem management and burnout from a deeper, personal perspective (Isenbarger & Zembylas, 2006). Hochschild's (2000 [1983]) work could additionally help explore the various 'feeling rules' that coaches and athletes learn during their socialisation experiences in the field and through formal coach education provision. Such a perspective locates coaches' emotions and emotional understanding not simply as physiological and psychological attributes but as products of the socio-political nature of the interactions that take place within the coaching context (Zembylas, 2005). (These are some of the issues explored by Phil Marshall later.)

A further way in which Hochschild's (2000 [1983]) work could inform our research endeavours in sports coaching invovles using her concept of emotional labour in examining the micro-level implementation of an 'athlete-centred' approach to coaching practice. The notion of athlete-centred coaching has gained huge popularity in the discourse of coaching and coach education. However, similar to the notion of 'caring' in educational literature (Isenbarger & Zembylas, 2006), our current understanding of athlete-centred activity has rarely gone beyond assuming a functional link between it and good coaching, and preconceived conceptions associating athlete-centredness with being 'nurturing, supportive, nice, inclusive, responsive and kind' (Goldstein, 2002: 2). Not only has there been a failure to underpin such rhetoric with a supporting theory, but the paucity of empirical enquiry that considers the emotional labour that may occur when coaches strive to implement such ideals in practice further undermines the notion as a truly practical one. For example, in the quest to express the emotions that are deemed socially acceptable within an athlete-centred approach, a coach may have to modify, induce, neutralise, inhibit and control a variety of positive and negative emotions, and act in ways that may be at odds with his or her personality. This needs to be addressed. Similar issues in relation to the actions of community coaches who are required to deliver social policy outcomes through sport (e.g., developing healthy and good citizens, promoting social integration) when working with a diverse range of individuals (e.g., disaffected youth, the unemployed) could also be researched to give the concept a stronger grounding. Hochschild's work could equally be applied to explore the emotional labour experienced by coach educators in the delivery and assessment of coach education certification and development programmes. Indeed, we believe that there are many areas of coaching practice and education that would fruitfully benefit from Hochschild's theorisations.

While we clearly recognise the value of Hochschild's thinking in terms of how it can help us examine and better understand coaching, it is important to acknowledge that her work has been subject to criticism. For instance, it has been criticised in relation to overestimating 'the degree of managerial ownership and control of workers' emotions' (Brook, 2009: 532), the dichotomisation of the distinction between the 'private self' and the commodified 'public self', and her emphasis on the negative aspects of emotional labour (e.g., Bolton, 2005; Isenbarger & Zembylas, 2006; Lynch, 2007; Simpson, 2007). With regard to the latter, it has been argued that Hochschild ignores the possibility that individuals, such as coaches, may view emotional labour as a rewarding, fun and exciting part of the job. Indeed, some coaches may be gratified by the emotional labour demanded in and by the job, especially if they consider it their role to provide opportunities to improve the performances, experiences and lives of athletes (Isenbarger & Zembylas, 2006). In this sense, emotional labour does not necessarily have to be detrimental or harmful. Despite such judgements, though, even her critics have recognised that Hochschild's work provides the 'greatest contribution to advancing an understanding of emotion in organisations' (Bolton, 2005: 48). As such, either in its own right or particularly when used in conjunction with alternative contemporary theorisations of emotions in social life (e.g., Bolton, 2005; Theodosius, 2008; Zembylas, 2005), Hochschild has much to offer coaching scholars, coach educators and coaches as we strive to come to terms with the emotional nature of coaching.

A coach's commentary by Phil Marshall

I am an athletics and strength-conditioning coach. I've been coaching track and field athletics for over fifteen years, and working as a strength conditioner for almost ten years. I currently coach a small group of both able-bodied and disabled track athletes, and work as a conditioner for British Fencing's National Academy and the Talented Athlete Scholarship Scheme at the University of Hull.

Before writing this piece, Hochschild's concepts of emotions and emotional labour were completely new to me. However, their relevance to the coaching environment made immediate sense. I have always been acutely aware of the need to put on a performance as a coach, to act out a role, based on a number of different factors. These include the needs of the athlete, the expectations of parents and the requirements of the club or organisation. The application of the concepts (mentioned in the chapter) offer a new perspective from which to view my own coaching practice. They help to explain some of the inherent emotions involved in the real world of coaching. These are emotions that I've experienced as a coach but haven't been able to articulate fully.

Hochschild suggests a number of ideas which lend themselves to the analysis of coaching practice. For example, the difference between our public and private spheres and the images we portray in those spheres are amplified in a coaching setting. In many ways, the coach becomes the focus of attention for not just the athletes but parents, officials and even, to some extent, onlookers. Hochschild's concept of emotion management has real significance here. As a coach, I am expected to have answers to the questions asked of me by everyone; I am expected to present myself professionally, to say and do the right things, to make the right decisions. In many cases, all of this is done under the watchful eye of those around you. Not all of those who observe your coaching are supportive. I am often aware of additional pressures placed on me as a coach by other coaches who may be critical of my methods or who would be only too pleased to see me fail. All of this brings with it additional pressure, pressure to manage my emotions and not to show what I am really feeling. These are emotions that all coaches will experience at some point in their careers: anger, boredom, frustration, disappointment. However, we're trained to hide these feelings and, in many cases, don't even fully acknowledge them anyway.

Much of what I do publicly is governed by what Hochschild calls feeling rules. These rules are learned through our socialisation as coaches. For me, this socialisation took the form of coach education, with my course tutors and supporting literature telling me not just how to behave and what emotions I could express, but even influencing my personal appearance and the clothes I wear when taking a training session. Being mentored by and working alongside other coaches further contributed to this socialisation process. I have been coaching for fifteen years now and as a result I've been exposed to a lot of learned behaviour and to the feeling rules of the coaching environment: I must be positive, I mustn't show my disappointment, I must be supportive. In many cases, this makes it difficult to separate my own emotions from those that I have learned over a period of years. The concepts of deep and surface acting are also things I can identify with. Deep acting is something I do in my day-to-day role. It has become difficult at times to separate the learned behaviours I've described from my own emotions in this day-to-day role. Surface acting is something I engage in much more consciously. When working with new athletes or those that I'm not that familiar with, particularly if they compete at a higher level, I've become more aware of the need to surface act. To some extent, this is an exercise in impression management, trying to give the right impression and ensure the athletes are confident in me as a coach. Often this performance conceals nerves or uncertainty when working in an unfamiliar environment, with unfamiliar people. The experience is usually very emotionally draining for me as a coach.

All of this equates to what Hochschild refers to as emotional labour. The coaching work I am doing has commercial and professional value. I am trying to give the right impression and to do the right thing through my coaching. My coaching becomes a commodity which I want the athletes I work with to buy into. To some extent this also leads to an inauthenticity of self. For example, when working with larger groups of athletes, I am aware of what I should be doing, of the level of service I should be providing. However, working with large numbers of athletes inevitably affects the quality of the interaction between athlete and coach, and the quality of the feedback I'm able to provide. It often leaves me feeling unsatisfied with my work and the standards I'm achieving.

To some extent this also applies to my day-to-day coaching. Even though numbers are much smaller, the pressures of everyday life mean that I struggle to provide the level of support I would ultimately aspire to. We're taught through experience and coach education that we should always have session plans in place, that our planning should always be up to date, and that we should set time aside to reflect on our practice and continually make improvements. I've always found it difficult to do this. Coaching isn't my day job, it doesn't pay the bills and, therefore, often comes second to more important aspects of life, like work and my family. At times, this does make me feel what Hochschild describes as deficient and insincere in my work; as though I'm not doing my job as effectively as I should, and that I'm letting down the athletes.

I become even more aware of this when dealing with disappointment. If one of the athletes I coach doesn't achieve their goals or experiences competitive disappointment, I inevitably begin to analyse the work we've done and the support I've provided. Have I done enough? What could I have done better? What if we'd tried this instead? All the time, emotion management is at work. I have to be supportive, to try to provide answers to the questions asked of me, and to put a positive spin on things. This often means ignoring my own feelings of dis-appointment or frustration. Engaging with Hochschild's writing has made me much more aware of the emotional cost of coaching. It has raised awareness of aspects of my work that I didn't previously consider. Much of what I do as a coach is almost subconscious. I can now see that, in fact, my actions have been learned over a period of years.

Overall, I feel that the emotional labour I invest in my coaching offers many positives. I coach through choice, and have done so for many years, because I enjoy it. While coaching does come with an emotional cost, it is also a hugely rewarding experience. By engaging in the emotional labour of coaching, I am able to support athletes more effectively, to help them develop and to achieve their goals and competitive ambitions. The reward is in seeing this happen, in watching those you work with enjoy their training, growing in confidence and ability. For many of the athletes I work with, their involvement in sport is the most important part of their lives. They desperately want to succeed. This brings with it a high emotional cost to the coach, in managing the emotions and expectations of the athlete. However, this also brings with it a huge feeling of satisfaction in a job well done when they do achieve.

Conclusion

The purpose of this chapter was twofold. On one level, it sought to provide an introduction to Hochschild's (2000 [1983]) work – *The managed heart*. In this respect, we believe her work helps us to recognise that 'emotions matter, and they matter not only in the domestic sphere but in the workplace – they are an essential, and rationally instrumental, part of the commodities produced and sold in our (ever-expanding) service economy' (Dillon 2010: 343). Similarly, Theodosius (2008: 26) has suggested that 'not only does she successfully identify and define the significance of emotional life, but also she shows how emotion can be shaped, even created (through inducing and exhorting) for social purposes'. The chapter also aimed to consider the relevance of her work for developing our critical understanding of coaching. Perhaps the most important lesson that we have taken from Hochschild's thinking in this regard is the need to recognise that the coaching community has much to gain from engaging with the inherently emotional nature of coaching practice. For example, her sensitising framework may help us to uncover and consider the self-alienation that can occur in coaching at all levels of sport, an issue that currently receives little acknowledgement in our theoretical and/or practical endeavours. Indeed, we would argue more generally that the challenges, tensions and dilemmas faced by coaches (and athletes) are not just cognitive or social in nature, but are emotional phenomena and need to be understood as such. Consequently, we firmly believe that it is time for researchers and educators to explore and construct representations of coaching that are rich in emotion.

6 Anthony Giddens: Acknowledging structure and individuality within coaching

Laura Purdy with Stephen Aboud

Anthony Giddens: a short biography

Anthony Giddens was born in London in 1938. He completed a bachelor's degree at the University of Hull, a master's degree at the London School of Economics, and a Ph.D. at the University of Cambridge. His early academic career took him from the University of Leicester, to Simon Fraser University (Canada), to the University of California at Santa Barbara. In 1985, he became Professor of Sociology at the University of Cambridge, where he worked for twelve years. In 1997, he was appointed Director of the London School of Economics, a position he held till 2003. In 2004, he was made a member of the House of Lords. In addition to his work in academia, Giddens has had a considerable impact within politics. With his advice being sought by political leaders from four continents, he is best known for his involvement in the evolution of Tony Blair's New Labour Party. He helped to popularise the political philosophy of the Third Way.

Giddens's work covers a range of topics but the most notable are his structuration theory, his thinking on globalisation and his Third Way political philosophy. While Giddens has published over forty books, this chapter draws on his earlier works: namely, *Central problems in social theory: Action, structure and contradiction in social analysis* (1979) and *The constitution of society* (1984). These two books focus on Giddens's theory of structuration. Structuration conceptualises the relationship between the individual (agent) and social institutions (structures) by considering structures as both the medium and the outcome of a person's actions. Here, 'the day-to-day activity of social actors draws upon and reproduces structural features of wider social systems' (Giddens, 1984: 24). While his most recent work has not been closely related to sport, his master's thesis focused on the development of sport in England in the nineteenth century. On a more personal level, Giddens is an avid supporter of his local football team, Tottenham Hotspur (McMann, 2007).

Introduction

This chapter draws upon Anthony Giddens's theory of structuration as a 'sensitising lens' through which we can better understand sports coaching.

Structuration theory is appealing because it provides an explanation of how social activity is produced and reproduced. Here, production is concerned with how social life becomes practised, while reproduction relates to how activity provides continuity and patterns in social life (Layder, 2006). Such a view of the combination of social production and reproduction contrasts with traditional theory. For example, symbolic interactionists have concentrated on the human actor as a centre of meaning, and have tended to neglect the influence of institutions. Structuration also contrasts with macro-sociologists' view of the individual solely as a product of the constraining influences of social structure, thereby disregarding the role of agency. Rather than viewing structure and agency as two independent phenomena, Giddens (1984) proposed the two as a duality, suggesting that human beings (agents/actors) create meanings and social reality from within social settings (structures) – a process termed the 'duality of structure'. In this case, structural properties consist of the rules and resources that people use in their daily interaction. These rules and resources mediate human action while, at the same time, being reaffirmed through their usage (Orlikowski, 1992). Basically, structuration marked an attempt to understand how social competencies work in what might be called the social unconscious (Lemert, 1997). According to Giddens (1979), structuration always presumes the duality of structure. In this way, all social action involves the existence of structure while, at the same time, structure presumes action. This is because structure depends on the regularities of human behaviour (Delanty, 1999). By treating structure and agency as a duality, Giddens (1984) acknowledged the enabling and constraining effects of social structure, and how individuals' action can create, reproduce and change that structure (O'Brien & Kollock, 1991). Hence, Giddens believed that humans are constantly involved in a process of making and/or remaking society.

In a sports coaching context, this means that agency and structure shape the roles and practices of coaches and athletes, and those who interact with them (Coakley, 1994). That is, an individual's behaviour is comprised of decision-making (agency) as well as being influenced by wider social factors (structures) (Jones *et al.*, 2004). In other words, coaches act as they choose as well as how they have been influenced to choose (Armour & Jones, 2000; Lemert, 1997). By using agency and structure, both organisational socialisation and the individuality of human action can be used to understand coaches' behaviour.

The purpose of this chapter is to use Giddens's theory as a means through which to study sports coaching. Emerging from the discussion are the concepts of interpretative schemes, resources and norms, which are subsequently described in relation to the coaching process. The chapter concludes with a critical commentary about the theory by Stephen Aboud, a coach with the Irish Rugby Football Union.

Structuration theory

According to Giddens (1984), there are three dimensions of structure – signification, domination and legitimation – and three dimensions of interaction – communication, power and sanctions. Additionally, all processes related to the structuration of social systems involve three elements (modalities): the communication of meaning (interpretative schemes); the exercise of power (facility/resources); and the evaluation or judgement of conduct (norms) (Giddens, 1979). As each modality operates differently within agential and structural domains, the modalities determine both how the institutional properties of social systems arbitrate or influence human action and how human action, in turn, constitutes social structure (Giddens, 1984). In essence, then, modalities refer to the mediation of interaction and structure in the process of social (re)production. For instance, at the macro or structural level, interpretative schemes comprise structures of signification which represent the semantic rules that enable, inform and inhibit the communication process (Orlikowski & Robey, 1991). The interaction that occurs between the communicators reproduces or changes the interpretative schemes which then impact on the structures of signification (i.e., the social rules that enable, inform and inhibit the communication process) (Orlikowski & Robey, 1991). Thus, the 'rules' that govern the interaction may change. In contrast, at the micro or agential level, interpretative schemes require people to draw upon stocks of knowledge to help make sense of their interactions. Stocks of knowledge are inherent in an actor's capability to go on within the routines of social life, and are used to interpret both behaviour and events in an effort to achieve meaningful interaction. Here, people rely on their previous experience interacting with others both to organise and to shape the encounter (Giddens, 1979).

The second modality, facility, refers to the resources one has at one's disposal. Giddens believed that power is generated in and through the reproduction of structures of domination, which include command over the material world (allocative resouces) and the social world (authoritative resources). From a macro perspective, power is the instrument of domination whose objective is to construct, coerce and control others. Meanwhile, resources, at the agential or micro level, are the means through which intentions are realised, goals are accomplished and power is exercised (Giddens, 1979). For example, the knowledge and skills of the agent (which are often taken for granted) can be viewed as resources. That is, when interacting with others, people draw upon the resources they have acquired during their lives through either formal (education) or informal (friends) means in order to make things happen. While facilities at the macro level produce and reproduce resources which influence the structures of domination, people are not powerless in changing such structures. This is referred to as the 'dialectic of control' (Giddens, 1984). That is, a subordinate group can exert power over a superordinate group. For example, a coach organises a training session for athletes, but the athletes ignore the session and do their own training, thus superseding the coach's power.

The third modality – norms – relates to the context and, hence, what is an appropriate manner for people to interact with each other. At a structural level, norms express and sustain the 'normative order' through tradition, rituals and practices of socialisation (Orlikowski & Robey, 1991). These norms are legitimised through social reproduction. From an agential perspective, humans draw on norms to sanction their behaviour (Giddens, 1984). For example, referees are able to sanction players who do not abide by the rules of the game. Such sanctions reaffirm what is considered expected behaviour.

To summarise, underpinning structuration theory is the duality of agency and structure. Here, by repeating behaviours, individuals reproduce structures (e.g., traditions, rituals and practices of socialisation) or change them by reproducing them differently. Modalities (e.g., interpretative schemes, facility/resources and norms) are the tools that make interaction possible. That is, interpretative schemes generate actors' modes of signification, facilities produce modes of domination, and norms create modes of legitimation.

Having provided an explanation of the duality of structure, the following fictional (coaches') vignette and subsequent discussion illustrate how structuration theory can be used to enhance understanding in a sporting context.

Coaches' vignette

Dave White is the head coach of a national rugby team. Granted a four-year contract to lead the country through the World Cup cycle, Dave was appointed by a committee comprised of the organisation's CEO, the National Coaching Director and three volunteer members. The pressure on Dave to develop a successful team on the field is considerable. While the committee appointed a manager to work with Dave, he had some input into the selection of his coaching staff. He requested two assistant coaches (i.e., a forwards coach and backs coach), in addition to fitness-training, medical and analysis personnel. While Dave was invited to put forward names to fill these roles, it was the committee's final decision to select Dave's support staff.

While the fitness trainers and medical staff are given opportunities to provide input into the programme, Dave has clear expectations regarding the role and function of such personnel. Although he recognises the experience they bring to the team and trusts their abilities to respond to the demands of their respective positions, Dave prefers to manage the group 'on his own'. Similarly, with clear ideas about how the players should perform, Dave provides his assistant coaches with daily programmes which outline the nature of each session and the players to be involved. Dave also observes the sessions first hand to ensure they go according to plan and to inform the content of future ones.

While the fitness-training, medical and analysis personnel are happy to follow Dave's programme, the assistant coaches have mixed feelings about it. The forwards coach, Rob, would prefer to have more say in the events that occur. Consequently, when Dave is focusing on the backs line, Rob adapts the work of the forwards to how he sees fit. On the other hand, Rick, the backs coach, is happy with the set training programme. He used to play rugby with Dave, and trusts his judgement.

Initially, the players appear happy with Dave and his methods. The role of the coach, in their eyes, is to challenge them; to take their game to 'another level'. To do this, the players are looking for innovative sessions, inclusive of strong technical pointers. Some of the squad also have previous experience of working with Dave; they know his methods and are generally comfortable with them. The players, however, are sceptical of the assistant coaches. The more experienced players see a conflict developing between Dave and Rob, as Rob changes the programme when Dave is not around. In contrast, because Rick follows Dave's instructions to the letter, some of the players view Rick as a 'yes man'. This has implications for their 'buy in' or engagement with Rick's coaching, as they doubt he knows what he is doing and why. This scepticism is sometimes revealed in the players' refusal to trust Rick's work, as they are unsure whether he is taking their interests into consideration or simply trying to keep his job.

The subsequent discussion of the vignette is organised as follows; first, the respective actors' interpretative schemes, which were evidenced in the rugby programme, are examined; then focus turns to the modality of facility or resources; finally, how the norms of the sport influenced the daily running of the programme is examined.

Interpretative schemes

Much of the taken-for-granted behaviour necessary to 'go on' in everyday life is not consciously accessible; rather it is practical in character (Giddens, 1979). This behaviour is learned through observing others. It is through these observations that people develop an idea of how they should behave (Bandura, 1977). These behaviours develop mutual meanings and understandings with the resultant shared knowledge called interpretative schemes. In turn, interpretative schemes, which are drawn upon to understand behaviour, are translated into routines. Over time, these social practices are either reinforced or changed (Giddens, 1984). In a coaching context, this means that when an individual assumes the position of a coach he or she engages in a set of behaviours perceived to be needed to fulfil that part (Mack & Gammage, 1998). These behaviours are either reinforced (by doing the same thing as previous coaches have done) or changed (engaging in new coaching behaviours). In relation to the vignette, it is of interest to explore how the coaches and players interpreted their own actions as well as those of each other to understand where the behavioural expectations of each party originated, and whether these behaviours enhanced or constrained the sporting environment.

With the goal of preparing players for a successful World Cup campaign, Dave (the head coach) drew heavily on his previous observations and experiences as a coach. After working for several years as the assistant to the previous head coach, he relied upon his stocks of knowledge to create an operational strategy, which included a training plan, for the current squad. This plan was the direct result of his experience with a previous (generally successful) approach. Consequently, the plan became increasingly formalised, encoded and standardised (Giddens, 1984). Dave also drew upon his stocks of knowledge in terms of what he believed to be acceptable head coach behaviour.

The same forces and process outlined above also applied to the assistant coaches (and staff). With Dave dictating the style of play and the content of the training sessions, his assistants were largely reduced to being 'technicians involved in the transfer of knowledge' (Macdonald & Tinning, 1995: 98). Such limited responsibilities created tension for Rob, who felt that the restrictions put in place did not allow him to react to the social context unique to each coaching situation. Furthermore, because the assistant coaches were obviously not taking charge of the training situation in any real sense, Rick, in particular, had limited credibility in the eyes of the players.

Interestingly, while the assistant coaches' actions were dictated by structural influence (i.e., by Dave's impositions), their behaviours were also a consequence of their agency. That is, the assistant coaches' relative compliance to Dave's practice could have resulted from a conscious decision related to responsibility abdication. Although Rob somewhat resisted the overall programme laid out by Dave, both he and Rick were, for the most part, unwilling to go against the behaviour that had been prescribed for them. Certainly Rick's unwillingness to amend the training programme in front of Dave could have been due to his desire to keep his job. In this way, Dave, as head coach, was able to control and sanction the assistant coaches' behaviour.

One way of understanding how the coaches were socialised into behaving in the ways they did is to recognise that individuals are continuously involved in the process of 'role making' (Callero, 1994; Raffel, 1998). The term 'role' generally refers to the varying positions people execute in their daily lives (Biddle, 1986). Giddens (1984), however, reinterpreted the term 'role' to describe social identity. He preferred to understand it as the positioning of actors. A social position held, for example, by a coach involves the specification of an 'identity' within a network of social relations (Giddens, 1984). This social position carries with it a range of prerogatives and obligations that an actor, who is accorded that identity, may carry out with certain prescriptions associated with that position (Giddens, 1979). For instance, coaches develop their social identities from the values and attitudes they carry with them from previous sporting experiences, from observing others (particularly within their sport), and from making sense of the meanings they associate with those experience(s). This explanation recognises that all social interaction is situated in space and time and is constantly reconstituted (Giddens, 1984).

Through their participation in the programme and by subscribing to Dave's expectations, the assistant coaches and support staff began to develop identities. By identifying themselves in their positions, engaging in behaviours they deemed to be necessary to fulfil their respective parts (i.e., working with the players), the assistant coaches and support staff were able to locate themselves in terms of what it meant to be part of the squad.

While the above discussion has focused on the actions of coaches and support staff, the players would be undergoing a similar process, as is illustrated in the following vignette.

Players' vignette

Having just finished his first year playing top-level rugby, Sean was invited to a two-day squad session which would conclude with a final selection of players to receive a national contract. Given his limited experience at such a level, Sean's focus at the session was to keep his nerves under control, and try to perform to the best of his ability. Unfamiliar with the rules and routines of such a context, Sean paid close attention to the behaviour of others in order to understand the actions acceptable for a 'new' person. Here, Sean was monitoring his own conduct as well as that of his fellow competitors. He also relied on a more experienced player to help him understand the events which occurred over the two days. The knowledge Sean acquired from monitoring his and others' ways and manners enabled him to become an active participant in constituting and reconstituting the routine of the contextual culture. Thus, he became increasingly secure in his position and the positions of others as well as in the operations of the (general) programme.

One of the driving but highly diffuse forces behind action is the desire to sustain ontological security, or the sense of trust that comes from being able to reduce anxiety in social situations (Boucaut, 2001). If a person is uncertain in a social situation (e.g., Sean, in his first national squad session), it is considered an 'experiment with trust', which has consequences for an individual's self-identity (Giddens, 1990). Uncertainty upsets the action–identity dynamic by making it difficult to act and, therefore, hard to sustain a self-conception (Giddens, 1991). Central to feelings of ontological security is a sense of reliability in persons and things (Giddens, 1990). This reliability is extremely important in the interactions that occur within a sporting environment. Here, athletes look to coaches to be a source of reliability which, in turn, heightens the athletes' ontological security. This is in keeping with the literature, where, according to Côté and Sedgwick (2003), building athletes' confidence in both themselves and their support structures is a very important characteristic of 'good' coaching behaviour.

In the players' vignette, an outcome of the more experienced player relating his knowledge or understanding of international squad trials to the 'new' athlete (Sean) was that the latter became educated about what to expect. Such behaviour is in keeping with Giddens's (1984) suggestion that people draw upon their stocks of knowledge in the production and reproduction of interaction when they are involved in social encounters. As Sean spent more time in the trial context he became more able to 'get by' as his awareness of the social rules which governed the players' behaviour in such squads increased. Knowledge of these rules helped him become more secure in the programme and to develop his identity as an elite rugby player. Sean's behaviour is in keeping with Giddens's (1984) thinking that awareness of social rules is the very core of 'knowledgeability' which characterises human agents. Here, Sean's development illustrated that he was becoming highly 'learned' with respect to the knowledge needed to apply in the production and reproduction of appropriate or contextual daily social encounters.

Sean's story demonstrates that people are continually constituting and reconstituting their identities (Giddens, 1991). The fluctuating nature of identity is a crucial aspect of Giddens's (1991) work, in which he suggested that, although people tend to identify with many social groups, based on factors such as gender, national origin and so on, these factors are salient or prominent at different times and in different ways, thus contributing to the fluid nature of identity construction. When an identity becomes significant at a particular time, the sentiments, emotions and behaviour of the person in question will tend to be affected and guided by the norms and aspirations of his or her group (Chaitin, 2004). According to Chaitin (2004), the degree to which an individual identifies with a given social category is associated with the internalisation of that category's goals, values, norms and traits, and with the degrees of cohesion, cooperation and altruism he or she feels towards other group members. This, it can be suggested, was what was happening to Sean.

Thus far, the behaviour of those involved in the rugby squad has been discussed in terms of their interpretative schemes. Another way of understanding the interactions in the rugby programme is through the modality of facility/resources.

Facility/resources

Power is an inherent feature of social relationships and of understanding social interaction within all settings, including sports (Jones *et al.*, 2004). Many of the processes that Giddens identified regarding power built upon, or reflected, ideas that had been discussed previously by Parsons (1951) and Foucault (1977). Drawing upon the work of these (and other) earlier theorists, Giddens developed his own views about the power relationships founded in social action, interaction, systems and structures. As mentioned earlier, Giddens (1984) considered that to have power was to have access to valued resources: allocative and authoritative. Allocative resources stem from control of material products: for example, the access players have to coaching, equipment and information. Authoritative resources, on the other hand, are derived from the activity of human agents. These could include the actions of administrators hiring and firing coaches, or how players and coaches are informally or formally placed in hierarchies.

Authoritative resources

Hierarchies, or ordering, provide one way for people to demonstrate power on a daily basis (Nyberg, 1981). By ordering people according to criteria, individuals are granted a certain level of authority by the person doing the ordering. A person's standing, relative to the order, influences the extent to which that individual can exercise his or her power (Nyberg, 1981). A simple examination of the roles in the coaches' vignette brings to light the hierarchies that existed in the programme. The rugby coaches' hierarchy was formally organised so that they could act in concert, but at the same time play separate parts (i.e., head coach, Dave; assistant coaches, Rob and Rick). As a consequence of the coaches' different responsibilities, their work required delegation and consent. That is, the effectiveness of the coaches' work was dependent upon Rob and Rick's acceptance of Dave as the leader.

In addition to a hierarchical ordering of coaches, players also have a pecking order, often in accordance with ability and experience. Such a pecking order could have consequences, as the ordering of squad members naturally affects the nature of an individual's interaction with his or her coaches and team-mates. Furthermore, hierarchies could also influence the perceptions participants have of what is considered to be acceptable behaviour for themselves and others. That is, being ranked in a high position permits players to act in certain ways, while a lower ranking leaves them open to increased scrutiny.

While the hierarchies evidenced in both vignettes reflected the players' and coaches' various roles, they were not always limited by the structures created. Here, Giddens (1979) believed that, because power is dialectical, actors in subordinate positions are never entirely dependent. Hence, they are often adept at converting whatever resources they possess into a degree of control over their conditions (Giddens, 1984). For example, when Dave was not present during a session, Rob would exercise his agency and change the session. Certainly, by amending the session to one which he considered more appropriate, Rob assumed more ownership of the training programme. While some players saw this as resistance against the head coach, which had a negative effect on their respect for Rob, the converse also occurred. This is because others viewed Rob's intervention as responding to their needs of the moment, resulting in an increased respect for him and his coaching.

Allocative resources

Giddens's theory also examines domination through the control of materials (allocative resources). If we build on the rugby scenarios given above, allocative resources are represented by, for example, player contracts. Once a player receives an international contract, he or she is bound by the policies and codes of behaviour of the national govering body. Each contract is also likely to contain performance indicators (i.e., skill and fitness specific) to be achieved by the player, while he/she is also expected to cooperate with support staff (e.g., medical, fitness, nutrition, performance analysts). Should a player not comply with the contract, disciplinary procedures can be put into effect. The same, of course, can be said of the appointed staff.

In summary, structures of domination are evidenced by allocative and authoritative control over resources. By holding and distributing resources, the committee that appointed Dave was able to control his behaviour. From there, the hierarchical positions of the support staff and athletes helped to determine which actors had (or were perceived to have) more power than others (e.g., the head coach had more say than the assistant coaches). Additionally, allocative resources, such as contracts, were also able to sanction players' (and staff) behaviour as they would (typically) be afraid to risk their positions in the programme, thus conceding to the requirements of the contract.

Norms

While the previous discussion suggested that coaches and athletes draw upon their interpretative schemes to understand what it means to be a member of any sporting programme, this section contends that to know the meaning of the terms 'coach' and 'athlete' is to get to know what the person does and how that position differs from others (Giddens, 1991). Here, the behavioural norms of contextual actors are created, disseminated and legitimated. For example, and again in reference to the coaches' vignette, by following the directions set for them by Dave, the assistant coaches learned their roles. Although their responsibilities in the squad differed greatly from previous rugby teams, Rob and Rick quickly determined their new stations. By subscribing to their new positions and doing what was expected of them, the assistant coaches legitimised their roles.

It is important to recognise that the components of structuration theory sometimes overlap. For example, both players and coaches in the vignettes drew upon their stocks of knowledge (i.e., structures of signification) to interpret each others' behaviours. This knowledge consisted of being familiar with the habits and routines that had been part of their previous experiences, and from which they developed ideas related to appropriate or acceptable behaviour for each other (i.e., structures of legitimation). Hence, by subscribing to 'familiar' coaching behaviours, coaches reconstituted traditional actions to which they were accustomed. However, if the coaches did not want to comply with such a 'traditional' approach, they could create new behaviours, thus changing expectations. New behaviours were always possible as the coaches were not constrained to behaving in the same manner as their previous coaches. That is, the coaches could use their agency and act as they chose as well as how they had been influenced (by structures) to choose (Armour & Jones, 2000; Lemert, 1997). Nevertheless, in reality, coaches are often compliant with traditional coaching practices. One explanation for this complicity is that it is what they are comfortable doing, thereby reinforcing their ontological security (Giddens, 1984).

Sean, being new to national trials, exemplified the modality of norms in practice. Upon arriving to join the squad, he paid close attention to the interaction and behaviour of the players and coaches. Here, he was trying to understand what behaviour was 'acceptable' for each party. By familiarising himself with the habits and routines of the squad's coaches and other players, he was forming ideas related to appropriate behaviours. By understanding the 'rules' and 'routines' that governed the squad's interaction, not wanting to 'rock the boat', Sean learned the 'norms' and found his place.

A coach's commentary by Stephen Aboud

I am currently the Irish Rugby Football Union's Technical Development Manager, responsible for providing direction to the elite player and coach development programme. I've been with the Irish Rugby Football Union for twenty years, as Regional Development Officer (Leinster), a National Elite Player Development Manager and National Coach Development Manager. I've served as Assistant Coach to the Ireland Under-20s, Irish Colleges, Ireland Students, Ireland 'A' and Leinster, in addition to being a Technical Adviser to the Irish national team.

I am always interested in new ways of thinking about coaching, which is why (I think) I was approached to review this chapter. While the language used to describe structuration theory is daunting, the theory itself is appealing as it provides a realistic three-dimensional view of the sporting environment. Rather than thinking about the sport as a 25-piece puzzle, this theory attempts to 'capture' the complexity and reveals that the puzzle has, in fact, 250 pieces – it is far more complicated than we have ever acknowledged. The traditional view that the sporting context is more simple than this hardly recognises the complexity of the coach's job, especially within the professional game. The theory reminds us not only to look at what is happening on the field, but to acknowledge the wider picture (i.e., political, historical and organisational contexts) in order to understand the events and interactions that occur.

As a part of my work remit lies in the development of rugby coaches, I see four principal benefits of encouraging coaches to engage with Giddens's thinking. First, as just mentioned, structuration theory raises 'awareness' of the multiple dimensions that influence each sporting context; things we often skip over or take for granted, like the roles we 'play'. Second, the theory can help coaches to see what issues are occupying their time (structural or agential) and which areas are being neglected. Third, the theory positions the coach as an active agent in the process, able to choose, strategise and resist (through the dialectic of control) as he or she sees fit. Fourth, the concept of ontological security (or the lack of it) helps to explain the processes players, new coaches and staff go through when they are new to a squad. Awareness of this is extremely beneficial to all team members in understanding behaviour.

The appeal of using this theory is that, although the coach is the centre of the discussion, there are many things going on in coaching, at many other levels. We can use this theory, then, to make sense of what is happening within the structures of the sport; for example, the 'structures of domination'. In a professional sporting context, the maintenance of the coaches' power is often based on the results that are achieved. However, it also rests on meeting the expectations of those in the system (e.g., committees, players/athletes). Both of these are somewhat linked. That is, positive results will increase the coach's individual authority in dealing with these and other stakeholders (e.g., the media, supporters and so on). On another level, the coach, as a structure, needs to acknowledge his or her influence on the support staff and players. Here, a coach should perhaps recognise the value of providing space for support staff and players to exercise at least some agency.

Whether they (i.e. staff and players) then use that freedom, depending on how comfortable they feel about it (their ontological security?), I suppose is up to them. In any case, what Giddens teaches us here is that social actors, be they coaches, support staff or athletes, can't behave too outlandishly as they are tied by norms and expectations (the social structures).

I'd never really thought about it like that before. More than anything, I suppose, the theory can give us, as coaches, an insight into why things are as they are in coaching contexts. Once we understand that, we can get a better feel for how we can change things for the better.

Summary

The purpose of this chapter was to use Giddens's theory of structuration as a 'sensitising lens' to help understand sports coaching. Giddens's work takes into consideration both agential and structural issues that characterise the complex interactions involved in coaches' work. Using examples from two vignettes, the dimensions of structures (i.e., signification, domination and legitimation) and agency (i.e., communication, power and sanctions) were highlighted. Translating structure and agency into action are three modalities: interpretative schemes, facility/resources and norms. While structuration theory has had limited use in sports coaching, its appeal lies in its recognition of how agency and structure shape the roles and practices of coaches and athletes, and those who interact with them (Coakley, 1994). This chapter, then, builds on, and clarifies, tentative work already undertaken in sports coaching from a Giddensian perspective (e.g., Purdy et al., 2008), particularly in relation to understanding the various degrees of compliance, cooperation and resistance evidenced in the coaching context.

7 Niklas Luhmann: Coaching as communication

Lars Tore Ronglan with Øystein Havang

Niklas Luhmann: a short biography

In some of the obituaries published in European and US magazines following his death in 1998, Niklas Luhmann was described as one of the most important social theorists of the twentieth century (e.g. Fuchs, 1999). Yet, he is virtually unknown in much of the Anglo-Saxon world (Arnoldi, 2001; Beckmann & Stehr, 2002). Luhmann was born in Lüneberg, Germany in 1927. Between 1946 and 1949 he studied law, before entering public administration and spending ten years as an administrative lawyer. In 1962, he received a scholarship to Harvard and started an extremely productive academic career. In 1968 he was appointed Professor of Sociology at the University of Bielefeld, Germany, where he worked until his retirement. At the time of his death, at the age of seventy, he had published over 14,000 printed pages – more than 50 books and over 400 articles (Andersen, 2003).

Luhmann's journey towards a theory of modern society took a dual approach. First, there was his development of a novel systems theoretical perspective – 'a kind of thinking which does away with the notion of system in all its traditional wordings' (Baecker, 2001: 69) – outlined in the book *Soziale systeme* (Luhmann, 1984; translated as *Social systems*; Luhmann, 1995). Second, there were his extensive analyses based on this framework, which included those of the scientific system, the political system, the arts system, the educational system, the system of justice, love and family as a system, the system of mass media and the system of economics, among others. Luhmann's ambitious project was fulfilled with his book *Die Gesellschaft der Gesellschaft* (*The Society of Society*), published shortly before his death (Luhmann, 1997).

Introduction

The preceding short biography may give the impression that Luhmann was a macro-sociological scientist. In one respect, he was. At the same time, however, his theorising can be read in numerous ways and related to different levels of society. Indeed, his developed theoretical framework was considered 'ambitious in its scope and relentless in its abstraction' (Knodt, 1995: xvi). Luhmann aimed to construct a theory marked by internal consistency, conceptual richness and analytical utility (Sevänen, 2001). According to Lee (2000), the value of Luhmann's work lies both in what it has and in what it does not have: it has structural form without specific content. The theory has often been compared to a 'labyrinth' (Andersen, 2003), possible to rewrite and experiment with in many ways.

Luhmann hoped to provoke sociologists into asking new kinds of questions. First and foremost, his approach invites us to observe in particular ways in order to understand social life and dynamics better. The starting point in observing society is perhaps the most unfamiliar aspect of this theory. Østerberg (1988: 264) has described it as 'a new conception of the world'; Lee (2000: 330) as 'a radical break from the past'. One of the radical breaks contained within the theorising is the replacing of individuals with communications as the fundamental unit of society. This communication-theoretical turn (Andersen, 2003) meant that Luhmann left the traditional notion of social systems as systems of action. Instead, society was understood as a number of self-organising systems of communication, consisting of and created by communication alone.

The aim of this chapter is twofold. First, given that Luhmann's sociology is complex and rather unknown in the English-speaking world, it is to introduce and discuss some of his fundamental notions. Here, we are not concerned with his many analyses of different societal systems, only with the Luhmannian eye for social systems as communication. The notions of observation, system/environment, communication and complexity will be outlined. This is necessary to understand a premise that has produced both vigorous criticism and extensive misunderstanding of his work (Beckmann & Stehr, 2002): that society does not consist of people but that people belong to the environment of society. The second purpose of the chapter is to apply Luhmann's thinking to sports coaching, briefly suggesting possible consequences of using such lenses. This second section, in turn, will be guided by two questions. How can researchers (i.e., external observers) utilise this approach to develop and refine our knowledge of coaching processes and contexts? And if coaches (i.e., internal observers) view the situations they are part of with Luhmannian glasses, how might this influence their way of acting and reflecting? The latter question will be discussed by the Norwegian handball coach Øystein Havang.

Unlike the work of most of the other sociologists presented in this book, Luhmann's theoretical framework has, to date, hardly been applied to sports coaching research. Additionally, within sports sociology in general, his thinking is almost absent, excepting some work analysing sport as a societal system (Cashay, 1988; Stichweh, 1990; Tangen, 1997, 2000), the use and non-use of sport facilities (Tangen, 2004), and a recent anthology using Luhmannian thinking to observe different sport phenomena (Wagner *et al.*, in press). Given the paucity of its application, the chapter can hopefully offer some new sensitising concepts to understand coaching practice. At the same time, we will underline the connections between Luhmann and other sociologists presented in this book, no matter how different the frameworks might seem at first glance. For example, the approaches of Luhmann and Goffman may productively complement each other when trying to grasp social interaction in specific athletic contexts. Furthermore, Luhmann's concept of system is related to Foucault's concept of discourse; they can both be used as discursive analytical strategies (Andersen, 2003).

Observations and distinctions

To grasp and understand the social reality we are a part of, we have to *observe*. What does that mean? It means that we have to separate something from something else, otherwise everything merges into an incomprehensible chaos. To be able to see (or observe) anything at all, we have to differentiate. This is one of the starting points in Luhmann's sociology. Inspired by the British mathematician George Spencer-Brown, Luhmann defined observation as a specific operation of creating distinctions. In the words of Spencer-Brown (1969: 1): 'We cannot make an indication without drawing a distinction.' By drawing a distinction, something comes to the foreground for the observer, against a horizon. The distinction possesses an inner side as well as an outer side; the inner side being the indicated side. For example, whenever there is observation, one side in the difference is 'the marked space' (the selection, the indicated side) and the other side is 'the unmarked space' (Baecker, 2001). A difference – for example, between man and woman, offside and onside, risk and security – is chosen, and one of the two sides of the difference is indicated: for example, woman (not man), offside (not onside), risk (not security).

From this, it follows that every observation is an act of distinction. Consequently, to observe gender, it is necessary to use distinctions like male/female or masculinity/femininity; the distinctions are premises on which it is possible to observe the phenomenon. For example, to observe power, it could be necessary to use the distinction superior/inferior, while to observe performance in sport one could use distinctions like win/lose or improve/worsen. These examples illustrate Gregory Bateson's statement that 'information is a difference that makes a difference' (Bateson, 1972: 457): that is, a difference applied by the observer that enables discrete entities to emerge. Luhmann's concept of observation as an act of distinction has inspired commentators to label his systems theory a theory of difference (Gumbrecht, 2001), while his shift from an ontological focus ('what is . . . ?') to an epistemological focus ('who says . . . ?') has been labelled *radical constructivism* (Luhmann, 1993; Reese-Schäfer, 2001). Radical constructivism does not deny the existence of a reality; on the contrary, it supposes it. It accepts that obviously there is something out there to observe. But reality, as such, the unity of the observer and his environment, 'the paradoxical sameness of difference, of inside and outside, remains inaccessible' (Knodt, 1995: xxxiv). That is, whatever is observed is observed by an observer, who cuts up reality in a certain way in order to make it observable. For Luhmann, then, without distinctions there would be no observable reality, as any observation (operation) is already an interpretation and, as such, always biased.

Luhmann describes modern society as comprising myriad communication systems – institutions, organisations and social interactions. Each of these systems constantly produces and reproduces itself on the basis of its own specific operations. Each system also observes itself and its environment, with each observation being marked by that particular system's unique perspective: that is, by the selectivity of the specific distinctions used for the observations. Luhmann's constructivist epistemology is defined as a theory about second-order observations. Hence, it holds particular relevance for sociologists (and other external observers) who observe the observer: that is, to enable an understanding of what kind of distinctions are used in the social world in terms of what is included and excluded (Tangen, 2004); to see the observer's 'blind spots' (Krause, 1996: 85), and what implications this might have. This is not to assume that second-order observations are not bound by their own distinctions, as there is no privileged position within society making it possible to take in the totality. Sociology is nevertheless viewed as communication, based on operations of observation. Hence, by using other distinctions, a sociological observation can see something that the observer does not see, thereby hopefully producing new knowledge.

System and environment

One of the most misunderstood aspects of Luhmann's sociology is his concept of system. Within sociology, 'systems have never really had a good press' (Baecker, 2001: 59). Usually, the term 'system' is linked to something fixed and stable, to order and control. Luhmann's concept of system, however, is quite the opposite: it is something 'non-linear, contingent and temporal' (Lee, 2000: 323). For example, when a group of friends meet and start to play football in a park, a social system (that is, communication) emerges. While the play is proceeding, much of the communication is bodily (e.g., movements and play actions), and the game is made possible due to a common agreement of what is going on, and negotiations on the way (e.g., rules, fouls, goals). The football communication may at any moment break up for several reasons (e.g., tired players, injuries or the fact that it is dinner time). As soon as the interaction ends, this particular system disappears. When communication connects with communication, social systems emerge because of the distinction between self-reference and external reference (Luhmann, 1995). That is, related to the above example, the football play is possible due to the border that is continuously drawn and redrawn between what is relevant to the game (self-reference) and what is not (external reference). By drawing borders – that is, selecting something (e.g., playing football) from a multitude of possibilities – a distinction between system (the actual: the self-reference) and environment (the possible: the external reference) is created. The boys or girls could have chosen to do something else, but by choosing to play football a specific system/ environment distinction is established, as long as the game continues.

According to Luhmann, a social system constitutes itself (self-reference) and its environment (external reference). Hence, the environment is a system-specific environment as it consists of that which is defined by the communication as its relevant surroundings. Applied to sports coaching, something and someone are included in a coaching situation (which constitutes the system; self-reference), in contrast to a specific environment that at the moment is not part of the process but is still significant to consider and to relate to (e.g., information, institutions, relations, persons). The environment is always more complex than the system itself, and represents a surplus of possibilities, not actualised at that instant. From moment to moment, selections have to be made – the coach chooses to do this rather than that – and thereby a distinction between system (what is chosen) and environment (relevant possibilities) is created. Hence, the distinction between system and environment is no fixed border; on the contrary, it is continuously produced by the selections undertaken.

Luhmann's systems theory might, therefore, be more precisely labelled a 'system–environment' theory. It focuses on how a border – and thereby a connection – between an inside (a system) and an outside (the system's environment) is produced through communication. The boundary has a double function of separating and connecting the system and the environment. The assumption in the very first sentence of *Social systems* – 'there are systems' (Luhmann, 1995: 12) – should therefore be understood as *there are system–environment distinctions*. The concept of environment is not a residual category; rather it is a presupposition for the system's identity, 'because identity is possible only by difference' (Luhmann, 1995: 177). By drawing a border, an inside (e.g., a team's identity, 'us') is defined in relief against an outer world ('the others').

The guiding distinction in Luhmann's sociology, then, is the distinction between system and environment. This implies a radical break with most sociological theories, which operate on the basis of another guiding distinction when observing social life: namely, that which exists between the individual and society. The basic point of view in these theories, and in common thinking about society, is that society is comprised of concrete individuals. It is this premise that Luhmann rejects. His society does not consist of individuals and actions, but of social systems (i.e., communication). Changing this fundamental difference in observing the social has been characterised as a paradigm shift within sociology (Stichweh, 2000). His social theory removes human beings from the centre of the social system, 'and throws them, body and soul, into the systems environment' (Lee, 2000: 322). This is a rather unusual conception, and must be understood in light of Luhmann's alternative conceptualisation of the individual. It is to this that we now turn.

Communication and the individual

Luhmann insists that one does not locate society inside individuals, but between them (Lee, 2000). In other words, communication is something going on between people. Subsequently, Luhmann established that the individual, his or her 'body and soul', is situated in the environment of the social. Of course, communication supposes individuals – it does not take place beyond, outside or separate from individuals. Individuals are necessary contributors to create communication. And because one human being cannot enter the consciousness of another, social interaction enforces communication. In the course of communicating, we can try to express ourselves in different ways and to interpret other people's responses, utterances, body language and movements. At the same time, we are free to think and reflect while we are communicating with others. If we want to express our thoughts, this has to be done by the means and possibilities offered by the communication itself, and with limited control concerning how our contribution will be interpreted and how it might influence the social situation. In this way, communication emerges as a circular and genuine social phenomenon that neither participant can determine alone.

This means that communication evolves as a much more complex process than a simple exchange of thoughts. Luhmann claims that consciousness ('psychic systems') and communication ('social systems') constitute two distinct types of system which are structurally coupled. That is, they stimulate each other and are necessary conditions for each other's development. Still, consciousness and communication operate differently: 'thoughts produce thoughts and communication produces communication' (Luhmann, 1995: 262). For Luhmann, communication is no simple operation between a 'sender' and a 'receiver'. It represents something else, a third dimension, which both parties observe while communicating, and through which they understand each other (Baecker, 2001). Communication is seen as a circular, three-way process of information, statement and understanding. For example, if a person wants to add something to a conversation in which they are a participant ('information'), they must choose a way to express this ('statement') and then wait for the interaction partner's response ('understanding') to interpret how their communicative act has been understood. Thus, when communications connect to communications, the understanding is confirmed communicatively (Shannon, 1989), not just in the minds of the interaction partners. This does not in any way suppose 'agreement', as the interaction partners are still free to think, reflect, interpret, disagree or misunderstand as the communication process evolves. Luhmann's social and conscious systems are distinct, and communication partners never merge into a shared consciousness: 'Consensus in the full sense, meaning total agreement, remains beyond reach' (Luhmann, 1997: 82). In this respect, he rejects the assumption that society is held together by a consensus between individual members about common moral values, ideas or interests.

According to Luhmann, then, until they begin to communicate, individuals are not in society (Lee, 2000). Furthermore, when they do communicate, individuals do so to a limited extent, never as 'whole persons'. Humans, consequently, are considered to be far more than communication; they are always more outside society than inside. When society is understood as communication, its limits become clearer (that is, it has the same limits as communication). In this respect, all that is not communicated remains outside society. For example, poisoned fish in the North Sea are not part of society – until they are brought into the social discussion. Similarly, disagreements or emotions among athletes themselves or between coaches and athletes are not part of the coaching process until they are communicated.

As individuals, we contribute to a range of social systems: face-to-face interactions, organisations and institutions. We move between social contexts that, in turn, operate on quite different logics: for example, the economic market, the educational system, workplaces, family life and maybe sport. Such differing system logics find expressions in social expectations (Tangen, 2004). Expectations have the function of orienting thoughts and communication (Baraldi *et al.*, 1997). In this way, specific expectations contribute to structure coaching situations and coach–athlete relationships within distinct frames of references. However, despite this obvious power, the 'force of expectations' (Tangen, 2004: 9) can only orient and never determine coaching processes as courses of communication. In this respect, it cannot remove the basic uncertainty created by the internal and external complexity inherent within coaching.

Complexity and contingency

Complexity is a core concept in Luhmann's social theory. He believed that modern society explodes in complexity. The world's complexity – the infinity of possibilities – enforces selectivity, but this has its costs: 'Complexity means being forced to select, being forced to select means contingency; and contingency means risk' (Luhmann, 1995: 25). Hence, our handling of the complexity problem has the important consequence of contingency (that is, a possibility or unforeseen event): each selection made could have been different; it can always be questioned and reversed. Luhmann stresses that a lessening of complexity never removes the contingency of social life: that is, the basic uncertainty (risk) that is created by the necessity to select. Applied to the coaching context: every day a coach has to make many selective decisions among a surplus of possibilities – training content, game strategy, player selection – that always could have been different and, therefore, can be questioned. The contingency marking coaching situations makes trust and confidence an important, though vulnerable, aspect of coach–athlete relationships.

As mentioned above, the reduction of complexity does not imply a movement from complexity to simplicity. On the contrary, it means bringing unorganised, incomprehensible complexity into another form: organised complexity. Within social systems, organised complexity should not be understood as a stable state. Communication always takes place in time, and from moment to moment selections are made. Over time, social systems build up more internal complexity: that is, they increase their internal relations and possible combination of elements. Greater internal complexity means increased sensitivity towards the (even more complex) environment. From the system's point of view, complexity also appears as indeterminacy or lack of information. This means that the system 'produces and reacts to an unclear picture of itself and its environment' (Luhmann, 1995: 28), like individuals (e.g., coaches) or groups (e.g., sport teams) who have to make decisions on very limited information.

To illustrate Luhmann's notion of complexity and link it to the concepts of communication, the individual, system and environment, this section ends with an example. It illustrates how this theoretical framework can be applied to observe group dynamics, and is given in response to the question: how might social interaction within a group of people, such as a sports team, look if we observed it through Luhmannian glasses (Ronglan, in press)? As we have seen, interaction on the group level creates communication. Communication is always about something and not everything, which implies an emerging system created through the establishment of borders. Each system is constituted thematically (what the communication is about), temporally (the use of time) and socially (who participates and contributes). When observing the development of a group over time it is possible to see whether certain topics or types of situation recur in the interaction. If they do, within such situations a greater internal complexity is gradually built, comprising a history, an inner logic, and the evolution of different roles, expectations and relations. If a range of such recurring situations can be observed in the interaction, the group may be differentiated into several social (sub-)systems. Each communication system originates from certain distinctions, and produces its own internal complexity and specific environment. In short, a sports team may, as a miniature society, develop multi-contextuality and several distinct communication systems. It may emerge as a performance group, as a group of employees, of learners, of footballers, of peers or of women, dependent on the participants' framing of the context.

To sum up: Luhmann's framework views the group as made up of communication rather than concrete individuals. It asks us to focus on differences rather than identity; on multi-contextuality rather than unity. It invites us to deconstruct the courses of communication, searching for underlying distinctions that include and exclude. It induces us to look at how complexity is reduced, and with what kind of consequence.

A critique of Luhmann

Luhmann's abstract and unfamiliar theoretical framework has naturally met resistance. Perhaps the most provocative part of the theory is his deconstruction of the human being and the subsequent removal of the individual subject from society. This 'radically antihumanist' (Luhmann, 1997: 35) perspective has been subject to a long-lasting debate in Germany. Led by Jürgen Habermas, the criticism has centred on the premise that Luhmann developed a 'social technological' theory consisting only of systems (Habermas & Luhmann, 1971). Habermas accused Luhmann of not acknowledging the individual human life-world as a contrast to the alienating societal systems in modern life. Luhmann's response was that society, as such, cannot be marked as more or less alienating, just more differentiated and complex, and that the concept of life-world corresponds to an individual's observation of himself or herself and his or her environment (a conscious operation). Despite the intense debate between Habermas and Luhmann, they were influenced by each other's perspectives and developed their thinking in dialectical opposition (Kneer & Nassehi, 1993).

A second criticism raised against Luhmann relates to his apparent denial of 'intersubjectivity', understood as a collective consciousness, as a prerequisite for social integration. This critique strikes at Luhmann's absolute distinction between communication and consciousness, meaning that 'consensus in the full sense, meaning total agreement, remains beyond reach' (Luhmann, 1997: 82). Luhmann's position is a logical consequence of his communication–theoretical turn (Andersen, 2003), but it collides with usual conceptions of social communities. This tension remains somewhat unresolved. However, sociologists engaged with developing Luhmann's perspective are working to overcome this apparent dilemma by integrating concepts of 'collective rationality' and 'solidarity' into the systems theoretical framework (Hagen, 2000).

How can Luhmann's framework inform sports coaching?

As stated in the introduction to this chapter, Luhmann's theoretical approach has hardly been applied to sports coaching research. Thus, the purpose of this section is to suggest how his work could be utilised to sensitise sociological observations (or second-order observations) of coaching processes. What might be gained by shifting the starting point from individuals and action to distinctions and communication? And what kinds of question would guide such enquiry?

Luhmann's core concepts of complexity, contingency and communication may be used to characterise coaching processes as well as the general society. In applying such a theoretical investigation to sports coaching it could be pertinent first to ask: how is complexity handled within the concrete social context of coaching? This question draws attention towards the selections made within the wider coaching process and the episodic coaching act. Observing the courses of communication may problematise the ways coaches and athletes reduce (external and internal) complexity. Any coaching process or action has to be about something and not everything, and has to include someone and not everyone. Searching for the internal distinctions that are applied within coaching may illuminate the system's boundaries of meaning: what kind of rationality and expectations structure the ways coaching situations are understood and handled? Similarly, and equally important, one could ask: what is excluded? That is, what kind of knowledge, information and incidents are not being thematised as part of the coaching that is taking place? Such questions point to a principal focus of Luhmann's system theoretical analyses. Why is this particular guiding distinction used? Why not use a different distinction (Andersen, 2003)?

Complexity within sports coaching finds expression in, among other things, inherent dilemmas. Examples of dilemmas are the extent of individualisation as opposed to team orientation, participation against performance, results in the short term versus development in the long term, and internal cooperation or competition, among others (Jones & Wallace, 2005; Saury & Durand, 1998). Such dilemmas cannot be absolutely resolved, but have to be addressed day by day through interaction between coaches and athletes. The contingency created by the necessity to select among a surplus of possible courses does not disappear by a single decision at one point in time. On the contrary, the contingency is embedded in inescapable dilemmas, continuously emerging as concrete problems to handle. A second-order observer (e.g., a researcher) may see to what degree the dilemmas are recognised and communicated, in which way they are communicated, the different points of view that are actualised and how selections and decisions are made.

Over time, complexity management via the selections that are done will structure coaching in certain directions. This may happen quietly, or be followed by disputes and conflicts. Observations of structuring processes may illuminate how dilemmas in coaching contexts are handled, and with what consequences. A recent system theoretical analysis of elite teams (Ronglan, 2000, 2010) showed that the coaching observed was structured according to a superior code: performance enhancement. A 'code' describes the marked side of a guiding distinction (Luhmann, 1995). The guiding difference of improve–worsen (of performance) resulted in a specific reduction of complexity. Here, the communicative process circulated around the basic, often implicit, question: how can we improve our performance even more? This open-ended – but still limiting – frame of reference constituted an inside (social system) and a specific environment (relevant to performance). The performance group constantly took part in new contests, which generated continuous preparations (training, etc.) and evaluations. These processes ran parallel to each other; preparations were evaluated in light of the contest, which gave direction and focus to new preparations for new contests, and so on. The preparations were geared towards improving performance, and the evaluations sought to determine what had been achieved. Within the performance communication, it was possible to observe mechanisms of inclusion and exclusion: how incidents were interpreted, what information was considered relevant, what kind of conflict were regarded as legitimate, and how actors (coaches, athletes) and relations were constituted. For example, roles, relations and group structure in the team 'on court' (performance group) and 'off court' differed significantly. As one player put it, 'you often get a totally different impression of a person on court as off court' (Ronglan, 2010: 203).

Although the above work was focused on performance, coaching can be structured according to other codes as well: for example, health, education and participation. Such a framework can lead us to question and observe the guiding distinctions that mark dominant interactions in a variety of contexts, and if several are operating simultaneously. It also enables us to see how possible contradictions are handled. Additionally, even in elite sport, performance communication does not occupy the entire social space. Informal team interactions can foster friendships, social communities or informal cliques; meaning that the team members do not relate to each other just as athletes (using the performance logic), but as friends or peers with personal likes and dislikes. The consequence may be an increase in internal group complexity: that is, an increase in the number of relevant social roles (athlete, friend, employee), relations (personal and impersonal) and perspectives, and all that entails.

Growing complexity often leads to internal differentiation. According to Luhmann, systems have the capacity to differentiate themselves into sub-systems. Within specific coaching contexts, then, we might catch sight of differentiating processes and sub-systems/environments. Viewing differentiation in this way means that an external observer has to choose systems or frames to see how complexity, identity and the environment appear from different locations. For example, the coaching process might be observed from the coaches', the athletes', the bench-players' or the club's point of view; each comprising different discourses, cultures and networks of communication. The 'team on the court' might be observed from the perspective of 'the team off the court', or vice versa. Or the internal performance logic ('performance enhancement') might be observed in contrast – although related – to the internal labour union logic: 'reasonable working conditions' (Ronglan, 2010). For an external observer, it is always possible to shift the point of observation 'and, in so doing, the observed communications emerge in new ways' (Andersen, 2003: 113). No description can cover the whole picture. What a second-order observer (e.g., a researcher) can do is choose a system of reference and explore the coaching process from that particular point of view. By changing the point of observation, so that what used to be a system now appears as an environment, more of the situational complexity of coaching can be unearthed.

So, what about the individuals involved in coaching? Although Luhmann's theorising has been criticised for making actors invisible in social processes, we end this section by suggesting how the approach can be utilised to illuminate the relation between the communication (the coaching process) and the human beings who comprise it. In Luhmann's system–environment theory, individuals emerge as persons performing social roles within a contextualised (e.g., coaching) process. Each person involved in coaching, athletes as well as coaches, can contribute in a number of ways and perform a variety of roles within the myriad situations that comprise it. The main difference between sociological action theories (e.g., Goffman, Blau and Wenger in this book) and Luhmann's theory is how the dimensions are emphasised. To put it simply, within action theory, actors and actions 'produce' communication; within systems theory, the course of com-munication 'produces' actions and actors. In line with this perspective, relevant questions guiding an observation of a coaching situation might be: how does George, a coach, try to influence the situation? And how does the social interaction constitute George as a part of the situation? To what extent and how is George marginalised or made an influential person in the situation? Within a system theoretical perspective, any individual initiative – an action, an utterance, a smile – has to be contextualised within the ongoing communication to spot its meaning and significance. This way, there are similarities between Luhmann's conceptual-isation of system and Goffmann's description of frame as 'a principle of organization that defines a situation' (Goffman, 1974: 11).

Following Luhmann, coaches, to be able to influence a social situation, should develop observational skills, social competence and communicative competence. Observational skills are about the coach's capability to see what is going on in and around the team, to ascertain who the important agenda-setters and situation-definers are, and how this is then reflected in the meaning-making and the relationships within the team. Social competence is based on the ability to read the situation, to see how social expectations structure the interaction, and to adapt to different language games in order to influence the process. Communicative competence requires taking the perspective of others (Mead, 1934), to observe and reflect how he or she as the coach is perceived by the interaction partners (Goffman, 1959). It is rarely possible for a coach not to take part in the communicative process, because silence, or the decision not to act, may be as influential as any shouting or energy. Indeed, the coach is continuously being observed by the athletes, and may influence face-to-face interaction merely by his or her bare presence. Communicative competence is about the ability to use the diversity of means given by the role, the expectations and the context flexibly. This way, coaches may make a difference even within Luhmann's world of systems.

A coach's commentary by Øystein Havang

I am a former Norwegian national handball team coach, currently coaching at an elite club. I start this commentary by relating to the last part of the chapter, which really made sense to me. My experience is that coaching is about communicating effectively; consequently, it requires good communication skills. As a coach, you also have to be humble enough to see that your influence is limited – you *can* make a difference, but you are far from being the only influential person in the team. The necessity of humility and adequate social skills is maybe the most important lesson I have learned after ten years as a coach in elite handball. When I ended my long career as a professional player abroad and started to practise as a coach in Norway, I had a rather naïve conception of the coaching role. I didn't recognise the skills needed, besides being a 'strong leader' and a 'handball expert'. Years of experience, though, have taught me that you have to observe and listen carefully, read the situations and take the players' roles and perspectives into consideration before taking action. Making the right moves at the right times requires the observation skills and behavioural flexibility that are discussed in this chapter. For example, keeping silent is a 'coaching act' I have found efficient in many situations, as it can both stimulate player activity and provide me with time to observe and reflect before intervening. In addition, keeping silent and 'passive' can give good opportunities to detect how role structure operates in the team – who are the dominating actors among the players? Silent observation, of course, has to be followed by interventions, but then you develop a better 'feel' for how you should approach players and problems to help get things back on track.

Communication skills? What is that about? As I see it, communication is so much more than just the words you are uttering. I think that attitude, engagement, body language, gestures and movements are as important as words to influence the processes in your team. For me, it has been important to use my humour actively in developing a personal and inspiring coach role. I use humour to make it all less 'serious', to calm down nervous players, to increase their effort, to solve problems, and to make fun of myself. This is not to say that humour should be as essential to all coaches as it is to me; my point is that coaches should use their own strengths and personalities in developing and applying a wide range of behaviours in their coaching. You have to be clear but flexible, and not take yourself too seriously. If the players get bored or sick of you, you won't survive long as a coach. I have seen colleagues quit because the players or important staff members couldn't stand them any more. And some of these coaches didn't even see it coming; they had no idea what was going on. This demonstrates limited communication skills on their part. To me, communication skills are about being able to use a variety of means, and developing a sensitivity regarding when it is time to apply this or that behaviour to influence a situation. In that respect, what was written in this chapter about the relationship between the individual and communication was an eye-opener for me. Viewing the individual as standing 'outside' the communication process, observing it and taking part in it at the same time, was a picture I could recognise. To develop as a communicator I think I have to increase my sensitivity when observing what impact my behaviour has, and how it is interpreted by players.

Another idea I took from this chapter was Luhmann's notion of 'reducing complexity'. Often we talk about 'choosing', 'deciding' or 'prioritising', but I think the notion of 'reducing complexity' more precisely describes what this process or action is about. There are so many elements (strategic, physical, psychological, technical, social, etc.) relevant to coaching that I find it impossible to argue that one specific strategy or content-directed means is the only way to do it. Several roads lead to Rome. Obviously, however, we have to 'reduce complexity'; meaning that I try to help players keep focused by sticking to the strategy and not opening all the boxes. Simplifying a complex game is one of the most important tasks for me, as a coach. From what I understood of Luhmann's work, internal complexity is built within the system. On the one hand, my handball team has to 'reduce external complexity' – that is, simplify – to be able to walk together in a certain direction. On the other hand, we have to 'build internal complexity' – that is, variety – when preparing the team to meet different opponents and situations. In other words, we have to balance simplification with flexibility. As a coach, I find this tension basic in developing a team. I have to clarify roles and relations on court according to a clear playing philosophy, and so make intra-team interaction more predictable and fluent. At the same time, the internal predictability should not be so strict to limit players' flexibility when that is needed on court. I have to allow and cultivate individual players' freedom of action within the overall playing philosophy.

This pressure adds to the inherent dilemmas within coaching discussed in the chapter. In addition to dilemmas related to individualisation as opposed to team orientation and results in the short term versus development in the long term, I find the tension between discipline and creativity challenging. As a coach within a team game, you want disciplined players who follow the game plan, but you also want players to be creative enough to solve the unforeseen game situations that always appear. But you cannot discipline players to be creative! Creative behaviour, as the counterpart of disciplined behaviour, has to be nurtured by the way the coach designs the training practices and the way he or she performs his or her coaching. The way I understand Luhmann's notion of internal complexity, I would say that I now (more than earlier in my coaching career) strive to increase internal complexity in my team. That is, I encourage more variety and tolerate more 'undisciplined' behaviour on court, because I think it is necessary to succeed in modern elite handball.

Luhmann's work has also made me think that a team can be viewed as consisting of several communication systems. This makes sense to me as a coach, as it restricts but also focuses my role in team interaction. I have gradually become more aware of how my role limits my relationships with the players in certain ways. I can certainly be their 'friend', but first and foremost I am their 'coach'. Even in informal situations, the players will not include the coach in all conversations and interactions. There are several things the players won't share with the coach – and shouldn't share – because they need to bond, to make jokes about coaches or staff, and to discuss their own interests without involving me in everything. This means that there are things going on in the team that the coach is not part of. However, that is nothing to be afraid of, and does not mean that you are opposed as a coach. What the coach is in charge of is limited to the coaching process that is going on. As I said before, you certainly have to develop the observation skills that are needed to discover potential conspiracy among players. Beyond that, my opinion is that you should respect the athletes' privacy and right not to be monitored all the time. In Luhmann's words, that would probably mean accepting and tolerating the development of several communication systems, not just the direct coaching act.

Finally, I have to admit that Luhmann's theory was hard to get into. I found the concepts of system and environment difficult to grasp. However, one thing I liked was its basic notions of observation, communication and complexity. In many ways, this sums up how I see the essence of the coaching role. Observation has become increasingly important to me as I have gained experience as a coach. The quality of observations often distinguishes the ordinary coaches from the really good ones. To be respected as a competent coach, I think that you first and foremost have to demonstrate that you are really capable of seeing what is going on both on and off the court. Additionally, precise observations make it a lot easier to 'reduce complexity', thereby focusing your communication. In this way, the coach can hopefully structure meaningful coaching sequences that 'make a difference'.

Conclusion

The purpose of this chapter was to introduce a few concepts related to Niklas Luhmann's social theory, and suggest ways in which they can help us better understand sports coaching. Although there is no obvious first concept in Luhmann's thinking, we started with observation, understood as an act of distinction, because that points to the constructivist foundation of the theory. For a constructivist like Luhmann, our observations of reality are dependent on frames of reference. Applying distinctions, making it possible to reduce complexity, is necessary in order to make reality observable. This applies both to first-order observers (actors in social life, like coaches) and to second-order observers (observers of observers, like researchers). At a basic level, this constructivist insight is of benefit when trying to understand coaching, regardless of whether we adopt other aspects of Luhmann's theorising.

A constructivist position means that the social world – including coaching – can be analysed broadly and from many sides. This implies an openness regarding levels of analysis and conceptual frameworks, as long as the point of observation is clearly made. In this way, Luhmann's approach is open despite its apparent restrictedness; for example, *Social systems* has structural form without specific content (Lee, 2000) in that it supplies instruments for observing a variety of social systems, such as societies, organisations and interactions. The theory's general character provides scope for developing rich empirical material within the principal framework.

8 Etienne Wenger: Coaching and communities of practice

Chris Cushion with Gary Denstone

Etienne Wenger: a short biography

Etienne Wenger first worked as a teacher before obtaining a Ph.D. in artificial intelligence. He then joined the Institute for Research on Learning in Palo Alto, California, where he developed his concept of communities of practice. In the course of his career, he has provided conceptual frameworks for two different fields. His first book on artificial intelligence in education shaped the domain known as 'intelligent tutoring systems'. Later, in the 1990s, he focused his efforts on 'situated learning' and 'communities of practice'. He was the co-author, with Jean Lave, of *Situated learning* (Lave & Wenger, 1991), where the term 'community of practice' was coined. Building on these original ideas, he wrote *Communities of practice: Learning, meaning, and identity* (1998) and *Cultivating communities of practice: A guide to managing knowledge* (co-authored with Richard McDermott and William Snyder, 2002). Since 1997, Wenger has been an independent researcher, consultant, author and speaker. He is currently an Honorary Professor at the School of Humanities, University of Aalborg, Denmark.

Introduction

Etienne Wenger places learning in the context of our lived world experiences. Learning is therefore assumed to be a fundamentally social phenomenon, reflecting our own deeply social nature as human beings capable of knowing (Wenger, 1998). Developed from Lave's (1988) initial thinking, Lave and Wenger (1991) and Wenger (1998) argued against a cognitivist approach to learning that separates cognition from the cultural context and activity (Rovegno, 2006). Instead, they support a focus on relations between sociocultural structure and social practice, and the indivisibility of body, cognition, feeling, activity and the sociocultural world (Lave, 1988; Wenger, 1998; Rovegno, 2006). In collaboration with Jean Lave (Lave & Wenger, 1991, 1996) and others (Wenger *et al.*, 2002), Wenger engaged in a conceptual shift from the traditional view of 'the individual as learner to learning as participation, and from the concept of cognitive process to the more-encompassing view of social practice' (Lave & Wenger, 1991: 43). The primary focus of Wenger's theory, then, is on learning as social participation, not just in local events with certain people, but a more encompassing 'process of being active in the practices of social communities and constructing identities in relation to these communities' (Wenger, 1998: 4). Contributing to a general theory of learning, Lave and Wenger (1991) used the concept of legitimate peripheral participation. Here, learners were believed to progress from less important tasks towards crucial 'core' ones, thus moving from peripheral to full, or central, participation. As this occurs, understanding unfolds, with the learner developing a view of what the activity entails. This process ensures that learning itself involves improvisation where the 'curriculum' unfurls in opportunities for engaging in practice (Fuller *et al.*, 2005). The individual is located within the community of practice and facilitates learning through mutual engagement in an activity that is defined by negotiations of meaning both inside and outside the community (Fuller *et al.*, 2005). The concepts of identity and community of practice were important to Lave and Wenger's (1991) original thinking, although Wenger subsequently (1998) suggested they had not been given adequate attention in relation to their centrality.

In response, Wenger's more recent work (Wenger, 1998; Wenger *et al.*, 2002) has attempted to highlight these concepts of identity and community of practice. His writings have therefore come to be most associated with a social theory of learning, using communities of practice (CoP) as its main entry point. Wenger's output with Lave, in addition to his own continuing development of ideas and concepts, has strongly influenced thinking in the field of learning across a range of domains, including coaching. Here, then, the construction of coaching knowledge through direct experience has increasingly come to the fore (Cushion, 2008).

This chapter first outlines and then critically discusses Wenger's ideas related to situated learning and legitimate peripheral participation. Although CoP acts as the main conceptual structure throughout, the chapter specifically considers this notion by examining its nature, structure and boundaries. Developing the underlying concepts related to CoP, the discussion moves to examine the importance of identity, alignment and repertoires. While links to coaching are made throughout, the 'Communities of practice and coaching' section looks specifically and critically at coaching-related CoP research. Finally, Gary Denstone provides a coach's commentary before a brief conclusion.

Social learning: situated learning and legitimate peripheral participation

Wenger's (1998) theory of social learning rests on the following assumptions: (1) humans are social; (2) knowledge is competence in a valued enterprise; (3) knowing is an active participation in that enterprise; and (4) meaning is the ultimate product of learning (Egan & Jaye, 2009; Culver & Trudel, 2008). As mentioned earlier, within this perspective participation involves active involvement in practice and identity construction in relation to the community (Wenger, 1998). Practice is similarly defined as 'doing in a historical and social context that gives structure and meaning to what we do' (Wenger, 1998: 47). Meaning is negotiated within practices through the ongoing interaction of that which is historical and that which is contextual (Culver & Trudel, 2008). In this sense, social practice, cognition and communication in, and with, the social world are situated in the historical development of ongoing activity (Lave & Wenger, 1996). This defines the learning process as the 'historicizing of the production of persons' (Lave & Wenger, 1996: 146).

The action of participating in social practice can be read as belonging to a community. Becoming a member of a community, in turn, allows participation and, therefore, learning to take place (Fuller *et al.*, 2005). Learners enter a community (e.g., beginner coaches enter coaching) at the periphery. Over time, they move closer to full legitimate participation as they gain knowledge, learn the norms of the community, and see themselves as members of the community (Cushion, 2006). Consequently, learning is viewed as distributed among many participants within the community in which people with diverse expertise (experts and novices and those between) are transformed through their own actions and those of other participants.

From this relational perspective of people within a socially and culturally constructed world, understanding and experiences are in constant interaction (Buysse *et al.*, 2003). Essential to this process, making CoP relevant to coach education, is the 'development of self through participation in the community' (Barab & Duffy, 2000: 35). The processes, relationships and experiences that constitute the participants' sense of belonging underpin the nature of subsequent learning, a phenomenon captured through the notion of legitimate peripheral participation (LPP) (Fuller *et al.*, 2005). LPP is a process characterised by both social structures and relations: 'Legitimate peripheral participation provides a way to speak about the relations between newcomers and old-timers, and about activities, identities, artefacts and communities of knowledge and practice. It concerns the process by which newcomers become part of a community of practice' (Lave & Wenger, 1991: 29). In this sense, learning through LPP takes place irrespective of the context 'or whether there is any intention for it at all' (Lave & Wenger 1991: 40). Situated learning, then, is more than learning by doing; a position that gives 'situatedness' a dynamic and theoretical perspective. In essence, learning is viewed as part of social practice (Cassidy & Rossi, 2006). Similarly, participation in social (communities of) practice by definition will involve learning, as the process of becoming a member of a community allows learning to take place. Being 'situated' means that people learn as they participate. They become intimately involved with a community or culture and, through interacting with the community, learn to understand its history, assumptions, cultural values and rules (Lave & Wenger, 1991; Fenwick, 2000). Hence, 'learning is situated in interactions among peripheral participants in a community of meaning. These interactions take place in the context or practice characterized by modeling of both mastery of practice and the process of gaining mastery' (Jacobsen, 1996: 23).

This notion of learning from more experienced members of a community in cultures of practice has particular resonance with the development of coaches.

Taking Lave and Wenger's (1991) argument more broadly – that social practice is the primary, generative phenomenon with learning as one of its characteristics – means that coaching should be analysed as an integral part of social practice. This seems to be analogous with the evidence of how coaching, as both a social system and the knowledge associated with it, evolves from that practice (Cushion, 2006). Indeed, the characterisation of coach learning as a social process has gathered momentum in recent times (Cushion *et al.*, 2010). For example, the notion of an 'informal apprenticeship' seems to be typical of the development of most sports coaches, with time spent as athletes and coaches providing a basis for future practice (e.g. Cushion, *et al.*, 2003, 2010; Saury & Durand, 1998; Trudel & Gilbert, 2006). The progression from assistant coach to head coach and through different levels of sport is a process that may be referred to as legitimate peripheral participation (Trudel & Gilbert, 2006; Cassidy & Rossi, 2006). Thus, coaches are situated and engage with 'others' as part of the social practice of coaching. Indeed, constant interaction with peers has been shown to be one of the best sources of learning for expert coaches (Cushion *et al.*, 2010) as elicited by Salmela and Moraes (2003: 289): 'Sharing of knowledge with other passionate coaches provides a rich forum for better understanding the complexities of coaching, as well as testing the effectiveness of one's particular ways of interaction and behaving in practice and games.'

In recent work, Cassidy and Rossi (2006) and Cushion (2006) argued the case for situated learning and CoPs to be used as frameworks to understand, and as a possible design for, learning. These authors focused on the 'newcomer and old-timer' relationship, considering it in terms of mentoring within a coaching community. The notion of a CoP is particularly helpful in this case as it challenges the perception of 'knowledge generators' as experts (Palinscar *et al.*, 1998). Coaching and learning can, therefore, be usefully viewed as a bi-directional relationship, with both mentor and protégé contributing to the community's knowledge base (Cushion, 2006). Here, the community of practice and situated learning framework recognise that knowledge is generated and shared within a social and cultural context. Within it, mentors are not viewed as working *on* but rather *with* the world of practice (Waddock, 1999); engaged in considerably more than merely passing on 'survival tips' or 'the tricks of the trade' or even in simply caring about coaches' well-being (Cushion, 2006). According to Lave and Wenger (1991), learning is particularly effective under conditions that a mentor is able to influence, such as providing access to different parts of the activity, enabling eventual full participation in core tasks, allowing horizontal interaction between participants, and ensuring that the structures and workings of the CoP are transparent (Cushion, 2006).

Utilising this framework as a tool for understanding mentoring means that, to be effective, mentors must not only command the appropriate knowledge and skills but must be full participants in the cultural practices of the community themselves (Cushion *et al.*, 2003; Cushion, 2006). As communities are social structures, they involve power relations, and the way power is exercised can make LPP empower-ing or disempowering (Lave & Wenger, 1991; Fuller *et al.*, 2005; Cushion, 2008).

Moreover, given the nature of coaching, its traditions and cultures, there remains a dynamic tension between continuity and displacement within a given community, thus impacting on the nature of mentoring relationships and their subsequent success or failure (Cushion, 2006). Despite these issues of negotiation and power, both mentor and protégé operate within an environment of shared enquiry and learning, with interaction revolving around ambiguity and dilemmas that emerge from practice settings (Cushion, 2006). Here, the mentor is often able to create meaning from protégés' lived experiences that, in turn, become reinforced. This is because the CoP is the practice environment. Finally, learning occurs within the context of social relationships with other members of the community, who have similar, if not identical, issues and concerns from the realm of practice (Cushion, 2006).

While considering coach learning in this way is a useful explanatory tool, the overriding assumption of situated learning and LPP is that learning takes place within a participatory framework. That is, rather than simply being in the learner's mind, meaning is mediated by the differing perspectives among co-participants; it is 'not a one-person act' (Lave & Wenger, 1991: 15). The learner belongs legitimately to the context. He or she is also peripheral, thus allowing change through participation and movement, ensuring that the learning enterprise is not static (Brockbank & Magill, 2007). Learning, then, does not occur in isolation but as part of a system of relations. This system is called a community of practice (Lave & Wenger, 1991; Brockbank & McGill, 2007).

Communities of practice (CoPs)

Nature and structure

Participation in social practice is a way of belonging to a community; similarly, participation in social (communities of) practice will inevitably involve learning (*Fuller et al.*, 2005).

> A community of practice is an intrinsic condition for the existence of knowledge . . . Thus participation in cultural practice in which any knowledge exists is an epistemological principle of learning. The social structure of this practice, and its power relations, and its conditions for legitimacy define possibilities for learning . . . A community of practice is a set of relations among persons, activity and world over time, and in relation with other tangential overlapping communities of practice.
>
> (Lave & Wenger, 1991: 8)

As the above quote indicates, a CoP is not merely a repository for technical knowledge and skills; rather, it is an 'intrinsic condition for the existence of knowledge, not least because it provides the interpretive support necessary for making sense of its heritage' (Lave & Wenger, 1991: 98). Therefore, participation in a cultural practice, the knowledge associated with it and its application are all connected, while the learner's location within a CoP also impacts on the negotiation of meaning related to the practice (Fuller *et al.*, 2005). In this respect, Wenger *et al.* (2002) argue that knowledge is an accumulation of practice and experience; a 'residue' of actions, thinking and conversation.

In coaching, coaches will interact with a range of people. These interactions have been described as networks of practice, informal knowledge networks or communities of practice (Trudel & Gilbert, 2006). In networks of practice 'most members are unknown to one another . . . and hardly meet face-to-face yet contribute and help each other regularly' (Nichani & Hung, 2002: 50). Informal knowledge networks are loose and informal; although people know each other and exchange information, no joint enterprise holds them together (Trudel & Gilbert, 2006; Allee, 2000). Such networks seem central to coach learning, but may not always indicate a community of practice, which has more of a shared understanding and a sense of mission (Trudel & Gilbert, 2006).

Communities of practice, then, are different to other sets of relationships: they contain selected groups of people who share a common sense of purpose and desire to learn and know what each other member knows (Lave & Wenger, 1991; Wenger, 1998). These groups can be somewhat informal in nature, being self-organised by the members themselves, while possibly existing within larger organisational structures. Wenger (1998) describes the dimensions of the relationships evident within communities of practice as several concepts: for example, as mutual engagement between the participants which allows them to do what they need to do while binding members into a social entity; as a joint enterprise resulting from a 'collective process of negotiations that reflects the full complexity of mutual engagement' (Wenger, 1998: 77); and as a shared repertoire of communal resources that belongs to the CoP and includes 'routines, words, tools, ways of doing things, stories, gestures, symbols, genres, actions or concepts that the community has produced or adopted in the course of its existence, and which have become a part of its practice' (Wenger, 1998: 83).

'Passion, commitment and identification with the group's expertise' (Wenger & Snyder, 2000: 42) is the glue that holds together these collectives. The group's life-cycle is subsequently determined by the worth these qualities provide to group members, not to organisational values or institutional schedules. The power within a CoP stems from the fact that it organises itself, sets its own agenda, and establishes its own leadership. Thus, members of a CoP may feel more connected to smaller communities than to larger organisational cultures. Wenger (1998: 125–126) proposed the existence of signs as evidence that a community of practice has formed. These include sustained mutual relationships, ways of communicating information facilitated by common understandings that may be unique to the CoP, forms of practice that assume shared implicit knowledge of processes and procedures, a sense of membership from experiences of working together, and the development of practice styles that are unique to the CoP (Egan & Jaye, 2009). These conditions can be applicable to communities that are continuous over time, inter-professional and/or integrated around perfor-mance. They could also apply to episodic and task-specific communities which disband on completion of a specific objective (Egan & Jaye, 2009). Thus, communities of practice can be represented very broadly or much more narrowly, making precise definitions problematic (Hodkinson & Hodkinson, 2004a; Egan & Jaye, 2009).

Despite illustrative examples of CoPs resembling close-knit groups of workers sharing knowledge, tasks, activities and a common physical location, the definitional divergence has led to ambiguity about learning in terms of applicability and scale (Hodkinson & Hodkinson, 2004a). For example, questions relating to the impact macro factors, organisation, structure and purpose, localised patterns of interaction and micro factors have on determining learning in different CoPs remain unanswered (Hodkinson & Hodkinson, 2004a). While these issues are worthy of consideration, it is important to remember that learning, as has been discussed earlier in the chapter, is considered an integral part of generative social practice in the lived-in world, not just merely situated 'in practice' (Lave and Wenger, 1991; Cushion, 2008). Therefore, participation in social practice is a way of belonging to a community, with the process, relationships and experiences that constitute the participants' sense of belonging underpinning the nature and extent of subsequent learning (Cushion, 2008; Fuller *et al.*, 2005). In other words, a CoP is an intrinsic condition for learning; we need to belong in order to learn, a point which is more significant than determining what a CoP specifically is (Hodkinson & Hodkinson, 2004a).

Wenger (1998) argues that practice influences identity, because the latter is produced as a lived experience of participation in specific communities (Egan & Jaye, 2009). Regardless of curriculum and discipline, then, transformative learning and the development of identities involve membership of and within CoPs (Wenger, 1998). However, as Egan and Jaye (2009) note, even though a CoP is often shaped by the (social and historical) conditions outside the control of its members, the day-to-day reality is nevertheless produced by participants within the resources and constraints of their situation. In a practical sense, this means that, although always mediated by the community's production of its own practice and discourse, individuals still have room for agency (Egan & Jaye, 2009). In short, people still have some power within social structures.

Boundaries

The discussion has thus far considered the nature and structure of CoPs. In coaching, it could be argued that two types of CoP exist. First, there is a formal CoP based on 'profession', organised with and by governing bodies, and empowered by legitimate regulation. Alternatively, there are much less formal groupings of coaches, sometimes a temporary configuration, often with other practitioners (e.g., strength and conditioning staff, performance analysts and physiotherapists, among others) brought together in a combined effort to generate improvements in athletes' performances. Within the latter group the boundaries are much less distinct and more permeable than those defined by professional scopes of practice (Goodwin *et al.*, 2005; Egan & Jaye, 2009).

The notion of boundary is significant for Wenger (1998) as, in the first instance, it is a 'potent signifier of difference, demarcation, and distinction between CoPs' (Egan & Jaye, 2009: 118). It also provides the means to elucidate and theorise the relationships between CoPs, and between members of CoPs (Wenger 1998). Boundaries can define the CoP as much as its practice (Wenger, 1998). Newcomers will be confronted by boundaries that can take physical form (for example, areas or activities from which they are excluded), or role boundaries and jurisdictions. Boundaries can also be marked by unique understanding and language. Coaches frequently have a particular linguistic style that has to be mastered to engage in effective practice. In addition, practices employed within a coaching CoP can often be described in terms of a boundary that distinguishes the CoP from other environments. The key here is that coaches need to learn to identify not only existing boundaries but which boundaries demarcate what from what. While in some cases these can be explicit, in others they can operate implicitly and might be difficult to identify. Wenger (1998) uses the concept of boundary objects to describe the role of artefacts in organising practice. Ownership of boundary objects can be distributed among CoPs and, consequently, can be seen as the meeting place between CoPs. For coaches, the curriculum to be delivered or the athletes themselves may represent boundary objects, in that they mediate and organise coaching practice. As boundaries can organise and mediate practice, in many ways they hold the capability to determine the constitution of a CoP by requiring certain forms of practice (Wenger, 1998; Egan & Jaye, 2009).

Identity and alignment

The lived experience of participation in specific CoPs means that practice will influence identity (Wenger, 1998). LPP leads to full participation within a CoP through the notion of alignment, which Wenger (1998) described as a sense of belonging or connectedness between members of a CoP. It is through processes of alignment that the enterprise of the larger group can become part of the identity of the participants within the CoP (Egan & Jaye, 2009). This notion of alignment in identity construction shares similarities with ideas related to socialisation. Indeed, Eraut (2000) argues that a person may be socialised into the norms of an organisation (CoP) without necessarily being aware either of the learning process or what those norms are; hence, they become 'aligned'. Through alignment, individuals will acquire norms, discourses and other aspects of occupational culture over time 'which implicitly add meaning to what are interpreted as routine activities' (Eraut, 2000: 126). This implicit learning and knowledge can become very powerful and may override explicit learning as the person develops (Eraut, 2000). The alignment with norms and cultures has been demonstrated well in coaching, as has the impact of the 'filtering' of 'new' knowledge from coach education through a lens that has been implicitly learned and developed over time (Cushion *et al.*, 2003; Trudel & Gilbert, 2006).

The process of alignment and identity construction within coaching means that becoming a coach is central to the learning of how to coach, and it is this process that articulates between practice and identity (Wenger, 1998). Indeed, Wenger (1998: 149) argues that there is a 'profound connection between identity and practice'. Building an identity in coaching means that coaches need to negotiate the meaning of their experiences as related to their membership of the CoP. Alternatively, practice entails the negotiation of ways of being a person in that context (Wenger, 1998). In this sense, Wenger's thinking addresses the agency–structure dichotomy, with identity as the bridge, allowing an approach that is neither individualistic nor structural. Practice, therefore, is negotiation. This is because being part of a coaching CoP enables participation as social practice, but also facilitates the negotiation required for that participation. Importantly, Wenger (1998) recognised that there may be tensions and conflicts as well as agreement and concession in this negotiation which will impact on participation in the community and learning. Lastly here, as identity, practice, participation and learning are connected, continual learning means that practice and identity are always under negotiation within a CoP. In this sense, the coach is never 'finished', with the learning extending well beyond that gleaned from specific developmental episodes (Cassidy & Rossi, 2006; Hager & Hodkinson, 2009).

Repertoires

A key characteristic of CoPs is that they generate repertoires of practice that include normative roles, behaviours and routines that may be both formal and informal (Wenger, 1998). At an organisational level, repertoires will be constrained by the scopes of practice as they are defined by different contexts (Egan & Jaye, 2009). However, at the interactional level of the coach and athlete, repertoires can consist of routine ways of behaving (who does what and when) that constitute the everyday practice of the community. This includes what is both said and unsaid. Indeed, coaching practice includes not only the explicit – language, roles, tools, documents – but the implicit – relationships, tacit conventions, subtle cues, untold rules of thumb, recognisable intuitions, specific perceptions, well-tuned sensitivities, embodied understandings, underlying assumptions and shared world views (Wenger, 1998; Cushion, 2007). While most of these implicit phenomena can never be articulated, they are unmistakable within coaching practice and, arguably, crucial to its effectiveness (Cushion, 2007).

The tacit is often 'taken for granted' and tends to fade into the background because it comes naturally or is instinctive (Egan & Jaye, 2009). These taken-for-granted aspects of a CoP's practice can be considered as 'hiding in plain sight' (Gair & Mullins, 2001). Interestingly, what is hidden from old-timers, even in plain sight, can be obvious to the newcomer: 'No matter what is said, taught, prescribed, recommended, or tested, new-comers are no fools: once they have actual access to the practice, they soon find out what counts' (Wenger, 1998: 156). In this way, repertoires may also require specific forms of dress and personal presentation, an order of ceremony (e.g., who talks when, and who asks questions), a local approach to practice, group attitudes to outsiders or other CoPs, and so on (Egan & Jaye, 2009). These sub-cultural norms or repertoires have been demonstrated in coaching where the CoP acts as part of a normalising influence for both coach and athlete groups (e.g., Cushion & Jones, 2006).

Communities of practice and coaching

Galipeau and Trudel (2004, 2005, 2006) studied university teams and concluded that each team should not be viewed as a single CoP. Rather, they should be considered as two distinct CoPs (one for the athletes and one for the coaches) involved in a constant negotiation process in relation to how to direct and lead the team (Gilbert *et al.*, 2009). However, as discussions around definitions described earlier in the chapter suggest, CoPs in coaching may not be as neat and tidy or indeed as easy to decipher as we would like (Cushion, 2008). Coaching practice and CoPs therein are not benign social structures. In fact, they may not be stable, cohesive or even welcoming (Cassidy & Rossi, 2006; Fuller *et al.*, 2005; Cushion, 2008). Importantly, within CoPs, power sets and relocates boundaries for learning. The power here (as everywhere else) is unevenly distributed, and stratified through complex social and cultural lines (Cushion & Jones, 2006). To understand CoPs, then, we need to engage not only with their structures and characters but with the complex interaction of power, position and disposition evident within them (Cushion, 2008).

In the first of two related studies, Culver and Trudel (2006) examined if CoPs form naturally. They found that CoPs in coaching will be ineffective unless elements of the setting are specifically designed to nurture and sustain them (Gilbert *et al.*, 2009). The second study contained an intervention designed to support a CoP within a Canadian alpine ski club (Culver & Trudel, 2006). The data revealed that those practitioners who participated appreciated the discussion opportunities, finding them to be both valuable and enjoyable, and that the process contributed to their development. However, follow-up interviews a year later found that the CoP from the intervention had dissolved due to the absence of leadership and structure (Gilbert, *et al.*, 2009). Similarly, Culver *et al.* (2009) recently documented the attempts of a technical director to foster a CoP within a competitive youth baseball league. Here, coaches were encouraged to share knowledge despite the environment being related to the notion of 'competitive advantage'. Although a cooperative learning environment was initially developed, this again failed when the technical director left the position.

In another related study, Lemyre (2008) attempted to establish a CoP in two sports contexts: in a community-based karate club, and with high school sports coaches. In the karate setting, despite attempts to facilitate interactions between the instructors, the hierarchical structure proved counterproductive to establishing a culture of negotiated learning (Gilbert *et al.*, 2009). In the high school setting, Lemyre worked with six coaches in facilitated meetings. These encounters allowed the participant coaches to see how others were thinking, to listen to others' opinions, and to experiment with new ideas in practice. The participants reported positively in relation to the opportunities provided to meet with the facilitator individually, and also acknowledged the importance of sharing their knowledge with peers (Gilbert *et al.*, 2009). However, subsequent interviews revealed that following the withdrawal of the facilitator, the group lacked leadership and direction; thus its effectiveness, as with the previous studies mentioned, became critically compromised (Gilbert *et al.*, 2009).

The findings from these studies suggest that the facilitator (learning architect) played a vital role in the group development process, adding a certain amount of structure to the learning (Culver & Trudel, 2008). The research cited here, however, seems to have adopted a narrow characterisation of CoPs. Although it may be useful to attempt to apply a tight definition of a CoP to small, coherent groups, it is more general notions of membership and social relations that underpin practice and learning. Therefore, participatory practices and relationships within a community seem more important than a criteria for establishing one (Hodkinson & Hodkinson, 2003). Indeed, the processes, relationships and experiences that constitute the participants' sense of belonging underpin the character and extent of subsequent learning (Fuller *et al.*, 2005). Therefore, it could be argued that the nature of 'manufactured' or 'facilitated' CoPs do not engage the coaches' sense of belonging, existing only in a superficial sense and thus inhibiting any meaningful learning (Cushion, 2008).

As discussed, learners enter a community at the periphery, and over time move closer to full legitimate participation as they gain knowledge, learn the norms of the community, and see themselves as members of the community. Consequently, learning is viewed as distributed among many participants within the community in which people with diverse expertise (experts, novices and those between) are transformed through their own actions and those of other participants. Essential to this process, and what distinguishes communities of practice, is the 'development of self through participation in the community' (Barab & Duffy, 2000: 35). Arguably, therefore, a manufactured CoP with a 'sample' of coaches is, in effect, a new community for those coaches – a community 'dropped into' an existing community of practice.

A coach's commentary by Gary Denstone

I am currently coaching at Warwickshire County Cricket Club, whilst also holding a coach development role with the England and Wales Cricket Board. I have been coaching cricket, primarily within the context of a state secondary school (due to my previous career as a teacher of physical education) and a local cricket club, for the last fourteen years. As a coaching practitioner, an acute awareness of learning as a process of 'social participation' located within Wenger's framework of 'communities of practice' is something that resonates with me clearly. The chapter and the ideas discussed within it provided me with tools to deconstruct and interrogate my career, learning and development as a cricket coach. Thinking about learning as a social phenomenon, I can share my experiences of informal learning that are constantly presented on a day-to-day basis, and reflect on some important considerations for the design and development of formalised governing-body coach education.

Although formal, informal and non-formal learning opportunities and experiences have helped construct my current status as a coach, attempting to unpick, measure and pinpoint the exact contribution of each is undeniably complex. An awareness of the 'development of self' via 'legitimate peripheral participation' in a community of practice is a useful tool to be able to begin to comprehend my evolution as a coach within a social world. I would certainly attach enormous significance to my constant interaction and work with other coaches within the various cricket communities of practice that I have participated in over the last fourteen years. Without doubt, my membership of and participation in each community (and associated collaboration with a vast array of coaches of varying experience and expertise) has provided countless influential learning opportunities. For me, these 'real-life' or 'in-field' experiences, in terms of observing other coaches (from cricket and other sports), co-coaching opportunities, countless professional discussions and the continual sharing of coaching practice, have had a powerful and long-lasting impact in terms of shaping and defining my personal coaching philosophy, pedagogy and behaviour. This contribution has been so considerable that it is fascinating to consider what my current coaching practice would look like without it.

Informal learning (via the process of legitimate peripheral participation) within a community of practice is not only something that strikes a pertinent personal note; it is something that is supported by other coaches with whom I have worked or come into contact. A recent conversation with Peter Moores (Lancashire CCC Head Coach and former England Head Coach) identified the countless hours spent working in conjunction with colleagues in coaching communities as a key determinant in his development as an elite coach. Therefore, one must not underestimate the impact of this social framework for learning across the profession.

My membership of a variety of different communities of cricket coaching practice has made me appreciate both the social and the practical realities that coaches experience as a result of the process of legitimate peripheral participation. The reality is that I have assimilated values, beliefs, an extensive subject knowledge base and good coaching practice not only from more experienced and qualified practitioners; even the most inexperienced or newly qualified practitioner has contributed to my personal learning. As coaches, we should also acknowledge that each interaction with our athletes might provide a significant developmental opportunity.

This highlights the crux of the potential contribution of Wenger's work. Indeed, my reflections on it have raised some significant issues for me as a coach, as it emphasises the central importance of viewing one's coaching as a journey of continual development, where each coaching interaction (with both coaches and players), session, observation or discussion should be seen as a priceless learning opportunity. For me, this is perhaps the key insight that I can offer to other coaches as a result of my analysis of the theory presented in this chapter.

I would also approach any social interactions with a critical social filter, recognising that not all learning within a community of practice is necessarily positive. I have found that learning may not always involve the development of good practice. I have seen that ineffective practice can permeate. This is because coaches may not have the ability to filter appropriate or non-appropriate knowledge, behaviour and practice. Alternatively, I have also witnessed first hand the scenario where a coach may feel forced to adopt certain values, practice or behaviour to uphold the status quo of a certain group and thus maintain their identity and subsequent membership within a specific community. Clearly, all coaches must have a critical awareness that the process of informal learning within any community of practice is not simply a passive, positive or power-neutral one. Instead, it is a process that is shaped by the inherent complexities associated with the people, the organisation and the sport.

Finally, as a designer and developer of coach education courses and resources, an understanding of Wenger's work reinforced the potential impact that formalised coach education can have upon the development of coaches. This is not to suggest that governing bodies of sport should attempt to control or artificially facilitate cricket coaching communities. Instead, I believe that effective coach education interventions could support and enhance potential learning in any coaching context via high-quality, context-specific, formal participatory programmes. Armed with an understanding that, for many coaches, formalised coach education courses may be their initial route to membership of a specific community of practice, it becomes the unquestionable responsibility of the coach educator to contribute positively to the establishment and development of that process. Therefore, the key for me as a coach educator is to maximise the effectiveness of formal coach education programmes to meet the needs of coaches at all stages of personal development, in an effort to enhance both their understanding of the players that they work with and their ability to align coaching practice with effective player development (whatever their performance level).

Conclusion

Coaching is a social activity, and coaching practice – that is, the interaction of coach, athlete and context – is a reference point through which individuals (coaches and athletes) give meaning to their activities and manage their identities (Allen & Pilnick, 2007). Coaching, coach and athlete learning, and curricula (coaching and training sessions) intersect in communities of coaching practice, with the CoP mediating principles and policies (rules, plans), conduct, skills and knowledge (Egan & Jaye, 2009). Because CoPs are where athletes and coaches encounter one another, and where 'normative' practice is demonstrated, Wenger's theorising on learning and the development of professional identity through LPP is a very useful framework for examining how coaches (and athletes) gather, generate and interpret knowledge.

Cassidy and Rossi (2006: 243) comment that the emphasis on a collective theory of learning, with the engagement in social practice as the central process by which learning takes place, 'is a more fruitful way to think about how coaches can come to know'. Consequently, Wenger's (1998) theorising on CoPs and the development of professional identity through LPP in those communities offers great potential for understanding learning within coaching practice. Such an approach also offers a viable alternative to theorising learning to the individualistic and cognitive/behavioural models that have traditionally held privileged positions in coach education (Cushion *et al.*, 2010).

Wenger's ideas point to a need to analyse and reflect on coaching settings and the nature of coaching practice as learning opportunities. To this end, there is a growing body of work in sports coaching that utilises the CoP framework. In addition, Lave and Wenger's (1991) and Wenger's (1998) work has a corpus of research examining situated learning in CoPs. However, there is no current universal agreement regarding its utility and application, with issues relating to power and the relationship between formal and informal learning remaining unclear. Nevertheless, Wenger's work remains an innovative way to consider learning as a social practice, and to understand and develop learning opportunities in coaching.

9 Peter Blau: Exchange, reciprocity and dependency

How coaches and athletes rely on each other

Robyn L. Jones with Jake Bailey

Peter Blau: a short biography

Peter Blau was born in Vienna in 1918. He emigrated to the USA in 1939, and gained a Ph.D. at Columbia University in 1952. From 1953 to 1970 he taught at the University of Chicago before returning to Columbia, where he remained until 1988. From 1988 to 2000 he taught as an emeritus professor at the University of North Carolina, Chapel Hill. His sociological speciality concerned an investigation of organisational and social structures. Although he is usually noted for his contribution to grand theorising, and, in particular, to organisational theory, Blau also developed a 'microstructural' theory of exchange and social integration (Blau, 1960). This work on social (as opposed to economic) exchange, including flows of advice, esteem and reputation, and its interaction with group power structures, led to his landmark book *Exchange and power in social life* (1964). His thinking here became important in the later formalisation of exchange theory by Richard Emerson. Such an analysis, however, was not at variance with his macro-sociological considerations, as he viewed individual-level outcomes such as competitiveness and cooperativeness as being at least somewhat derivable from 'structural effects'. In this respect, his attraction to exchange theory lay partly in his belief that it could provide a means to forge a link between micro- and macro-sociological perspectives. In 1974, he served as president of the American Sociological Association.

Peter Blau died on 12 March 2002, aged eighty-four.

Introduction

Within a later introduction (to the Transaction edition) of his book *Exchange and power in social life* (1986), Peter Blau explained how his thinking moved to embrace the notion that macro- and micro-sociological analyses need not be incompatible. Through academic interaction with the sociologist George Homas, Blau came to realise that his work was as much about informal group relations as a study of bureaucracy. This rekindled his 'interest in the study of social exchange' (Blau, 1986: x), which Blau envisaged as providing a nexus between macro- and micro-sociological analyses. The ultimate result was his aforementioned book *Exchange and power in social life*, first published in 1964, from which this chapter draws heavily. Here, an attempt was made to connect the everyday theories of Erving Goffman and Georg Simmel to the broader thinking of Max Weber and Talcott Parsons. The basic idea of social exchange had occurred earlier to Blau, during his Ph.D. work involving a case study of government officials. Here, he observed a practice of informal consultation among colleagues, where 'each gains something while paying a price' (Blau, 1986: viii). For example, an individual requesting and receiving help from a colleague without having to expose his or her difficulties to a supervisor pays the debt through giving the consultant respect which is implicit in the requesting of the advice (Blau, 1986). The consultant's status is subsequently raised at the cost of devoting time and effort to dispensing the advice. If properly reciprocated, the social rewards received by the consultant serve as inducements to assist further, creating a social bond between the two actors. Consequently, quoting the noted seventeenth-century French author François La Rochefoucauld, Blau (1986: 1) asserted that 'we pay our debts, not because it is right that we should discharge them, but in order more easily to borrow again'. For Blau, exchange theory was an attempt to explain how social life becomes organised into complex structures of associations. In particular, he was concerned 'with the microsociological [principles and] processes of reciprocity and imbalance that govern social life and relations among people' (Blau, 1986: vii); or, put another way, with the direct process of give and take between two or more people.

According to Sabatelli and Shehan (1993), the exchange framework contains a number of core assumptions about the nature of relationships. These include that, when interacting with others, individuals seek to maximise profits for themselves while minimising costs. They also, within the limitations of the information they possess, calculate these rewards and costs, and consider alternatives before acting. Exchange relationships, then, are characterised by interdependence, and regulated by norms such as reciprocity and fairness. Although guided by reciprocity, social exchange also has the potential to give rise to differentiations of power, and the legitimisation of such arrangements. Furthermore, the stability of relationships derives from the levels of attraction and dependence experienced by the parties who comprise them, as opposed to any notion of precise equality or balance. Indeed, it is this force of social attraction that stimulates exchange in the first place; a point which holds great relevance for coaching.

Lest he be accused of one-dimensionality, Blau was quick to point out that not all human action is guided by considerations of exchange. Rather, such behaviour 'must be orientated towards ends that can only be achieved through interaction with other persons, [while] seeking to adapt means to further the achievement of those ends' (Blau, 1986: 5). The actions of social exchange, then, are contingent on rewarding conduct from others that cease when such reactions are not forthcoming. From an exchange perspective, individuals could be posited as rather rational beings working towards conscious objectives. On the other hand, locating his thinking within the often seemingly irrational social world, Blau believed that such objectives are firmly rooted in cultural symbols and expectations; there is, consequently, no predictable sequence in human exchanges.

The aim of this chapter is to illustrate and discuss the work of Peter Blau and, in particular, his conceptualisation of human behaviour as social exchange. The principal theoretical notions explored within it include social relations as manifest in the exchange of rewards, reciprocity and balance; impressing others, unspecified obligations and trust; and differentiations and legitimation of power. Following the established pattern, the chapter progresses to the thoughts of Jake Bailey, an elite trampoline coach, who implemented aspects of exchange theory into his coaching practice in preparing his critique. Finally, a short conclusion summarises the principal points made.

Social rewards, reciprocity and balance

Blau believed that social life rested on the associations (themselves part of a broader social matrix) between people. In his own words, 'much of human suffering as well as much of human happiness has its source in the actions of other human beings' (Blau, 1986: 15). Subsequently, the central task of his sociology was to analyse such associations, the processes that sustained them, the forms they took and how they became organised into complex social structures. His work started to focus on exchange transactions and power relations which were constituted as social forces in their own right. In this respect, he was aware that the rewards obtained by some from their social associations entailed a cost to others. Rewards in this context were defined as the pleasures, satisfactions and gratifications enjoyed from participating in a relationship (Thibaut & Kelley, 1959). Such a position, however, did not mean a zero-sum or an all-or-nothing contract. On the contrary, Blau considered that people associate with each other because they all potentially derive profit from the association. The point was that people do not all profit equally, in that there is always more of a cost for some. The costs could vary from the energy invested in a relationship to the rewards relinquished from not engaging in one course of action as opposed to another (Blau, 1964).

For Blau, the term 'balance' within the context of social exchange was ambiguous, because we talk of both 'balancing the books' and having 'the balance in our favour'. The principle suggested here was 'that balanced social states depend on imbalance in other social states' (Blau, 1986: 26). The example Blau gave to explain this apparent anomaly was that of a boy who spends much time and money making himself attractive to a girl. Although the attraction becomes reciprocal, the 'reciprocity has been established by an imbalance in the exchange' (Blau, 1986: 27). That is, for the boy, the girl's company in itself is enough to secure satisfaction; while, for her, his ability to make their dates enjoyable through continuing to make special efforts is what keeps her interested. As Emerson (1962: 34), that other prominent exchange theorist, was quick to point out, 'balance does not neutralise power'.

On the other hand, Blau was fully aware that some social associations are inherently rewarding: for example, the pleasure derived by friends from being with one another. Social associations could be rewarding in another sense, however. The example given by Blau here was that of the motorist who stops and helps another whose car has stalled. The expression of gratitude received from the stalled motorist is the social reward obtained for the favour. A person who fails to reciprocate is accused of ungratefulness, an allegation which indicates that reciprocation is expected although seldom articulated. The accusation also serves as a social sanction that discourages people from reneging on their obligations; the social debt, then, is usually repaid. For Blau, the fact that some people go to great lengths to assist others was explained in terms of the social rewards subsequently received. This is not to say that all such human acts possess dark ulterior motives (although Blau did concede there is an underlying 'egoism' in human conduct), but that we require at least some incentive for unselfish acts, 'even if it is only the social acknowledgement that we are unselfish' (Blau, 1986: 17). Such acts are grounded in the belief that humans are largely driven by their desire to seek social rewards, with the resulting exchanges responsible for shaping the structures of social relations. As previously mentioned, however, this is not to advocate a rationalistic conception of such transactions. Rather, Blau was at pains to emphasise that it is *not* assumed that people make such decisions on the basis of complete information, that there are no existing obligations which limit alternative choices, that preferences are always consistent, and that people only pursue one specific goal to the exclusion of all others. Hardly linear, logical decision-making, then. Furthermore, the need to anticipate the likely rewards for initial favours in advance introduces additional elements of uncertainty, ambiguity and errors of judgement, 'making perfectly rational calculations [and actions] impossible' (Blau, 1986: 19).

Impressing others, unspecified obligations and trust

According to exchange theory, social attraction is the force that induces associations between people. Although Blau drew a blurred distinction between intrinsic and extrinsic attraction, he generally believed that such attraction is generated by the expectation that associating oneself with another will be rewarding; it is the interest in that social reward that draws one to another. Similarly, the person who is attracted to another is interested in proving him- or herself as attractive to them. Both parties seek and anticipate associations from which they can mutually reap benefits. Such action can often be seen in the behaviours of both coaches and athletes as they embark on a continual process of acceptance and progression ('Their attraction to him, just as his to them, depends on the anticipation that the association will be rewarding' [Blau, 1986: 21].) According to Blau, to arouse this initial anticipation, a person consciously tries to impress others. The subsequent mutual attraction draws people to establish associations, with future actions (depending on whether they are rewarding or disappointing) dictating whether the association continues.

The strategies used to impress others vary widely and are contingent on a number of things, not least what the other might find impressive: for example, athletic quality, insightful knowledge on a particular topic, sophisticated wit or artistic talent. Similar to Goffman's work discussed in Chapter 2, then, the aim of such behaviour is to create a 'good' (or desired) impression in the quest for social acceptance. This impression management naturally entails risks, such as being conceited, although, conversely, 'taking risks is a method of impressing others in its own right' (Blau, 1986: 40). Blau quotes Goffman's (1961a) notion of 'role distance' here in explaining how people engage in behaviours that 'risk disapproval yet successfully meet the challenge' in the quest to generate attractiveness and respect from others. Such behaviour is based on the social performance that the demands of the given role are beneath an individual's capabilities and thus can be impressively performed with ease: for example, the surgeon bantering through feigning incompetence before nurses. However, Blau also pointed out that such concern with impression could not be continuously dominant, as this would prohibit the individual from fully concentrating on his or her task. The conscious mask could also be dropped due to a perceived security within the group – the individual performer being sure of the collective approval.

A crucial way that social exchange differs from economic exchange is that the former entails unspecified obligations, and 'the trust both required for and promoted by it' (Blau, 1986: 8). Whereas in economic dealings the terms are agreed upon at the time of transaction, in social exchange, although there is a general expectation of some future return for a favour done, the exact nature of the response is 'not stipulated in advance' (Blau, 1986: 93). The original favour carried out, then, creates a diffuse obligation. Additionally, because the terms are not specified in advance, the nature of the return gift cannot be bargained for; rather, it is left to the discretion of the one who has to make it. Consequently, as 'there is no way to assure an appropriate return for a favour, social exchange requires trusting others to discharge their obligations' (Blau, 1986: 94). Trust refers to an individual's belief that he or she will not be exploited or taken advantage of by the other in the relationship or association they have entered. This happens when relationships conform to the norms of reciprocity with the pattern of exchange being perceived as fair (Blau, 1964; McDonald, 1981). Trust is proposed to be important in relationship development because it allows individuals to be less immediately calculative and to see longer-term outcomes (Scanzoni, 1979). Social exchanges usually evolve slowly, beginning with minor transactions for which little trust is required because little risk is involved. If favours are recip-rocated and obligations discharged, if only to induce further favours or assistance, individuals start to prove themselves as trustworthy. In this way, a mutual trust in social relations is generated and expanded as individuals, through reciprocation, confirm themselves worthy of further credit. When such an experience of trust is facilitated, commitment is seen to develop within a relationship, which involves individuals' willingness to work for the continuation of the relationship (Sabatelli, 1999; Leik & Leik 1977; Scanzoni 1979). According to Cook and Emerson (1978), commitment builds stability into relationships by increasing partners' dependence on each other. Commitment, which also reflects a neglect in developing other relationships or associates, additionally gives an individual another reason to trust that the partner will not evade his or her obligations in their relationship.

Differentiations and the legitimation of power

Although the language of exchange is littered with notions of reciprocity, Blau believed that social exchange tends to give rise to differentiations of status and power. As touched upon earlier, people in associations do not all benefit equally from them. Indeed, providing needed benefits which others cannot easily do without, perhaps akin to the guidance and insight an expert coach gives to athletes, 'is undoubtedly the most prevalent way of attaining power' (Blau, 1986: 118). Conversely, situations arise where in order to secure the assistance of a particular other, a person must subordinate himself or herself to the other. This is usually because he or she cannot force the assistance from the other, cannot find the assistance anywhere else or cannot work things out alone, while recognising that they have little or nothing that the other needs to reciprocate for the help. The reward given, then, is power over him- or herself; the willingness to comply with given demands. In this respect, a person who commands the services of others receives his or her compliance or dependence in return. That is the bargain that is struck. This, of course, clearly resonates with athletes' experiences in the relationships they develop with coaches. Taken as such, exchange processes 'give rise to a differentiation of power' (Blau, 1986: 22).

The degree of dependence evidenced in such relationships is determined from the outcomes derived from it. That is, dependence and subordination can often be tolerated in highly rewarding relationships. However, staying in a relationship is not simply a matter of how rewarding that relationship is, as it also seems to be contingent on the alternatives available. This notion of a comparison level of alternatives (CLalt) was developed by Thibaut and Kelley (1959) to help explain individuals' decisions to remain in or leave a relationship. Such a perspective also conceptualised power as a more complex phenomenon than that existing in a dyad, with one party simply having more than another. Alternatively, the CLalt refers an individual's assessment of the outcomes available in an alternative to the present relationship. When such outcomes exceed those available in a current relationship, the likelihood increases that the person will leave the relationship. This was a point that both Blau (1964) and Emerson (1976) were very keen to make.

Consequently, the power a dominant actor holds over subordinates is not absolute, as it can wane if those subordinates consider that they have (equally) good alternatives. It can also diminish if the subordinates think they can do without the benefits the principal power-holder confers or if the demands made on them are perceived as excessive, 'arousing feelings of having to render more compliance than the rewards received justify' (Blau, 1986: 22). According to Blau, social norms in relation to acceptable and appropriate actions define and guide behaviour and subsequent judgement here. Such norms refer to the broader cultural consensus that exists about how relationships should be structured and how individuals should act within them.

It has been suggested that the bases of power within exchange relationships lie with the constructs of resources and dependence (e.g., Huston, 1983). Here, it is assumed that dependence and power are inversely related, as those who are least interested in their relationships tend to have the greater power because they are less dependent on the relationships. Although, at first glance, this seems pretty straightforward, Emerson's (1962) insightful analysis of the position highlighted that it was anything but. For example, if a more powerful partner demands a 'higher price' from the less powerful for the continuation of a relationship, he or she becomes increasingly dependent on the relationship, thus becoming somewhat less powerful within it. The opposite, of course, becomes true for the less powerful. In demanding more, the individual becomes less powerful. Hence, the relationship generally moves towards balance, unless (there always seems to be an 'unless') 'there are limits set on the demands exchange partners can place on each other' (Powers, 2004: 200). Such limits can be based on law, norms or myriad social ties (e.g., the coach–athlete relationship). On the other hand, and perhaps more obviously, resources and power within exchange theory are also (to an extent) seen as being positively related (Huston, 1983; Thibaut & Kelley, 1959). This is because the partners with the greater resources tend to be those with the greater power, as they have relatively greater control over the available outcomes.

To achieve power over others, a person must prevent others from choosing alternatives, 'thereby compelling them to comply with his [*sic*] directives' (Blau, 1986: 121). This involves remaining indifferent to the benefits subordinates can offer. The strategies employed here include encouraging competition among the suppliers of the service, and securing benefits from outside sources, thus not leaving the dominant power-holder in hock to the more powerless. Additional means to sustain power include barring access to alternative suppliers from which the subordinates may draw (a tactic manifest in service monopolies), and discouraging coalitions among subordinates that would enable them to extract demands. Finally, power also depends on the needs of the subordinates, 'their needs for the benefits that those in power have to offer' (Blau, 1986: 122). As pointed out by Emerson (1962: 32), 'the power to control or influence the other resides in control over the things he [*sic*] values'. However, as previously mentioned, this power is never absolute, because if the demands are too severe, relinquishing the desired benefits may be preferable to succumbing to the demands.

Within the framework of exchange theory, 'authority appears quite naturally [as] legitimised power vested in roles'. The process of 'legitimation', in turn, is seen as a development or 'coalition through which norms and role prescriptions are formed' (Emerson, 1962: 31). The resulting collective approval by subordinates leads to legitimation of the power exercised over them. Here, people consider that the advantages gained from subordination outweigh the hardships of compliance. In other words, a positive imbalance of benefits generates feelings of legitimate power towards the leader (Blau, 1986: 30). According to Blau, the developed consensus provides further group pressure to comply, thus increasing or promoting the power of control and the legitimation of authority. Such legitimate authority becomes the basis for organisation, which makes possible collective effort towards a given objective. Without this developed legitimacy, any organ-isation operates on highly precarious ground. Indeed, collective disapproval of power leads to opposition, a feeling often generated by the perceived insufficient rewards received by subordinates for their efforts.

How can Blau's concepts inform sports coaching?

Recent work by Jones (2009b) has begun to portray coaching in terms of an exchange relationship. Here, it is suggested that coaches bring the social gifts of knowledge, expertise, direction and assistance to the coaching context, while athletes bring a willingness to learn, a degree of compliance and best effort. This is not to portray the relationship in exclusively functional terms, as Jones's auto-ethnographical (2006a, 2009a) accounts have highlighted. Here, difficult and dysfunctional moments within coaching relationships are described in terms of 'contracts' being broken and 'bargains' not kept. Indeed, the inherent aspect of power within coaching always contributes to messy, awkward interactional problems and issues.

The problematic nature of coaching relationships was also well illustrated in d'Arripe-Longueville *et al.*'s (1998) investigation into the working practices of top-level French judo coaches. The interactions of these coaches were characterised by stimulating interpersonal rivalry among the players, provoking them verbally, displaying indifference, entering into direct conflict with the players, and openly showing preferences. A disciplined, authoritarian regime was established by the coaches, where negative feedback was commonplace. So why did the players stay in the context? Why did they comply with the abusive climate to which they were subjected? Echoing the earlier discussed notion of the degree of dependence being determined from the outcomes derived, the players tolerated their subordinate status due to the potential rewards gleaned from it. They perceived themselves to be in a culture which could help them secure their ultimate sporting goals. Blau would explain such actions in terms of a legitimation of the coaches' power deriving from the benefits generated. The negative interactions to which the players were subjected, then, were deemed the price to be paid. Such a position illuminates the difference between satisfaction and dependency (O'Brien & Kollock, 1991), more realistically explaining why athletes (and people in general) stay in apparently punishing relationships. On the other hand, the athletes' acquiescence could also be explained by the lack of available alternatives, a notion which draws on Thibaut and Kelley's (1959) comparison level of alternatives. Emphasising the complex nature of power, although the coaches' demonstrated a high degree of authority, it was still not absolute here as they also made 'made tacit concessions when faced with the autonomous objectives of successful athletes' (d'Arripe-Longueville *et al.*, 1998: 328). There was always a balance to be struck.

In a similar vein, Seifried (2008) contentiously argued that coaches' utilisation of discipline and punishment should not necessarily be viewed as negative actions. This is because they could be productively used 'for censuring and deterring behaviours and restoring the balance between victims, offenders, and the greater society (i.e., the team)' (Seifried, 2008: 382). In this way, the use of punishment holds the potential to recreate and maintain order and stability for the potential benefit of all. Such work is at considerable odds with other coach–athlete literature which posits the relationship between both parties as almost universally (or desired) 'comfortable collective works, based on collaboration [and] social support' (Seifried, 2008: 329).

As with the judo players in d'Arripe-Longueville *et al.*'s (1998) study, the young footballers in Cushion and Jones's (2006) work appeared to be complicit in their domination. Both groups were able to justify their choices when questioned, giving some credence to the rational element of exchange theory. Hence, there appeared to be some short-term decisions made by individuals which reinforced the longer-term 'oppression of their social group[s]' (Cudd, 2006: 21). Such an interpretation, however, has been criticised for failing to locate the decisions taken in context: that is, within a culture ridden by particular normative commitments on which other individuals and groups have staked their identities (Taylor, 2006). Whichever way one leans on the structure–agency debate, it is nevertheless evident that the agency apparent within social exchanges takes place within bounded cultural contexts. Such a play between structure and agency was plainly seen in Cushion and Jones's (2006) aforementioned case study. Here, the coaches' harsh authoritarian discourse was collectively accepted, resisted and managed in numerous ways by the boys who were subjected to it. Like d'Arripe-Longueville's judo players, they considered it was done in their best interests. It was expected and rationalised as part of the culture. It was the price they had to pay for a (hoped for) career in professional sport. Seen through the lens of exchange theory, we can thus begin to understand why, as individuals, we submit to 'the normative expectations of others' (O'Brien & Kollock, 1991: 147). Additionally, by submitting so, despite both parties agreeing that the relationship is mutually beneficial, because the cultural context of the interaction (i.e., coaching) gives greater credence to the coach's role within it, the danger exists that athletes will become increasingly disenfranchised and dependent. Such was the story of Anne (Jones *et al.*, 2005), an elite swimmer whose reverence for and ensuing dependence on her coach left her increasingly fragile and vulnerable. Her brittle, over-invested athletic self-identity subsequently broke following a seemingly casual comment from the venerated coach about her weight. Indeed, McDonagh (1982), in developing her thesis on social exchange and moral development, cited the often severe consequences of punishments within social exchange, particularly where such punishments attack the foundation of the victim's self-image.

Lest a one-sided view of coach domination be presented here, Purdy *et al.* (2008) recently cited an example where athletes' discernment of poor-quality coaching led them to undermine the coach, who, in turn, resigned from her position. The perception here was that the coach was not performing as she should; was not fulfilling the social obligation tied up with the coaching role. Hence, she was subject to sarcasm and derision from the athletes which resulted in a loss of respect for her and her methods. An initially promising relationship had turned into a dysfunctional one, where no purposeful exchange eventually took place.

Recent work has also highlighted how coaches try to portray desired images in a quest to make themselves attractive to athletes. The objective here, of course, is to secure athletes' respect and, hence, compliance. Although such work has been theorised from a Goffmanian perspective (e.g., Jones *et al.*, 2003, 2004), the parallels with exchange theory are clear. For example, Bob Dwyer, a World Cup-winning rugby union coach, and Steve Harrison, a top-level football coach, both engaged in a form of role distance through making light of some of their coaching behaviours (Jones *et al.*, 2004); social performances to demonstrate that they could meet the complex obligations of the position with humour and relative ease. Again, drawing from this body of work, the actions of former England football coach Graham Taylor (Jones *et al.*, 2004), who made a conscious effort not to forget his players' wives' birthdays, marked a clear attempt to build trust. Such actions, in encouraging unspecified obligations, can be seen as endeavours to develop others' faith and belief in him as a caring person, as a coach who will not abuse or exploit players and is thus worthy of their loyalty. Finally, in this context, the functionality of trade within coach–athlete relationships was highlighted by Sánchez *et al.* (2009: 351), who found that, in exchange for coaches' accessibility and approachability, athletes were expected to provide a high work ethic and to sacrifice their 'individual interests in favour of the team'.

A coach's commentary by Jake Bailey

As a former competitive trampolinist I always had a vague notion that I would become a coach. I tinkered a little while a student and then, in 2000, in the midst of my postgraduate studies, I started my own club. By a serendipitous occurrence, at the same time a highly ranked trampolinist came to study at the university I was attending and, in the absence of any better alternatives, I became her coach. My association with her brought me into contact with other prominent athletes and coaches. Soon, I was completely hooked. I've continued to work hard to build the club, which is now nationally successful (in 2009 we had sixteen qualifiers to the British Championships and took six podium places). Since beginning my coaching career I've done a great deal of development work with other clubs in Wales, which culminated in the honour of becoming the National Coach of Wales in 2006.

Once I read the chapter, I couldn't stop thinking about everything (not just my coaching) in terms of this theory. Even writing this piece is an example of exchange in practice: I give my time and energy to put some observations and thoughts together in exchange for my name at the start of a book chapter. Within this commentary, after outlining the process I went through to construct it, I'd like to share some thoughts on my practice, as viewed through the lens of exchange theory. I then provide detailed reflection on a critical incident where my actions were directly informed by this chapter, before a concluding section ties together some main points.

I was initially surprised at how accessible the theory was. Every concept seemed to 'hum' with resonance. The question for me then related to how I could usefully apply the notions outlined to my practice without being overwhelmed. To avoid 'theoretical drowning', I carefully read the chapter again, highlighting what I thought were the most important parts. I then reflected on my practice in light of these selected aspects, generating examples to help me make sense of them, and to start bridging the troublesome theory–practice divide. I've thought and said on many occasions that one of the hardest things to do is turn understanding into action. This exercise was no different. Even though I could identify with many of the presented notions, the most difficult part for me was using the theory at the most basic micro-level to influence what I did as a coach. While there are so many possible practical applications of exchange theory to coaching, I chose one particular aspect of it to highlight this perceived relevancy. That related to reciprocity. Hence, it provides the focus for this commentary.

When I learned that exchange theory was 'an attempt to explain how social life becomes organised into complex social structures of associations', I was immediately struck by its closeness to the way 'my' trampoline club operates. Social associations between participants, participants and coaches, coaches and coaches, coaches and parents, coaches and administrators, administrators and parents, among others, are all necessary and inevitable to maintain the operation of the club. These associations or relationships invariably depend on the 'social rewards' derived, and allow the club to maintain a stable structure. As the person ultimately responsible for the club, I could view part of my role as trying to mediate stable relationships between key stakeholders to maintain their dependence on the club in terms of providing them with rewards (social, financial, etc.) that they perceive to be desirable. However, at the same time, it is also evident that my agency, or individual action, in fulfilling this role is variable and limited.

At the more micro level, phrases such as 'exchange relationships are characterised by interdependence, and regulated by norms such as reciprocity and fairness' made me think. No doubt, the athletes I coach need me and I need them; we both must offer something to the relationship (reciprocity), with the exchange perceived as being a fair one. When I was an athlete, I thought that my coach had favourites and this was, for me, a pivotal reason for the breakdown of our relationship (an unbalanced and unreciprocated exchange?). Because I perceived that others were getting more from him, my expectations of reciprocity within our own relationship were not met: he didn't give me what I needed or wanted. I have always worked hard to offer something, something good, to the athletes I work with. However, exchange theory cast my own perceived fairness into a more troublesome light. As the athletes I work with have developed, they have improved; our commitment (mine and theirs) to their efforts has increased. I now realise, though, that my commitment to some may have resulted in the relative neglect of others within the club. How awkward that an engaged reading of theory presented a few 'nasty surprises' along with a refreshed perspective and a deepened understanding of practice.

Another aspect that immediately struck me when reading the chapter was the level of power that being National Coach and the director of the most successful club within a 100-mile radius affords me. The lack of contingent alternatives available to people who want to be high-level trampolinists means that their dependence on me is high. However, perhaps because high-level trampolinists offer me greater social status within the practice community due to the results that they produce, means that my dependence on them could also be high. There seem, then, to be factors that balance, at least to some extent, the power relations between myself and the athletes I coach. I realised also that athlete choice was not simply limited to the selection of trampoline clubs. One athlete I coach is a high-level performer in track and field; consequently, she has the option to follow a different path to realise her sporting desires. Was I aware of this before I read the chapter? Yes, I think I was. But the chapter certainly gave me a more explicit understanding of how the choices available to this athlete influence the dependence and power differential within our coach–athlete dyad. I suppose the question that this brings up for me is: do I treat this athlete differently from the rest because she has other good alternatives? I suspect that in some ways I do. Exchange theory, however, helped me conceptualise why my behaviour is different: that is, because she is less dependent, it is incumbent upon me to make her more satisfied with her trampoline experience in order that she perceives that the benefits gained justify her continued engagement with me and the club.

Legitimation is another central concern for me as a coach. If people don't collectively 'buy in' to my programme then I'm lost. Blau's (1986) statement that a positive imbalance of benefits (as perceived by 'followers') generates feelings of legitimate power towards the leader resonates with the way I go about conducting my business. My approach sits very much in opposition to the judo coaches described in d'Arripe-Longueville *et al.*'s (1998) paper. Rather than creating a situation where 'the advantages gained from subordination outweigh the hardships of compliance', I try to create a situation where, if athletes are living up to their part of the bargain (e.g., displaying a willingness to learn, providing a degree of compliance and best effort) then they are rewarded with my best effort to create a positive and encouraging coaching and learning context. Proceeding in this way, I believe, creates more opportunities for athletes to gain a positive imbalance of benefits and makes the likelihood of their continuing in my programme greater. However, this reflection is offered with the caveat that Robyn mentioned earlier in this chapter: that there are still difficult and dysfunctional moments that need to be negotiated along the way (although, in my experience, by trying to maintain a milieu which is positive makes these moments more manageable).

While reflecting on the contrast between my practices and those of the judo coaches in d'Arripe-Longueville *et al.*'s (1998) article, I must admit to wondering about the utility of their tactics. Am I too nice? Do I rely too much on using my social skills to hook the athletes into a relationship with me? Does my being generally 'pleasant' and 'reasonable' with them leave them too soft to develop their full athletic potential in a sport that is tough and unforgiving? So, my final reflection is: could I make more use of the power that I have to help the athletes I coach reach their goals? This would place greater emphasis on the exchange I offer them in terms of instrumental performance. I don't think that I'm ready to test this reflection in practice quite yet, but I'll hold on to it for future reference.

The following section is illustrative of a critical incident that occurred and was explicitly influenced by my reading of this chapter. I then provide a related reflection some time after the incident which continues to influence my practice.

Exchange theory in practice

It's the third training session since a two-week Christmas break. I've patiently watched the athletes over the previous two sessions get back into their 'trampoline bodies': their stiff limbs moving mechanically in the air, with little of their usual grace and certainty. I'd expected this. I even feel some responsibility for it because, with my newborn baby not three weeks old, I couldn't organise extra sessions. But now, in their third session back, it feels like they're taking the piss. If I'm here, giving my precious time when I'd love to be home, then I expect more than they're giving. This is it: this is an example of exchange theory in practice (or not!). I'm not getting what I want here: they're not giving me the enthusiasm, the engagement, the degree of compliance or anything even close to the best effort I'd like. Why should I be giving them my time, assistance and patience if they're not prepared to live up to their part of the bargain?

I feel empty; dissatisfaction grows as the session proceeds. I prod and cajole them, but it's not working. My enthusiasm correspondingly decreases. There's only so much you can give when you don't feel you're getting anything back. At the same time, a fascination takes hold; it's so interesting to see this drama unfold and be able make sense of it, to see theory explicity in the moment of action. A sense of excitement returns; I'm going to share this understanding with the athletes.

I sit the three of them down in a semicircle. I sit on the floor with them, something I've done for a long time (I don't feel the need to bring extra emphasis to the uneven power relations that we all know exist). I know what I'm going to do is risky, and I need to make sure they don't perceive that they're being blackmailed. I just want to share my thoughts with them to help them see our relationships, our arrangements, with new eyes, as I just have. I tell them my truth at that moment, right as I'm experiencing it:

> I want to be here with you, but my effort, my presence comes at a cost. I've been patient over the last three sessions, but today I asked myself: 'What am I doing here?' I could be at home with my wife and baby, not watching you giving me effort far below your best. If you want my best, I expect yours. We're in this together, and we all have responsibilities. This can be exciting for us, but we have to work hard to make this happen, to get something from it. Next session I expect more.

They listened. Although I could sense they were relating to my words, I wondered what their reaction would be. Still, I felt more buoyant after the meeting, my expectations raised. Although I scolded them, I also gave them something. I was 'real'; I had taken a risk and had shared a part of myself. That had to be worth something.

During the following session I'm surprised. Not so much by their reaction, even though they trained much better. I'm surprised at how much more *I* have to give: I have more energy, more sparkle. We have a great session: we all give; we all play our part in the complicated exchanges that make the environment we've constructed work.

Reflections

The legacy of this exchange has brought me some deeper insights that I feel are worth sharing here. One of the athletes involved in the above scenario spoke to me very recently, citing this incident as pivotal in changing his attitude. He explained that, as a consequence, he began to see his responsibility to training (and to me) in another way. The other two athletes reacted somewhat differently. There was a short-term increase in effort, followed by a decline back to familiar training habits. The athlete who changed his behaviour has, in my estimation, greater social awareness than the others, who struggle to see beyond themselves. This high-lighted to me that the reciprocity which is so important in making relationships work is entirely at the mercy of the perceptions of the people involved (both mine and the athletes').

My final reflection, then, is that it is important that I should attempt to increase the sociological awareness of the athletes I coach (while also working on my own) in order that they can appreciate and more successfully navigate the complex exchanges in which we are involved.

Concluding thoughts

The thinking of Peter Blau presented in this chapter is, in large part, contained in the broader concept of mutual dependence. In Blau's (1986: 315) words, 'the prototype is the reciprocal exchange of extrinsic benefits'. The chapter's principal significance is subsequently twofold. First, in articulating how micro-interactions (through the notion of exchange) can contribute to our understanding of social relationships and (sometimes) eventual trust. And, second, in conceptualising opposition as a regenerative force. Rather than being viewed as dysfunctional (as in most sports coaching literature), disagreement and conflict are thus considered as catalysts for social change. Indeed, if it were not for 'conflict of interests . . . unequal dependance . . . there would be no need for interpersonal dispositions' (Kelley, 1986: 15). Consequently, we consider notions of (in)equality when related to exchange to have considerable relevance to appreciate relationships better within coaching; in particular, those between coaches and athletes. Certainly some current research points to their salience (e.g., Jones, 2009a). This empirical work, echoing Emerson's (1962) earlier call, should now be further developed to examine the factors leading to both power and dependence within coaching, in addition to the conditions under which such power can be actively employed by both parties.

10   Jürgen Habermas: Communicative action, the system and the lifeworld

Critiquing social interaction in coaching

Paul Potrac with Stephen Barrett

Jürgen Habermas: a short biography

Jürgen Habermas was born near Düsseldorf in Germany in 1929. He was educated at the Universities of Göttingen, Zurich and Bonn before becoming a research assistant to Theodor Adorno at the University of Frankfurt in 1959 (Edgar, 2006; Outhwaite, 2009). He subsequently held a number of academic positions at a variety of German and American universities before returning to the University of Frankfurt as Professor Emeritus in Philosophy (Edgar, 2006). He is perhaps best known for his work addressing political emancipation. Here, he critiqued the misuse of positivist models in the social sciences and, perhaps more importantly, social policy (Edgar, 2006). This work is best illustrated in his *The theory of communicative action: Reason and the rationalisation of society* (1984), *The theory of communicative action: Lifeworld and system: A critique of functionalist reason* (1987) and *Moral consciousness and communicative action* (1990).

His prolific academic output during the past fifty years has covered a diverse range of topics, such as the philosophy of language, accounts of the state and history, law, contemporary political developments in Germany, the moral problems of genetics, and, more recently, the debates on the supposed 'war on terrorism' (Edgar, 2006). Given the broad and interdisciplinary nature of his writing, students of sociology, philosophy, legal theory, cultural studies and politics have all come across his name at some point in their studies, making him one of the most widely cited and influential social theorists and philosophers of his generation (Edgar, 2006; Finlayson, 2005). In addition to his academic work, Habermas is recognised as a leading European public intellectual who has made frequent contributions on matters of political, cultural and moral concern (Finlayson, 2005).

Introduction

The purpose of this chapter is to explore how Habermas's critical theory can be related to sports coaching. While Habermas has not written directly about coaching and sport, his focus on grounded accounts of labour, power and communication (or interaction) as the main sources of human action and knowledge provides fruitful analytical tools for researchers in coaching, practising coaches and coach educators alike (Edgar, 2006; Outhwaite, 2009). Interestingly, Habermas distinguishes between what he terms 'strategic action', whereby an individual utilises 'sanctions or gratifications, force or money' to persuade another individual or individuals (Habermas, 1982: 269), and 'communicative action', which brings people together on the basis of developing a shared understanding through rational reasoning (Layder, 2006). Additionally, Habermas believed that we are not hamstrung by culture, as postmodernists suggest, but that, regardless of our life experiences and cultural background, our ability to communicate through language enables individuals to reach out to each other and across cultural divides (Jones, 2005). Given the recent recognition of the importance of 'influence', 'persuasion', 'conflict' and 'social interaction' within the coaching literature (e.g., Jones *et al.*, 2004; Cushion & Jones, 2006; Purdy *et al.*, 2008; Potrac & Jones, 2009a, among others), we believe that Habermas's work could usefully contribute to the advancement of our current theoretical understanding of social relationships and interactions within coaching environments.

In terms of structure, this chapter initially focuses on Habermas's writings in relation to communicative action, the lifeworld and the system, communicative rationality, and discourse ethics; key concepts that lie at the heart of Habermas's critical theorisations of social life. Following this discussion, the chapter shifts to a consideration of how these concepts could be related to sports coaching. Finally, a commentary regarding the value of Habermas's thinking for coaching practice is provided by Stephen Barrett, a coach at Scunthorpe United Football Club. It should be noted that while this chapter provides a basic introduction to Habermas's theory, it does not claim to provide an exhaustive overview of it. We therefore recommend that readers seeking to advance their understanding of his work engage directly with it (e.g., Habermas, 1984, 1987, 1990) and some related commentaries (e.g., Finlayson, 2005; Layder, 2006; Outhwaite, 2009; Mouzelis, 1992).

Communicative action I: Habermas's early theorisations

Habermas began to develop his theory of 'communicative action and universal pragmatics' in the 1970s and 1980s (Edgar, 2006). Within the resultant body of literature, he presents humans as essentially communicative beings and, as such, his work focuses on exploring how people use their communication skills to create, maintain and develop social relationships. He has been concerned with examining how people talk to each other in order to find common ground and establish a consensus over meaning. Indeed, Habermas believes that our ability to establish relationships with people from other cultures and generally to coexist at all can be attributed to the degree to which we are capable of being reasonable and rational in these social encounters. Subsequently, it is through rational communication, something which is unique to humans, that differences can be overcome (Jones, 2005). The prime purpose of communication from this perspective, then, is 'to bring about an agreement that terminates in the inter-subjective mutuality of reciprocal understanding, shared knowledge, mutual trust, and accord with one another' (Habermas, 1990: 3).

In particular, Habermas's work has suggested that, when individuals and groups engage in a communicative exchange where they treat each other as equals in genuinely seeking agreement (and have an equal opportunity to state their views), reaching such an agreement should be achievable (Outhwaite, 2009). Similarly, the likelihood of coming to an accord is significantly reduced when the social exchange becomes very one-sided, or if one or more of the actors engaged in the interaction has a fraudulent desire to reach an agreement with a third party. For example, we are probably all familiar with communicative encounters where one person has humiliated or subjugated another, or when people have talked *at* each other with no genuine intention of listening *to*, let alone reaching an agreement *with*, the other party. For Habermas, such social encounters are problematic if we are to create a society that is shared not just physically but morally with other people (Jones, 2005).

Within our everyday communication, be it through statements, accusations or questions, Habermas suggests that four validity claims are raised upon which the speaker could be challenged. These relate to truth, rightness, sincerity and meaning. The first claim (truth) is to do with the nature or reality of the world around us. In this respect, our view of the world could be wrong and subsequently challenged by the other party in the interaction. The second claim (rightness) focuses on the speaker's right to speak or to say what he or she says. For example, one party may question the other person's right to make a particular assertion, order or request. The claim to sincerity refers to whether a speaker may be accused of lying, teasing or irony. Finally, the claim to meaning refers to the coherence and comprehensibility of what is said. In an ideal speech situation, Habermas suggests that every individual engaged in a conversation is able to challenge what is said by the other speakers in terms of these four perspectives without fear of coercion (Edgar, 2006; Outhwaite, 2009).

In practice, Habermas (1970) recognised that everyday social encounters and exchanges fall some way short of this ideal. This is because, more often than not, they are distorted by the goals, motives and, not least, the power relationship that exists between the individuals engaged in the communicative exchange. Here, Habermas (1979, 1982) distinguished between communicative action and what he termed 'strategic action'. While the former is concerned with developing a genuine and mutual understanding, the latter occurs when one or more of the social actors participating in a dialogue view(s) the others as objects to be treated in an instrumental fashion. That is, the goal for the person engaging in strategic action is to cajole, persuade or coerce the other party to acquiesce to their purposes, regardless of whether that other party understands the rationale presented or agrees with it (Edgar, 2006; Layder, 2006). Such an engagement might entail using a number of obvious (e.g., threats of violence, bribery or blackmail) or more subtle (e.g., appearing sincere and genuine when exploitation and manipulation are the real motives) means to achieve their desired outcomes: for example, the use of rhetoric, emotive language and/or gestures that pressure the other to take the desired action, while simultaneously concealing the weaknesses of the arguments that are being put forward (Edgar, 2006; Layder, 2006).

In his discussions of strategic action, Habermas used the term 'systematically distorted communication' to refer to the failure to achieve mutual understanding due to shortcomings in the conceptual communicative abilities of the individuals involved in the conversation. Of particular interest is the suggestion that systematic distortion prevents people from questioning political inequalities by manipulating the ideas that are available in the dominant culture (Edgar, 2006). Here, Edgar (2006: 148) noted that:

> Systematic distorted communication suggests that the [dominant] ideology works, not by simply offering a legitimation of the existing political structure, but rather by preventing people from perceiving, talking about, and criticising that inequality. Systematic distortion blinds people to the inequalities of repression in which they are entwined. The task of the critical theorist is, therefore, akin to a psychoanalyst, helping society become aware of its blind spots, of the actually meaningless gestures that clutter everyday communication.

While the notion of distorted communication was important to his early theorisation, it was eventually abandoned by Habermas. He subsequently revised and modified some of his initial assumptions and terminology as he refined his theory of communicative action in the late 1970s and 1980s. In particular, he turned his intellectual endeavours to exploring how communicative action is impacted upon by the intrusion of the mechanisms of social organisation systems into everyday life (Edgar, 2006; Layder, 2006). This work will be addressed in the following section.

Communicative action II: the lifeworld and the system

In advancing his theory of communicative action, Habermas utilised the concepts of 'the lifeworld' and 'the system' to refer to two complementary accounts of the nature of the social world (Edgar, 2006). The lifeworld refers to the 'social world as it is constructed and maintained through the taken-for-granted social skills and stocks of knowledge of its members' (Edgar, 2006: xvi). These stocks of knowledge and cultural recipes inform not only how we perceive and understand the social world generally, but how we see the behaviours of others and subsequently respond to them in particular settings and situations. From this perspective, people's actions can be responded to because they make sense; they are part of the process of communication. Indeed, it is through our experiences of living in a particular society that we acquire views and knowledge that influence our attitudes and, subsequently, our actions. And it is through language, Habermas argues, that people establish, maintain and, where necessary, repair social relationships. The lifeworld, then, is the source of individual socialisation and carries the traditions of the community (Layder, 2006; Edgar, 2006).

In contrast to the lifeworld, the system is comprised of the economic and productive operations in which humans engage to maintain their physical survival.

Unlike the lifeworld, which is governed by the rules of communicative action, the system is overseen by instrumental rationality (Outhwaite, 2009). Instrumental reasoning and action have their roots in the natural sciences and involve choosing and implementing the most appropriate approach(es) to achieve a desired goal. They are concerned with knowable facts, causal relationships, and the identification and utilisation of the most efficient actions (in terms of the speed of delivery at the lowest cost) to achieve stated outcomes. In this regard, Habermas noted how scientists throughout history have carried out experiments on the natural world in order to identify universal laws, which have then been used to predict the consequences of particular actions. He believed that such experimentation, evaluation and reasoning have led to great advances in modern science and technology. For Habermas, then, in order to survive and flourish, we must be able not only to communicate effectively but to control our natural environment.

Given the above, Habermas did not view instrumental rationality to be problematic *per se*. Instead, he suggested that instrumental reasoning could be complementary to communicative reasoning (a feature of the lifeworld). However, he was critical of instrumental rationality when it was inappropriately applied to the social world. This was specifically when the system presents 'the individual as a meaningless, seemingly natural force' (Edgar, 2006: xvi). Drawing upon the classic work of Weber, Habermas argued that instrumental rationality continues to be the dominant way of thinking not only in science and technology but in the culture and organisation of many capitalist societies (Edgar, 2006). He also proposed that within social science there is a strong preoccupation with calculation, efficiency and predictability, but little concern for the notions of right and wrong, good and bad (Jones, 2005; Layder, 2006). This is most evident in forms of strategic interaction, where one person takes an instrumental attitude towards another. For Habermas, human rationality should also be concerned with how 'we *should* live, how we *should* behave, with what kinds of people we *should* be' (Jones, 2005: 169). He consequently showcased his position concerning how we have allowed instrumental rationality to guide our thoughts and actions regarding matters of values, something he considered to be quite wrong. In this regard, Habermas argued that contemporary capitalist societies have allowed the lifeworld to become colonised by the system (Jones, 2005; Outhwaite, 2009). Sloan (1999) provides an example of this colonisation of the lifeworld in describing how 'an established urban neighborhood might be destroyed, rather than renovated, in order to build a more profitable shopping mall or industrial plant. The voices of the many who care about community and sense of place are drowned out by the few who perform the calculus of profit and practicality.'

Habermas's discussion of the colonisation of the lifeworld also draws attention to how the system is increasingly subjecting people to the processes of management and objectification. It is suggested that through such socialisation processes we are trained to adopt an instrumental view towards our social and emotional lives, which deprives us of the capacities needed to communicate our subjective needs and, in turn, to understand the emotional needs of others (Sloan,

1999). This has a detrimental impact upon our opportunities to engage in social interaction that is genuine, mutual and has its basis in interdependence. Hence, the colonisation of the lifeworld has led to people viewing others as simply a means to an end, with little consideration and attention given to others' thoughts and concerns. Instead, the emphasis is on one party getting another to act in the way that is expected or desired. According to Sloan (1999), the colonisation of the lifeworld has led to the development of a continuum of problems in living, 'with, at one extreme, narcissistic manipulation, overt coercion, sociopathy and other power-seeking styles, and at the other extreme, depression, anxiety, fear, and a variety of states that sustain submissive postures'.

Importantly, Habermas's critique enables us to consider how those who possess legitimate power in the capitalist system (bureaucrats, judges, politicians and so on) can both compel others to behave in a certain way and delegate power and authority to other people in a way that is largely unchallenged and unquestioned by the majority. Here, Habermas notes, we are socialised into accepting inequalities in power relations as being an entirely natural, deserved and just way of being and living. Conversley, an emancipatory analysis of social life should seek to expose the political interests that are being served by 'the apparently meaningless or inevitable ideological appearance of society' (Edgar, 2006: 16). It is only through such critical examinations of social life that we will fully come to appreciate the extent to which our individual freedoms are being undermined through the illegitimate, and often subtle, use of power (Edgar, 2006).

Perhaps the two most significant concepts to emerge from Habermas's critical theorisation of social interaction in society are discourse ethics and communicative rationality. Discourse ethics is concerned with the ethical critique of the processes that people use to justify their actions, as well as the requests and demands they place on others. Habermas not only considered that no one individual should be excluded from participating in a social exchange but (as touched upon earlier) that all speakers in a conversation should expect to be challenged by the other parties during that particular social interaction. Importantly, when challenged by another individual in the exchange, a speaker should be able to justify his or her actions and viewpoints through rational responses that are grounded in underlying moral values and principles (Edgar, 2006). By encouraging us to explore the normative principles that underpin the interaction, Habermas believes that it becomes possible for us to question and revise not only the taken-for-granted rules that guide and govern our everyday interactions, but also the goals that we pursue both individually and collectively (Edgar, 2006). Hence, open dialogue, or communicative rationality, is the best means for human beings to resolve the problems that we encounter in social life.

Habermas: a critical approach to coaching

As stated in the introduction to this chapter, Habermas did not write directly about sports coaching. Similarly, his work has yet to be directly applied to coaching practice by other scholars. However, we believe that his writings on communicative rationality, instrumental rationality and strategic action offer a valuable theoretical framework for our critical reflections upon, and understanding of, social interaction within coaching. Indeed, the utilisation of Habermas's ideas could have a potentially transformative impact on coaching practice as a consequence of emphasising the development of more egalitarian relationships, where individual and collective freedoms can be practised (Morrison, 2009).

Specifically, Habermas's work could be used to help us better understand, and subsequently challenge, the dominant ideologies that underpin and guide communicative actions within the coaching process. In this sense, Habermas invites us to explore the dominant values, beliefs and practices that are inherent features of the coaching environment and to consider who is advantaged and disadvantaged as a consequence of their operation. His work allows us to dig beneath the natural appearance or surface veneer of coaching, not only to consider whose vested interests are being served under the mantle of the 'general good' but to interrogate the legitimacy of those interests (Morrison, 2009).

In terms of challenging the ideologies that underpin coaching practice and facilitating a movement towards more egalitarian interaction, we believe that Habermas provides us with a valuable analytical framework for guiding both the research endeavours of coaching scholars and the critical reflections of coaches and coach educators. In this respect, Habermas's critique consists of four phases: (1) a description and interpretation of the existing situation; (2) a penetration of the reasons that led to the creation of the existing situation; (3) the creation of an agenda for changing that situation; and (4) an evaluation of what is achieved by the changes that are implemented (Morrison, 2009).

As a starting point for critical enquiry, Habermas's thinking suggests that researchers and practitioners should begin the process of ideological critique (i.e., phase 1) by seeking to make sense of the everyday nature of coaching in different settings and environments through interrogating the apparently asymmetrical power relationships that have traditionally characterised the coach–athlete relationship. We may find that this type of relationship, which has tended to position the coach as the knowledgeable expert and the athletes as obedient followers, is something that is expected by coaches, athletes and their respective employers and sponsors alike (Cassidy *et al.*, 2009). Indeed, there is evidence to support the assertion that the socialisation experiences related to the pressure on coaches to succeed in top-level sport have led many coaches to seek to control as many aspects of athletes' lives as they possibly can (Cassidy *et al.*, 2009; Cushion & Jones, 2006; Jones *et al.*, 2003). Similarly, the personal motivations and goals of the coaches and the demands placed upon them by their respective employers (e.g., obtaining and maintaining a high win–loss ratio, winning championships, and accumulating significant amounts of prize money) have led coaches to engage in activities that are not necessarily in the best interests of the athletes with whom they work (Coakley, 1982; Johns & Johns, 2000).

For example, Roderick's (2006) exploration of everyday life in the lower leagues of English professional football illustrates Habermas's notions of instrumental rationality and strategic action in practice. Roderick's interpretive study revealed how players were frequently pressured by coaches into playing when injured, even though doing so could have a potentially detrimental impact upon their playing careers. The work highlighted how managers and coaches used a variety of subtle and more direct strategic actions that led many players to experience strong feelings of guilt at their inability to contribute to the team's efforts. Such feelings of guilt were reinforced when injured players interacted with the fit players, who questioned the seriousness of injuries and injured players' desire to play again and thus help the group as soon as they could. As such, it could be suggested that many of the (injured) players accepted the dominant instrumental values related to the importance of making a contribution to the team and 'not letting anybody down'. It is, therefore, perhaps not surprising that many of the players interviewed by Roderick (2006) described how they frequently succumbed to the mental pressures that accompanied such interactions and, subsequently, chose to continue to train and play 'through' injuries as much as possible.

The second phase of Habermas's framework focuses on 'a penetration of the reasons that brought the existing situation to the form that it takes' (Morrison, 2009: 216). It seeks to illuminate the ideologies and interests at work in a particular situation and to provide an evaluation of their legitimacy in both micro- and macro-sociological terms (Morrison, 2009). Again, using professional football as a context, the purpose of such investigation would not only be to highlight the distorted and oppressive conditions that players (and coaches) may experience within it but to be emanicpatory by stimulating action to bring about social change (Morrison, 2009). Such work might not only challenge the dominant discourses underpinning the behaviours and ethics of coaches at a variety of levels but also help players (athletes) to understand how their own 'views and practices are perpetuating a social order or situation that works against their democratic freedoms, interests, and empowerment' (Morrison, 2009: 217).

While the issue of empowerment is an important one in Habermas's work, we do not believe that it suggests all athletes should have unfettered freedom to determine their actions and goals in the sporting setting. Indeed, such a suggestion has been subject to increasing critique in the academic literature (e.g., Jones & Standage, 2006; Jones & Wallace, 2006). Instead, the emphasis relates to coaches (and athletes) considering the 'rightness' and the 'goodness' of their choices and behaviours, the impact that they will likely have on other individuals, and subsequently engaging in 'non-distorted' (or non-strategic) communication (Habermas, 1979).

Given the sentiments for promoting social change expressed above, it is perhaps unsurprising that the final two stages of ideological critique presented by Habermas focus on setting an agenda for changing the situation and evaluating subsequent impact and achievements. In this respect, the emphasis for researchers, coaches and coach educators would be not only to identify potentially more equitable practices but to implement them and subsequently examine their impact on the creation of a more even-handed and moral environment (Morrison, 2009). Far from being utopian, it should be noted that Habermas's mission was and is practical in nature. That is, 'it aims to bring about a more just, egalitarian society in which individual freedoms are practised' while eradicating the use and impact of illegitimate power (Morrison, 2009: 217).

Habermas's work, however, does not suggest that power is always bad or negative in nature. Indeed, like many of the other theorists in this book, he recognises that power can be used positively to redress inequality and oppression, and to serve collectively agreed goals. In this sense, power is viewed as potentially holding the promise for constructive, as well as destructive, change (Clegg *et al.*, 2006).

A coach's commentary by Stephen Barrett

I am a skills development coach at Scunthorpe United Football Club. My role principally focuses on leading a development centre for talented young local players aged between nine and twelve. I also provide sports science assistance to the youth team squad (players aged sixteen to eighteen) here at Scunthorpe. I have to admit that I hadn't really given much thought to sociology and sociologists in terms of my coaching practice. It would be fair to say that I had a number of reservations about accepting Paul's invitation to work with him on this chapter. On one level, having never really studied sociology, I wondered what I could bring to the partnership. On another level, I was also a bit sceptical as to what sociology can do to help me in my role as professional football coach. From my experiences as a former sports science student, I could see where physiological, nutritional and performance analysis principles could really help what I did. But I just couldn't fathom how sports sociology would fit into helping me produce young footballers good enough to play for the senior team at the club. Still, I was persuaded to 'give it a go' by Paul and to see how things went.

My engagement with Habermas has led me to reflect critically upon how coaches and players interact within a football club. In terms of the young players I work with, reading Habermas has led me to give serious consideration to the fact that they are, practically all of the time, told what to do, how to do it and when to do it by us, the coaches. It would also be fair to say that a player whom we consider to have a 'good attitude' is frequently one who works hard, does what we ask with maximal effort and never questions. To query a coach's commands and directions would be frowned upon, to say the least. When I think about why football coaches often communicate in this way I can't give an answer, other than it's how it has always been done. When I was a young player, the coaches never had to explain or justify their decisions to us (the players) and we certainly didn't expect to engage in a conversation about it with them. I have to admit that, while I found this quite an alienating and mentally demanding state of affairs, it was one that I accepted as normal. I certainly didn't resist it. Not to the coaches' faces anyway! While I wouldn't say that I now engage in the ideal interaction pattern championed by Habermas, working on this chapter has led me to reconsider the input I allow players to have in the coaching process, particularly in terms of justifying what I ask the players to do. I'm also making more of an effort to find out how the players are experiencing their time at the club and their views on how things are done. This is not an easy task, especially given the coach-led environment that many of them have become used to.

In addition to considering the nature of my face-to-face interactions with the players, my engagement with this chapter has led me to question the culture (or instrumental rationality, as I think Habermas defines it) that underpins how coaches tend to work at professional football clubs. We often talk about 'budgets', 'working efficiently' and 'maximising outcomes'. Everything we do is about getting maximal reward from minimum investment. While this might make sense from a financial perspective, such language and ideas have also permeated into how coaches talk about players. The pressure is on youth coaches to make players good enough to play in the first team or sold to another club for a profit. If we don't do this, then it could be argued we are not doing our job 'efficiently', that we are 'wasting resources' and certainly not justifying the 'investment made in the programme'. I think the pressures on youth coaches to 'produce' has seen them tending to view the players instrumentally: as objects that can be mechanically worked on to produce the desired performance levels. We drill them, we instruct them and we train them, we grade their performances, we judge their attitudes and then we throw out the ones that don't meet the (very subjective) quality levels. Reading Habermas has made me question if humanity is missing from what we are doing. The kids who come in are full of dreams and ambitions, they are emotional beings, but in many ways they all end up as objects on the football factory conveyor belt, with most of them inevitably destined for the 'reject bin'. I don't think coaches and football clubs have intentionally set out to do things in this way. Rather, it is the unconscious consequence of the instrumental rationality that we are socialised into accepting in today's capitalist world. Well, that's what I think Habermas would have to say about it, at least.

While there is certainly not a professional playing contract available for every talented young boy who comes to the club, Habermas's work has made me think about the experience they are provided with in terms of caring for their individual development and the provision of affirmative learning during their time with us. This may not make up for the feelings of disappointment that many will have when we have to release them, but it may help in terms of them getting something positive from their experience with us.

To conclude, I would say that my involvement with Habermas's thinking in this chapter has been challenging, not least because of the intellectual depth of his work. Perhaps more significantly, though, it has led me to question some of the taken-for-granted aspects of football coaching and the ethics that underpin them. Indeed, my engagement in this project has made me think critically about how I interact with the young footballers, what input they have in the coaching process, and how they are viewed and treated during their often short time at the club. While this has not been an easy process for me to engage in, I believe that is what Habermas ultimately wants us to do.

Conclusion

The purpose of this chapter was to outline the value of the work of Jürgen Habermas to coaching and coaches. We have sought not only to provide an introductory overview of Habermas's essential critical concepts and views on social life but to highlight how these concepts could be used to influence how we think about, and make sense of, coaching practice. As was admitted in the introduction to this chapter, we do not claim to have provided a complete explanation and exploration of Habermas's work. Rather, we invite readers to explore his work further and deepen their own understanding and interpretation of Habermas's theoretical endeavours. Perhaps the key lesson that Habermas teaches us is that communication between coaches and athletes should entail more than just talking at, and making demands of, each other. Instead, the focus should be on the creation of working relationships that are based upon mutuality and a genuine attempt to reach agreement.

A second aspect of Habermas's work worth mentioning here is its ability to help us recognise that the examination of ideology is not simply a theoretical concern but one that has direct relevance for enhancing coaching practice. In this respect, his framework for ideological critique enables us to reflect upon dominant coaching practices not as natural phenomena but as outcomes or processes wherein interests and powers may be protected and suppressed (Morrison, 2009).

Part III
Coaching and the social

11 Power in coaching

Paul Potrac and Robyn L. Jones

Introduction

[A]ll social relations are relations of power.

(Touraine, 1981: 33)

Acknowledging the significance of the above quote, the attempt to theorise and understand power has been one of the principal concerns of sociological analysis. Indeed, power is considered an omnipresent feature of social life, with even the most basic interaction being 'tinged by issues of power differences' (Snyder & Kiviniemi, 2001: 133). Despite acknowledgement of its pervasiveness, agreement on a common perception of power has not been forthcoming. The purpose of this chapter is to locate some of the conceptualisations of power introduced in Part II within the field of sports coaching. It builds on earlier discussions of coaches' power and how it is evidenced (e.g., Cassidy *et al.,* 2009; Jones *et al.,* 2004). Some of this previous work has tended to view power as a finite resource, part of a zero-sum game, where one party has power and the other does not (e.g., Jones *et al.,* 2005; Johns & Johns, 2000). It is analogous here to a football game where one team has possession of the ball and the other does not (Westwood, 2002), emphasising notions of repression and coercion, and power as 'power over'.

A second view of power utilised within coaching research has seen it as inherently linked to manipulation and strategy (Potrac & Jones, 2009a, 2009b). This is a perspective related to a Machiavellian or Weberian (Weber, 1946) perception of power as the ability of an actor to realise his or her will in a social action even against the resistance of others. To return to the football game analogy, it is interested in the competing teams' strategies and tactics, suggesting a much more fluid recognition of the phenomenon (Westwood, 2002). It is a view which gives primacy to the process of power, the ways in 'which alliances are formed and the processes of legitimation are secured' (Westwood, 2002: 135). It is also an account of power framed by notions of a contested hegemony. As with the previous perspective, although often presenting power-full portrayals of coaching practice, some theorists also believe this to be a limited view. As encapsulated by Michel Foucault (1978: 94), they believe that power is not a thing to be grasped, 'seized or shared, something that one holds on to or allows to slip away'. Rather, power is relational: it is everywhere and always present, even in our day-to-day interactions. Foucault, then, saw power as diffuse, which could be productive as well as repressive. Seen in this way, power is not located in one place, institution or person, but is constantly reinvented and renegotiated through social actions (Westwood, 2002). However, theorists like Westwood (2002: 3) are equally quick to point out that this does not mean 'that power is just free-floating' as there are definitive modalities and sites of power. Modalities refer to the forms in which power is exercised and through which it is enacted, while sites are the social spaces where it is exercised. As well as being de-centred, then, power can been seen to be somewhat structured.

Taking account of power's considered omnipotent nature, Westwood (2002: 17) believes that 'emancipation' is a flawed project as there can be 'no social space beyond authority'. Alternatively, the best we can hope for is 'the achievement of rationally defensible forms of authority' (Casell, 1993: 228). Naturally, such a view has implications for the current trend towards athlete-centred development and empowerment; but more of that later. It is enough to say at the moment that the various definitions of power are treated in this chapter (and elsewhere in the book) as being intersectional: that is, they interact with other each to create and mirror the social context of coaching. In this respect, in terms of conceptualisation, we lean heavily on Westwood's (2002: 25) position that 'there is no social without power'.

The organisation of this chapter takes account of this ongoing fluidity between the differing definitions of power offered by sociological theorists. It does so by organising the discussion around the power wielded by individual coaches and athletes, and by the more general coaching context. For example, the chapter will initially focus on offering an explanation of why coaches act as they do within the coaching environment in terms of the power they utilise, principally from an agential perspective. The same is then done for athletes, examining issues of compliance and resistance. Finally, a structural or macro-sociological approach to an exploration of how power operates at a contextual level within coaching is undertaken.

Coaches' power

Earlier work (e.g., Jones *et al.*, 2004; Cassidy *et al.*, 2009) has theorised the influential role of coaches using a framework of power developed by French and Raven (1959). The focus here involved interpreting coaching from six different bases or sources of power used by people to get others to do their bidding. These included legitimate, expert, informational, reward, coercive and referential sources. This work highlighted how coaches considered that the power afforded to them by athletes was not a simple static capacity emanating from their position as coaches within the social structure of the environment. Instead, they drew attention to how the 'trust' and 'respect' that athletes demonstrated towards them was fluid and dynamic, with the athletes' perceptions of their decisions and actions perhaps being the critical deciding factor in this regard.

The use of legitimate, expert and informational power was also evident in the practice of elite soccer coaches researched by Potrac and colleagues (Potrac, 2001; Potrac *et al.*, 2002; Jones *et al.*, 2003). Here, coaches seemed concerned to demonstrate their knowledge and 'expertise' to maintain the perceived all-important respect of the players. The coaches considered it vital for them to act 'like a coach'; to fulfil the obligations of their role which would grant them legitimacy within it. Indeed, an inability to fulfil the athletes' expectations of the role in relation to demonstrating practical proficiency was considered to be tantamount to failure. This sentiment was described by one of the coaches thus:

> They [the players] usually pump you with questions. They'll say they've never done that before, and if I can't say why I want it done that way, if I can't give a good reason, then I've got trouble. You can't afford to lose players. If they have no respect for your coaching ability then you've had it, you've lost respect and coaching sessions become very difficult.
>
> (Potrac *et al.*, 2002: 192)

In addition to the application of French and Raven's framework, the power of coaches has been examined from a Goffmanian perspective (e.g., Potrac *et al.*, 2002). As mentioned in Chapter 2, Goffman's thinking has traditionally not been considered in light of power relations. This would appear to be something of an oversight, as his work was undoubtedly grounded in the political process by which rules of social engagement are established, enforced, challenged and broken: that is, with how power is enacted in real, micro-contexts (Dennis & Martin, 2005). The framework was able to shed interesting light on the actions of Brian, an elite football coach, whose concern with presenting an 'appropriate' coaching persona to develop and maintain the admiration and regard of players lay at the core of his coaching practice (Potrac *et al.*, 2002). This persona consisted of a largely authoritarian style where the players had little input into the decision-making process. Brian justified his approach by the need to ensure that he was perceived to be in control of things; that he knew his 'stuff'. To ask the players for input was too risky as it held the potential for him to be seen as indecisive and lacking in knowledge. It is a strategy which echoes those of coaches featured in the aforementioned work (e.g., Potrac and colleagues) in the context of demonstrating expertise in the training environment.

Such a dramaturgical perspective on power relations in coaching was also evidenced in the work of d'Arripe-Longueville *et al.* (1998). This study provided further evidence of coaches engaging in contrived actions to present certain self-images deemed necessary to drive athletes to ever higher levels of performance. In contrast to much of the existing literature outlining how coaches portray a caring image to achieve desired outcomes (e.g., Jones *et al.*, 2004; Potrac *et al.*, 2002), the coaches here engaged in quasi- (and outright) hostile strategies, such as aggressively provoking and stimulating interpersonal rivalry between players, exhibiting favouritism, displaying an intentional lack of interest in players and even entering into direct conflict with them. For example:

Sometimes when they didn't do what they had to to win, when they have been beaten, I say nothing. I do this intentionally. I force myself to leave them in their mess. In fact, when the system doesn't work, when you define a tactic in advance and they are completely turned around, in bad times like these, I leave. I wait until they come back to have a discussion. I'm not going to take the first step. The principle works . . . if you have to wait five minutes, three days, a week, a month, it's all the same. In any case, the principle works.

(d'Arripe-Longueville *et al.*, 1998: 323)

The coaches here believed that such interactions were required to obtain the respect not only of the players in their charge but of the other key stakeholders in the French Judo Federation. That is, such interactions were expected of them in the subculture of French judo. We will return to this issue in the final section of this chapter.

Further work by Jones (2006a) also used a Goffmanian frame to locate his coaching auto-ethnography. Again, issues of 'face' and impression management lay at the heart of his coaching practice – a need to hide weakness and be perceived as the confident, knowing expert. Jones's story provides some insight into the emotional nature of power relations in coaching, as he describes the anxieties and fears of being exposed as a dysfluent ('not real') coach in the unforgiving environment of semi-professional football. His auto-ethnography illustrated how he was actively engaged in 'the management of feeling to create a publicly observable facial and bodily display' (Hochschild, 2000 [1983]: 7). In addition, Jones's (2006a: 48) work explores the little-understood world of how coaches construct their identities; how they use a number of social strategies, such as feigning ignorance and self-depreciating humour, to protect the 'evidentness' and reality of their personas. Jones's (2006a) auto-ethnography, then, provides some insights into the performative nature of social power within the coaching environment.

The notion of coaches using self-depreciating humour as a strategy to gain the 'buy-in' of their athletes was also evidenced in the earlier work of Jones *et al.* (2004). For example, Bob Dwyer, the Australian Rugby Union World Cup-winning coach, was candid about his conscious use of such a ploy. In his own words:

The players get enjoyment out of being able to mimic the things I do and say, so I leave them in my repertoire. I know they think some of the expressions I use are right funny, but I'm happy about that because they'll remember it. I think it's all part of the psychology of coaching.

(Jones *et al.*, 2004: 127)

Such actions can be explained by Goffman's notion of role-distance. Here, Goffman used the example of a surgeon who sings ditties while wielding a scalpel, so as to assure co-workers that there is an emotionally stable human being beneath his professional role – someone to whom they can relate. According to Goffman, such actions also form a kind of bribery to ensure that his 'team keep their heads during an operation'. Here, through his actions, the surgeon seeks 'a guarantee of equability from his team in return for being "a nice guy" – someone who does not press his rightful claims too far' (Goffman, 1969b: 75). This aspect of coaching behaviour can, of course, also be theorised in terms of social exchange. Specifically, it could be suggested that coaches use such interactions to gain 'attractiveness' from athletes by showing that they can undertake the complex roles of the activity with humour and relative ease (Blau, 1986). It is how they try to generate reverence and compliance.

It would be wrong, however, to see such strategic actions as dark, cynical deeds. Rather, as Potrac and Jones (2009a, 2009b) have pointed out, they should be viewed as more akin to the 'logic in use' within coaching practice: that is, how coaches manage the micro-relations inherent in the context, be they with other coaches, managers or athletes. In supplementing Goffman's writings on the performative nature of coaching practice with the micro-political frameworks of Ball (1987) and Kelchtermans and Ballet (2002a, 2002b), Potrac and Jones (2009a, 2009b) shed light on the contested nature of the pedagogical workplace and what it really means to be a coach. Like the study by d'Arripe-Longueville *et al.* (1998) cited earlier, such work has questioned some of the 'sanitised' and 'functionalist' depictions of coaching by providing gritty insights into the everyday micro-political nature of the activity. For example, Potrac and Jones's (2009a) empirical exploration of semi-professional football portrayed the coaching context as an 'arena for struggle', a poorly coordinated, ideologically diverse place 'riven with actual or potential conflict between members' (Ball, 1987: 19).

Such enquiry has highlighted how coaches work with a diverse range of individuals (such as athletes, assistants and administrators), who may not only bring different traditions, goals and motivations to the workplace but would often not hesitate to act on these beliefs if the opportunity to do so presented itself (Potrac & Jones, 2009a). It is important, then, to recognise that coaches frequently have to navigate their way through contexts where individuals and groups may choose to ignore official consensual organisational goals and, instead, pursue interests that serve to maintain and advance their own positions. From this micro-political perspective, in order to obtain and advance the support and 'buy-in' from key stakeholders, coaches may be required to engage in careful acts of negotiation and orchestration as they attempt to achieve their desired ends (Jones & Wallace, 2005). This could entail elements of struggle, conflict, collaboration and coalition-building. It is a sentiment which echoes the work of Kelchtermans and colleagues in education (e.g., Kelchtermans & Ballet, 2002a, 2002b; Kelchtermans & Vandenberghe, 1998), who asserted that we should not view micro-political practice as being dysfunctional or pathological. Instead, practitioners such as coaches should develop their 'micro-political literacy' if they are to engage successfully with the negotiated and contested aspects of professional practice. This necessitates coaches not only learning to 'read' the micro-political landscape of the coaching setting but 'writing' themselves into it and responding appropriately to situational concerns (Potrac & Jones, 2009a,

2009b). As one coach noted, such concerns should be at the heart of our understanding of coaching:

> Sometimes I'm worried that I'm guilty of portraying an overly political view of what goes on here. I mean it's not all politics. But then the more I think about it, the more I see the politics of it as an everyday part of what goes on too. In order to do well at this level I think you've got to be ready and willing to play the political games.
>
> (Potrac & Jones, 2009a: 572)

Considerable work has also emerged dealing with the power that coaches have and how they sometimes wield it inconsiderately over athletes. An early example was Deborah Shogan's (1999) study of the homogenising effect of modern sporting technologies, and what happens to athletes when they fail. Adopting a Foucauldian perspective, she examined the ethical issues and dilemmas that present themselves when athletes, coaches, sports scientists and administrators have to make decisions regarding how far to push the physiological and psychological limits of sporting performance. In particular, she provided an insightful critique into the normalising processes within high-performance sport and the impact these can have on athletes. The analysis highlighted how the discourse of expertise located within a culture of conformity can lead to athletes adopting an unquestioning, dependent and compliant role within the coach–athlete relationship (Shogan, 1999; Jones *et al.*, 2005). Here, the coach becomes regarded as the provider of knowledge, while athletes are positioned as the willing recipients of such knowledge, which they need to enhance their sporting performances (Jones *et al.*, 2005).

In a similar vein, Habermas's discussion of the colonisation of the lifeworld by the system could also be used to make some theoretical sense of asymmetrical coaching relationships and practices. In this regard, it could be argued that coaches, administrators and sports scientists come to treat athletes 'instrumentally', with timely production of required performance outcomes dominating process concerns. As such, athletes may frequently be subjected to the processes of management and objectification, with little attention given to their thoughts and feelings. Habermas urges us to take action against this state of affairs by critically examining who is advantaged and disadvantaged by the dominant beliefs, values and practices that exist in contemporary society (Morrison, 2009).

In addition to Shogan's (1999) theoretical treatise, a number of empirical studies have drawn upon Foucauldian concepts to examine not only the ways in which coaches influence athletes but the issues and problems that can subsequently arise (e.g., Johns, 1998; Johns & Johns, 2000). For example, Jones *et al.*'s (2005) case study sought to explain how an athlete's eating disorder could be understood in relation to her compliance to a culture of slenderness and norms within top-level swimming and, significantly, the coach's role within that culture. The findings were analysed in relation to Anne's (the swimmer's) wish to please her coach in a sport where her body was on public display. It highlighted how she 'bought into' the coach's ideas, methods and knowledge without question. In her own words:

My new coach promised exciting things and had a lot of new ideas and philosophies. He showed a lot of enthusiasm about my potential, so I [put in] a lot of effort to please him. It was expected that we would eat, live, and breathe swimming. It was tough, and we all had to keep log books for each session to record our training miles, sprint times, weight and other stuff . . . he kept putting pressure on us by lowering our [target] times and telling us what we should be eating and stuff.

(Jones *et al.*, 2005: 383)

The coach's subsequent criticism of Anne's physique had a significant impact upon how she viewed her body:

and I remember feeling really down; it really affected me. I wanted to do so well for him [the coach] and I thought that I was . . . [but] my performance became something to do with my body, that was the reason I wasn't doing good enough. My body was the problem . . . I was judged by my body shape not just how good I could do in the pool. It made me aware that other people looked at my body shape, and looked at me. I became very conscious of it.

(Jones *et al.*, 2005: 384)

Anne was no doubt influenced by the normalising gaze of her coach (and, subsequently, others), a form of surveillance that 'makes it possible to qualify, classify, and punish' (Foucault, 1979: 184–185). Such a gaze can lead athletes to engage in self-disciplinary practices and sometimes (as in Anne's case) to acts of excess as they strive to live up to the dominant norms and ideals.

Similar findings were reported by Johns and Johns (2000), who focused on the training and eating habits of middle-distance runners, rhythmic gymnasts and wrestlers. Excesses here included compulsive exercise, excessive weight-training, the consumption of ergogenic aids, and aberrant eating habits to conform to the sporting culture and the coach's 'normalising gaze'. For example, one gymnast described how public weighing sessions were used by coaches to force conformity:

One coach would weigh us four times a day. We had to weigh in before each practice and it made us really self conscious. And then she would say, 'You're fat, why do you weigh more than you weighed this morning? What did you eat this afternoon that made you weigh more?' It was an interrogation and it was terrible.

(Johns & Johns, 2000: 228)

More recently, Denison (2007) used Foucault's work on disciplinary power to offer a critique of the influence he wielded as a coach over a cross-country athlete. Denison described how he initially blamed the athlete's lack of 'mental toughness' for a poor competitive performance. Foucault's writings on how disciplining techniques can gain hold of an individual's movements, gestures and attitudes led him subsequently to question his practice as a coach and develop an alternative explanation for the athlete's apathetic performance. Denison explained how he had become an 'agent of normalisation' through his control of the athlete's training environment, timetable and race tactics. He believed that this ultimately contributed to rendering the athlete docile, as the latter's sense of self was removed from the act of being a runner. He noted:

> getting Brian to talk about his tactical awareness, and specifically his weaknesses, became a way for me, the expert, to control his race: The more he confessed what he did or did not know about tactics the easier it was for me to prescribe techniques and interventions; to mould him according to my vision of a productive competitor. It was in this way that I might have stripped Brian of his athletic identity such that he entered the race with little or no sense of why he was running and who he was running for.
>
> (Denison, 2007: 378)

Denison's power as a coach, then, was manifest not through violence or direct authority but through seduction – a Foucauldian example of how power and knowledge both depend on and produce each other.

Athletes' power

As outlined above, most of the work examining power within sports coaching has positioned athletes as rather passive actors who are subjected to it (e.g., Jones *et al.*, 2005; Johns & Johns, 2000). If sociology teaches us anything, however, it is that there is room (albeit quite limited in some cases) for agency. Indeed, Giddens (1984: 14) held that 'an agent ceases to be such if he or she loses the capability to "make a difference"; that is, to exercise some form of power'. This belief is shared by Layder (1996: 137), who drew upon prisoners' 'dirty' protests to pressure authorities as an example of how subordinates always have some resources at their disposal to alter the balance of power relationships. Similarly, Foucault (1982) believed that in order to understand power relations we should investigate forms of resistance against it. In this regard, even Shogan (1999) acknowledged that while coaches can exercise considerably more power than athletes because they are supported by organisational contexts that largely endorse their decisions, athletes are capable of acts of resistance. While such resistance may rarely manifest itself in revolutionary ways, like deposing a coach, it can occur more frequently in other ways, including making gestures behind a coach's back, refusing to train outside formal practice times, and discussing a coach's decisions and methods with team-mates and friends (Shogan, 1999). Such struggles are usually characterised by a search for the immediate (as opposed to an underlying chief concern), an opposition to the effects of power as linked to knowledge and competence, and a questioning of the status of the individual (Foucault, 1982). Although it may not be instantly obvious, then, athletes always have some power in their dealings with coaches.

Recent work by Purdy *et al.* (2008, 2009) highlighted the abilities and means through which athletes (rowers, in this case) resisted coaches' authority. Such a conceptualisation firmly defines power as relational, where the dominated are never truly without power. The rowers under study were seen to flex their authoritative muscles in opposition to what they felt were poor coaching practices. Resistance took the forms of derogatory nicknames for one coach in particular ('Seagull', on account of her seemingly constant squawk-like instructions), open verbal challenges and general scorn. The brittleness and breakability of power, particularly when confronted by scorn, is, according to Tawney (1931: 229; cited in Blau, 1986: 115), what power fears most: '[Power] is both awful and fragile. [It] can dominate a continent only to be blown down by a whisper. To destroy it, nothing more is required than to be indifferent to its threats. Nothing less, however, is required also.'

This sentiment was echoed by Nyberg (1981: 53), who believed that the ultimate act of confronting or dissipating power occurs through laughter, as 'authority fears no threat more than the laughter that comes from scorn'. According to Willis (1977), such actions as sarcastic humour and banter directly question authority by subverting the language in which it is normally expressed (Purdy *et al.*, 2008). Similar practice was evidenced by the young football players in Cushion and Jones's (2006) study, who, while not daring to be so vocal or active as Purdy *et al.*'s (2008) rowers, still occasionally withdrew best effort as a means of exercising a degree of control over their environment and a harsh coaching discourse. In this respect, resistance – especially scornful, sarcastic, discursive resistance – has the capacity to 'transform' the circumstances in which those usually subject to power (e.g., athletes) find themselves (Giddens, 1984).

But what can make athletes behave in such seditious, resistant ways? The rowers in Purdy *et al.*'s (2008, 2009) work lost respect for their coaches due to the latter's actions, which consisted of not behaving in ways the athletes expected or wanted, being too authoritarian, too inconsistent and too general, all without justifying what they did. By overly threatening the rowers' 'ontological security' (Giddens, 1984) which was, in turn, shaped and constructed by previous experiences and current expectations, the coaches lost the athletes' respect. The contract between the parties had been somewhat broken, a situation which Blau would have interpreted as a dysfunctional exchange. This sentiment is also in keeping with recent work by Jowett and colleagues (e.g., Jowett, 2005; Jowett *et al.*, 2005; Jowett & Cockerill, 2003), LaVoi (2004) and Poczwardowski and colleagues (Poczwardowski, Barott & Peregoy, 2002; Poczwardowski, Henschen & Barott, 2002), which has suggested that coaches' and athletes' behaviours, thoughts and emotions are causally and mutually interdependent. That is, athletes can influence coaches and the coaching environment as much as coaches are commonly understood to influence athletes.

An interesting point that arose in the studies by Purdy *et al.* (2008) and Cushion and Jones (2006) is that, while the athletes engaged in acts of resistance, the large majority of them chose to remain in the coaching environment. The resulting question here is why athletes choose to continue in coaching settings they find oppressive and/or unfulfilling. This issue could, in part, be understood in relation to Bourdieu's notion of the complicity of the dominated. For example, in the work of Cushion and Jones (2006), the minimal levels of resistance provided was explained in terms of the players regarding the abusive and severe discourse of the coaches as being motivational. This situation was fed by the players' perceptions of their coaches as the 'gatekeepers' to a future professional football career. It is perhaps not surprising, then, that the players opted not to voice any dissatisfaction with the working climate they experienced openly. As a consequence, the players' efforts to pursue their own personal goals led them to engage in social practices that helped to reproduce the existing culture. In this respect, those who appeared to accept the legitimacy of the dominant values were more likely to receive positive experiences, which Bourdieu encapsulated in his notion of 'submission [as] liberating' (Bourdieu, 1987: 184). For anyone involved in the struggle for capital and standing, like the players in Cushion and Jones's (2006) study, it is essential that they abide by 'the rules of the game': that is, 'they must accept the often implicit presuppositions that everyone else in the field takes for granted and shares' (Kim, 2004: 306). These include what to honour, desire, avoid and so forth (Kim, 2004). Seen in this light, people become somewhat knowing subjects in their own seduction, with a politics of identity coming to the fore (Westwood, 2002).

Similar findings were evidenced in the study by d'Arripe-Longueville *et al.* (1998), which highlighted that even in positions where athletes look as if they have no authority, they still have agency. The authors found that, despite being subject to their coaches' bullying, the players chose to remain within the elite judo programme. They did so because, while they may have considered the coaches' actions to clash with their need for self-determination, they recognised that the coaching system was effective and produced the results that they were striving to achieve. D'Arripe-Longueville *et al.* (1998) suggested such behaviour could be explained in terms of the notion of 'tacit cooperation' (Lacoste, 1991). Here, cooperation is not characterised by collaborative elaboration or negotiation but is rather based upon the power balance and strategic actions related to shared interests. It could thus be suggested that the athletes engaged in forms of 'strategic interaction' (Goffman, 1959) by manipulating the coaches' perceptions of them and the social situation in their quest to achieve their goals. Similarly, their actions, and those of the players in Cushion and Jones's (2006) study, could also be understood in relation to exchange theory in terms of the athletes accepting the negative interactions to which they were subjected as the price to be paid for achieving success in sport. The players' acquiescence could also be explained by the lack of available alternatives, a notion which draws on Thibaut and Kelley's (1959) comparison level of alternatives. As highlighted in Chapter 9, this (exchange) theory illuminates the difference between satisfaction and dependency (O'Brien & Kollock, 1991), and offers a realistic understanding of why athletes stay in apparently punishing relationships.

As stated in the introduction to this chapter, if power is considered pervasive, it must always be present in the social and 'intrinsic to all interactions' (Giddens,

1984: 14). Hence Westwood's (2002: 17) belief that 'emancipation' or empowerment is a flawed project as there 'is no social space beyond authority'. This is a perspective which grounds Jones and Standage's (2006) critical account of shared leadership in challenging the rhetoric and generalist statements regarding the benefits of an 'empowering' or 'athlete-centred' approach to coaching. Here, Jones and Standage highlighted a number of contextual considerations that appear to have received little attention in the given discourse. They argued that a need exists to understand the utilisation of empowering approaches within coaching in relation to the political and social conflict embedded between change and tradition. It is important to consider that it may not be possible to implement an empowering coaching philosophy cleanly, due to the incompatible beliefs and values that exist within the coaching environment. For example, some athletes may not wish to become involved in the decision-making process, especially if they have experienced success from a more prescriptive coaching style. Indeed, athletes who have been socialised into the role of follower within the sporting culture may not only prefer not to accept more responsibility but may consider the coach not to be doing his or her job properly by using such inclusive strategies.

Jones and Standage (2006) further argue that a traditional authoritarian culture has taught coaches to take control of each and every situation. This is perhaps unsurprising when the hierarchy of responsibility in many sports sees the coach as having to answer for everything that goes wrong. As such, the rather simplistic promotion of shared leadership and empowerment in coaching needs to recognise the uneasy coexistence between athletes who may or may not want more power, and coaches who may or may not want to devolve power. This is not to say that shared leadership approaches should not be used in coaching; rather that the discourse should be more realistically grounded in issues of power, social obligation and hierarchy, thus increasing its everyday relevance and usefulness for practitioners.

The power of context

If power is not merely endowed in individuals but dissipated within and soaked through the social environment, it stands to reason that the context exerts much influence on how power is understood, manifested and practised within coaching. For example, Foucault believed that power resides in knowledge and discourse which can, in turn, be reproduced or contested in a range of settings. Recent work by Denison (2007), as mentioned earlier, has examined the predominant rationalistic discourse of coaching and how it served to shape his practice. He described how the dominant discourse of the 'coach as expert' influenced him to control virtually every detail of the athlete's training, from the surface upon which he ran, to training loads and schedules, through to race tactics employed in competition. Such a practice echoes the records and accounting practices of modern-day states in which people are simultaneously 'individuated and objectified' (Westwood, 2002: 134). It is concerned with the disciplining of the body, with techniques to gain hold of individuals' 'movement, attitudes and rapidity' (Foucault, 1979: 137). For Foucault, this also extended to individuals policing themselves while they are being policed by others – a sentiment often heard in coaches' repeated calls for athletes to 'take responsibility' over what they do. As a principle, such a request often has merit; but when used without consideration it holds the potential to lead to multiple identity-related problems. It is through such cultural discourse that power-knowledge is enacted. Similarly, Jones's (2006a) auto-ethnographical account draws on anxieties to act as expected, in ways he perceived that the players and the context demanded; to become a knowing, fluent expert coach, someone whom the players could trust to 'call the game'. He subsequently feared that his dysfluency would be perceived by the players as a stigma that would disqualify him from full social acceptance within the environment (Goffman, 1963). In short, the context, or his perception of it, dictated his feelings.

Much other work exists documenting the principal knowledge source of coaches as a process of social learning (e.g., Jones *et al.*, 2004; Gilbert & Trudel, 2001). Bourdieu describes such a course of action as 'induction into the field', a term related to a structured system of social positions that defines the situation for its occupants (Jenkins, 1992). Because coaches learn predominantly from experience (Cushion *et al.*, 2003), coaching provides an almost perfect practical apprenticeship for the transference of habitus, another Bourdieuian concept. That coaches become influenced or socialised by their habitus is undeniable. The dominant knowledges feeding the habitus are, of course, instrumental in deciding what is learned and how it is learned, marking a clear relationship between power, interaction and learning. The point to be made here, however, is that the power inherent in the context, as manifest through dominant ideologies and common-sense acceptance of the 'way things are done around here', exerts considerable influence over coaching. Such findings have been evident in the work of many researchers, from Sage (1989) to Cushion and Jones (2006). They mark the 'hidden curriculum' of coaching (Cushion, 2001). Much of this later work also points to the nuanced influence of context, in that agents do not mechanically follow social norms but interpret them in ways likely to bring the most amount of possible capital (Bourdieu, 1990b). For example, the football coach Steve Harrison was determined to 'be himself', to coach in a way that suited him, thus developing his individual coaching sincerity. Such agential actions, of course, did not represent unencumbered freedom as, like other coaches, Steve could operate only within the 'space of the possible' (Bourdieu, 1990b).

As well as being created by context, Bourdieu's notion of capital is a great shaper of context. Capital is described by Bourdieu as being the capacity to exercise control over one's own future and the future of others. It is, then, in effect, a form of power. The many different forms of capital, including social, cultural, symbolic and physical, can all contribute to the social hierarchy, structuring the context for both coaches and athletes (Cushion & Jones, 2006). The capital afforded coaches gives them a sense of legitimate power within the context. Such power is normalised within coaching – that is, with coaches behaving like individuals in power – a concept related to Foucault's notion of the 'discourse of right'. In many ways, then, coaches come to be agents of legitimate authority, a position which, if not carefully considered, can lead to excessive authoritarian behaviour (as witnessed by the coaches in d'Arripe-Longueville *et al.*'s (1998) study, among others). The result for athletes and those subject to such behaviour is often a form of social trauma where the ethical norms associated with interactions are destroyed. According to McDonagh (1982), victims often cope with such trauma by taking responsibility for it themselves – in terms of their own motivation. This was evident in Jones *et al.*'s (2005) study of Anne, cited earlier, who adopted a drastic self-critical response to a comment by her coach. The point here is not singularly to criticise uncaring coaches, although greater consideration and sensitivity in this instance could certainly have avoided much pain. Rather, it is to highlight the strength of social norms to drive actions, inclusive of coaches' power and athletes' often docile responses.

A final explanatory framework to be considered in this regard is that of socialisation. It could be argued that, through the process of organisational socialisation (Sage, 1989), coaches not only learn the technical aspects of the coaching role but the norms and values associated with the position within a particular sporting culture. Various socialisation experiences provide a form of induction into the culture of coaching by providing practitioners with 'maps of meaning' (Sparkes, 1993: 111) that help to make the sporting environment intelligible to them (Jones *et al.*, 2003). Such learning is, of course, inclusive of the power relationships that exist between coach and athlete and, specifically, how these relationships should be structured and enacted (Jones *et al.*, 2003; Potrac *et al.*, 2002).

Recent work examining coaching behaviour and power relations in professional football (e.g., Cushion & Jones, 2006; Potrac *et al.*, 2002) has highlighted how context and culture dictated coaches' actions. In particular, the coaches described how their previous experiences as players and neophyte coaches, combined with the current expectations from employers and athletes, led them to coach in a particular way. The coaches asserted how they felt compelled to adopt a largely authoritarian and prescriptive approach in order to avoid being seen as 'not doing the job properly'. For example, Cushion and Jones (2006) drew attention to how a number of aggressive and belligerent coaching practices in top-level youth football were understood in relation to the traditional institutional discourse about how best to prepare young players for the demands and rigours of the professional game. Here, one coach noted, 'Threatening people has been the traditional way of doing it. It's "do as you are told" stuff' (Cushion & Jones, 2006: 149)

Similarly, the judo coaches interviewed by d'Arripe-Longueville *et al.* (1998) emphasised how their engagement in a number of aggressive and apparently 'uncaring' practices towards the athletes was influenced by their understanding of the culture and demands of the French judo system. In the words of one coach:

> The athletes that are successful know the best ways around the system, in a game that is a little bizarre. They know the necessary collective effort with rules based on very old tradition, and the self-sacrifice. You shut your mouth and go through the days.
>
> (d'Arripe-Longueville *et al.*, 1998: 323)

Such sentiments can be understood in relation to the work of Goffman (1959), who has suggested that social actors, such as coaches, are not able to choose freely the images of the self that they would have others accept; instead, they have to conduct themselves in ways that are in congruence with the roles, statuses and relationships that are accorded by the social order (Branaman, 1997). In drawing upon Goffman's (1974) work on frame analysis, which focuses on how social actors perceive and organise experience, it could be argued that coaching behaviour is influenced by coaches' understandings of the social context within which they work, and how they consider the necessity of their actions to fit with the dominant norms and values of that context.

While it is important to recognise how power relationships within the coaching environment are shaped by how coaches interact with the culture, they are not the only actors who are subject to the socialising power of context. The work of Cushion and Jones (2006) again provides some fascinating insights into why athletes accept the often severe coaching discourse to which they are subjected. The findings demonstrated that although resistance to the coaches' methods was evident, it was minimal, as the players had internalised the culture of the club, perceived it to be legitimate, and, consequently, accepted their position within the social hierarchy. As mentioned earlier, Bourdieu calls this process the 'complicity of the dominated'. In this respect, 'the players bore the indisputable imprint of their habitus that was formed in the context of their social position at the club' (Cushion & Jones, 2006: 156). Cushion and Jones suggest that such actions could be understood as a form of 'symbolic violence', which explains how order and restraint are established and maintained through indirect cultural mechanisms rather than through direct, coercive control (Jenkins, 1992). They argued that 'symbolic violence' kept players 'in their places' due to them 'misrecognizing' their role as unquestioning of authority. In their quest to become professional footballers, then, the players engaged in social practices that not only contributed to the existing structure but helped to reproduce it (Cushion & Jones, 2006).

Such explanations and understandings are also in keeping with the recent work of Roderick (2006), who studied the working lives of 'ordinary', lower-level professional footballers. Of particular interest is the players' understanding of the 'working culture' of professional football in relation to the social stigma attached to injury. Roderick's data revealed how players often felt compelled to hide injuries and continue to participate in training and matches whenever possible. Such actions were not only influenced by individuals' desire to remain in the team but by their reluctance to be seen to be letting down the manager and their team-mates. For example, one player described how the social isolation and guilt experienced while recovering from injury often resulted in an early return to training, against medical advice:

> Because the contact is minimal, whatever the manager says to you, you sort of take it to heart. Like if he comes in one day and says, 'How are you getting on? Come on, you should be getting fit,' you think, should I be getting there? Should I be getting fit? And because he's the manager and it's his decision

about you at the end of the day, you might start questioning yourself. I don't feel right but, you know, should I be getting fitter?

(Roderick, 2006: 81)

In keeping with Habermas's work on the dominance of instrumental rationality in organisational settings (Jones, 2005), the players in Roderick's study highlighted how this sense of guilt frequently stemmed from their perceptions, and the perceptions of significant others, that they were considered to be 'dead money' and a drain on the club if they were not able to participate fully in training and matches. This was articulated by a club physiotherapist in an exchange with an injured player:

I said, '[The manager] doesn't mind whether you're absolutely pathetic working in the gym as long as you're out there on Saturday . . . he wants players out there on the pitch.' And the young player thought because he was working hard in the gym he was earning his money. Which is not the case. You earn your money by going out there and playing on the pitch.

(Roderick, 2006: 78)

Interestingly, the players also mentioned that feelings of guilt were magnified by the humour that is a critical cultural component of professional football. Here, it was noted that the frequently injured players were often the target of banter from their team-mates. While the players suggested that such humour could help lift morale, they also said that it was 'alternatively recognized as veiled insults . . . which implied that the injured player was either lazy or soft' (Roderick, 2006: 72). The injured players, then, were anxious to avoid being seen as 'shammers', as having 'bad attitudes', and, as such, they accepted the need to conceal injuries and/or play in pain. No doubt the contextual pressure exerted on the injured players to recover acted as a means of social control through which the dominant working culture was internalised, enacted and reproduced (Collinson, 1988; Roderick, 2006).

Conclusion

The aim of this chapter was to provide some insights into the multifaceted, dynamic and fluid nature of power within coaching. By drawing on a range of theorists (e.g., Foucault, Bourdieu, Giddens, among others) and their various conceptualisations, we have highlighted not only the ubiquitous nature of power within interactions, practices and contexts but its centrality to understanding the complexity of coaching. To date, the interplay between coach, athlete and context presented in coach education provision has largely been grounded in a somewhat simplistic and functionalist account of human relations. If we are to prepare coaches better for the realities of practice, it would appear that a more in-depth understanding of the multiplicities, workings and potential consequences of power is essential. In order to achieve this, more empirically grounded investigations into the various ways in which power manifests itself and operates within coaching practice are required. By underpinning research with the conceptualisations of power discussed in this chapter, it becomes possible for us to recognise the practical value that sociology has to offer, not only because it can challenge the taken-for-granted nature of power relations in coaching, but because it has the potential to offer new ideas, improvements and outlooks for coaching practice and coach education.

12 Social interaction in coaching

Lars Tore Ronglan

Introduction

The idea of a coaching process is that coaches, in various ways, try to stimulate athletes' learning and progressive performance. Naturally, to have an impact and achieve this, coaches have to interact with athletes. Thus, social interaction can be viewed as the essence of coaching, with coach–athlete relationships being at the heart of the activity (Jones *et al.*, 2004). Other relationships also impact on successful coaching: for example, those between athletes, between coaches, and between coaches and other contextual actors (parents, additional staff members and administrators, among others). A principal challenge for coaches, then, is to handle different individuals and groups, and to be able to utilise the possibilities offered by the environment. This supposes flexibility and social competence: that is, the ability to engineer and shape face-to-face interactions productively.

The aim of this chapter is to highlight social interaction in coaching as viewed from the perspectives of the coach, the athlete and the context. In terms of structure, a brief discussion of roles, expectations, interdependency and trust within coaching is given first. As demonstrated by the theorist chapters, these concepts refer to fundamental aspects of face-to-face interaction. This is followed by an examination of coaches' and athletes' respective communications, guided by several questions. Which expectations are connected to the coaching role? Which competencies and behaviours can be useful within coaches' interactions with athletes and other actors? What marks athletes' social interactions within sport groups as communities of practice? And which strategies can help athletes to cope and develop within the coaching context? The latter part of the chapter explores how face-to-face interaction is embedded in societal contexts which, in turn, impact upon coaching in different ways. Specifically, it addresses the question of what characterises different sporting contexts and how culture-specific environments may influence the interaction going on within them.

Having read about power in the previous chapter, it should be obvious that social interaction implies, and produces, power relations. Interaction and power, then, are definitely not separate social things, because a coach's ability to influence athletes and vice versa is reflected in the interaction between them.

Similarly, an evolving coach–athlete relationship comprising fluid interactions constantly changes the power relations between the parties. A similar intimate and dynamic relationship exists between social interaction and the upcoming themes in the next chapter, which deals with coach and athlete learning. Power, knowledge and learning, then, are dimensions of social interaction: that is, conditions necessary to initiate and keep interaction going while at the same time being products of the proceeding interaction. As stated in Chapter 1, overlap between the theme chapters should not be seen as a problem; rather, it makes it possible to address the principal issues in coaching from different angles.

Roles and expectations

As was demonstrated in Part II of this book, the concepts of roles and expectations are fundamental to the sociological understanding of face-to-face interaction. If we imagine a social situation where we do not have any idea of what kind of behaviour is expected from us, interaction will obviously be difficult and will result in many misunderstandings and considerable personal frustration. Thankfully, this is usually not the case because, as social beings, we internalise informal rules and norms for behaviour that help develop and maintain interaction in everyday situations. Such rules appear as general guidelines, regulating and structuring our courses of communication. In some social encounters the rules are quite indefinite; hence, participants have a greater need to define or frame the situation (Goffman, 1974). For example, when a coach accidentally runs into two of his or her players in a pub at night, it is unclear whether they should relate to each other as acquaintances, as friends or as coach-and-players. Such a situation is more 'open' – that is, it comprises more vague expectations – than a meeting in the locker room the following day, when the same actors encounter one another before a match. The latter represents a particular type of coaching situation: the situation is quite defined, with the reciprocal obligations and expectations being less ambiguous to the participants.

The concept of social roles refers to shared expectations for behaviour in specific contexts: for example, in social encounters like that of a doctor and a patient in a hospital, a teacher and a student at school, or a coach and a player on a football pitch. Shared expectations and common interpretative schemes (Giddens, 1984) contribute to structure social processes and make courses of interaction more predictable. This does not mean that coaches and athletes are socialised to fulfil fixed and unambiguous roles mechanically. Individual action can never be reduced to such compliance (Goffman, 1959). Hence, it can be considered that both coaches and athletes are actively involved in the process of 'role-making' as opposed to merely passively 'role-playing' (Callero, 1994). Roles, then, are not just played; they may be adjusted through an interplay between individual personalities and intentions (agency) on the one side, and role demands and social expectations (structure) on the other (Giddens, 1984). This doubleness was demonstrated by the elite coaches interviewed by Jones *et al.* (2004) in articulating how they balanced their acting between playing and making the role(s) they adopted; between adjusting their behaviour according to contextual and athlete expectations, to using individual humour and intense personal involvement in an effort to create charismatic leadership.

While recognising the individual ability to form the coach role, we should, however, be aware of 'the force of expectations' within the athletic context (Tangen, 2004: 9). Research illuminating how coaches learn to coach shows that observing and learning from experienced coaches, as an athlete or assistant coach, is highly influential in the development of practice (Cushion *et al.*, 2003; Gilbert & Trudel, 2001; Gilbert *et al.*, 2006; Jones *et al.*, 2004). Similarly, learning from role models and through apprenticeship is an essential part of athletes' development. In this respect, both athletes and coaches can be taken as parts of communities of practice where extensive socialisation processes take place (Culver & Trudel, 2008). As the coaching context is characterised by experience-based learning and continuations of traditional (often ritualised) practices (Cushion & Jones, 2006), the actors involved usually draw upon extensive shared stocks of knowledge to guide their actions (Giddens, 1979), including clear expectations of how to behave in different situations. Typical courses of interactions, such as the pep-talk in the locker room or a usual training session on the pitch, are scripted: that is, they are marked by a set of appropriate behaviours within a certain interaction pattern. Consequently, a coach who seeks to form his or her personal coaching role should do so by carefully taking into consideration how the coaching environment, not least the athletes, dictate (or not) behavioural expectations. It would appear necessary for a coach to uphold the standards of conduct and appearance expected of someone in that position (Potrac *et al.*, 2002). This, of course, relates to athletes' ontological security within the coaching context in that they expect coaches to behave in certain ways to fulfil their side of the social bargain. This was clearly expressed by one of the coaches interviewed by Jones *et al.* (2004: 123), who admitted that his actions were somewhat dictated by his perceptions of what the players expected from him: 'Players like to have a structured framework; they like to be worked. So that's what I do.'

Although Goffman allowed freedom for the individual through role-distance, his basic theme was that the self was more or less an image cast by (ever-changing) social arrangements. Far from allowing the individual unfettered freedom, then, this was an attack on the Western belief of the self-contained individual, thus giving some credence to social context in determining action. Similarly, the strategies employed by the coaches studied by Jones and colleagues (e.g., Jones *et al.*, 2004) confirmed that their actions were often dictated by situational issues and aspects: when to be directive, when to show a 'human' face, when to speak to the individual alone and when to do so through the collective were all factors needing careful reflection before action was taken. For example, not being able to 'read' the nuances of the situation and the athletes' expectations turned out to be a problem to the elite rowing coach examined by Purdy *et al.* (2008), to such an extent that she was eventually forced to quit the job. Despite strong technical knowledge and an ability to structure a good training regime, she caused 'frustration and confusion' (Purdy *et al.*, 2008: 326) among the rowers because of her unpredictable behaviour. This illustrates that limited social competence may very well cost coaches their jobs. Following Niklas Luhmann's work (1995), a lack of communicative competence will significantly reduce a participant's influence on a social situation; instead, he or she will be at the mercy of others' definition of the situation. This is not to say that coaches always have to fulfil athletes' expectations. Sometimes it might be more effective for coaches not to do so: that is, to surprise them or to 'push them out of their comfort zones'. However, such action requires a conscious, sensitive understanding of both the expectations embedded in the context and the consequences of not meeting them.

A further issue to be considered here relates to the emotional nature of performing the coaching role. It could be argued that recognising, and responding to, the dominant expectations of the coaching environment is not only a cognitive but an emotional activity. For example, in order to present the necessary 'front' (Goffman, 1959) in a particular situation, coaches may have to manage, mutate, falsify, augment or suppress their emotional understandings and expressions, in addition to managing their verbal and physical behaviours. In Hochschild's (2000 [1983]) terminology, a coach's social interactions with athletes and other key contextual stakeholders may necessitate them engaging in various degrees of 'deep' and 'surface' acting. As illustrated in the preceding chapter focusing on Hochschild's notions of emotional labour and management, such interactions are capable of having a significant impact upon how coaches come to understand themselves and also how such personal understandings may impact upon their engagement with coaching. In this regard, Hochschild's work may help us examine not only the 'feeling rules' that coaches may perceive to govern their performance of the coaching role but how the quest to achieve organisational goals through the production of specified coaching performances may lead them to experience a number of issues related to the inauthenticity of the self, self-worth management, scepticism and exhaustion. Indeed, it could be argued that the development of an emotional sociology of coaching is crucial if we are to be in any way successful in our quest to put the 'person' back in the study of coaching (Jones, 2009).

Interdependency

'Athlete' and 'coach' constitute interdependent and complementary roles. First, they both depend on each other (as Blau's [1986] work points out). The coach is, for example, completely dependent on athletes in the sense that, without athletes, there is, in essence, no need for a coach. In addition, the parties complement each other in the sense that coaches often 'get the athletes they deserve' and, albeit to a lesser degree, athletes 'get the coaches they deserve'. This points to the reciprocity that exists between athletes and coaches, meaning that a certain conduct from party A stimulates or provokes certain responses from party B, again strengthening the typical conduct from party A, and so forth. For example, and generally speaking, a talkative man may foster a quiet-mannered partner, leading to him maintaining or even increasing his talkativeness. Within long-lasting relationships constituted of complementary roles, like those of a child and a parent, a student and a teacher, and an athlete and a coach, this kind of circularity may create stable interaction patterns, leading to more or less unintended outcomes. An example of this circularity is when a coach who always dictates to her young players exactly how to act and move on the court ends up with 'robots' who are completely dependent on her. This happens despite her intention, by acting like an 'expert', to create competent and independent problem-solvers. Similarly, an athlete who, due to modesty or natural shyness, never approaches or visibly responds to comments by the coach might gradually receive less attention from the coach because of his 'lack of engagement'. Stable interaction patterns, then, are not always functional.

Complementary roles mean that coaches' and athletes' sensitivity regarding how their behaviours appear in the eyes of the other are decisive in the creation of productive face-to-face interactions. According to George Herbert Mead (1934), social interaction depends on the ability to place ourselves in the position of others; to anticipate their responses to our own action before we carry it out; and to use this anticipation continually to regulate and adjust our own conduct. Meaningful coach–athlete interaction, then, could be taken as being based upon the parties' abilities to *take the perspective of the other*, to use Mead's terminology. Perspective-taking is basic to social competence. It is a premise which underpins many of the sociological theories presented in this book: namely, the impression management of Goffman (1959), the social exchange theory of Blau (1986) and the communication theory of Luhmann (1984). Here, Goffman's role-players, Blau's 'gift-bringers' and Luhmann's communicators all anticipate how their interaction partners will interpret their behaviour. Similarly, by placing themselves in the position of the athletes, coaches can become more aware of how athletes frame various situations, including their motives, their interests and the way they perceive the coach's conduct. Likewise, athletes can take the perspective of the coach and thus get sight of some of the dilemmas and contradictory interests with which he or she has to deal. This way, both parties may develop their sensitivity regarding how the situation appears to their co-actors, and thereby more competently contribute to purposeful interaction.

Trust

Trust is basic to the constitution of society in general, and confident face-to-face interaction in particular. According to Simmel (1978 [1900]: 379), trust is the mutual 'faithfulness' on which all social relationships ultimately depend; thus, it can be seen as 'a main theme within sociology' (Lewis & Weigert, 1985: 967). Trust is a relational and dynamic concept, marked by interdependency between the interaction partners. Hence, when we see others acting in a way that implies that they trust us, we become more disposed to reciprocate by increasingly trusting them. Conversely, we come to mistrust those whose actions appear to violate our trust or to distrust us. Thus, mutual trust in social relations is generated and expanded as individuals prove themselves to be trustworthy (Blau, 1986).

Focusing specifically on professional–client relationships within the work life, Lewis and Weigert (1985) argued that trust is basic to social interaction because of the 'competence gap' that exists between two parties. Since the layperson cannot validate the competence of the professional, he or she has no other option than to rely on the professional's judgement. The inescapable insecurity that this creates makes it even more important that the professional behaves in a way that proves him- or herself trustworthy. In this way, ontological security (Giddens, 1991) – that is, a sense of reliability in persons and things – can be maintained in the situation, allowing trust to be activated by the appearance that 'everything seems in proper order' (Luhmann, 1979: 107).

The sociology of trust is highly relevant to social interaction within coaching, especially as the context is marked by contradictory goals and values, and a high degree of uncertainty (Jones & Wallace, 2005). The coach, as a professional, is expected to bring order and direction to situations that seem 'chaotic and ambiguous' (Gilbert & Trudel, 2006). Within this context of trust, and given the perceived need to display impression management (Goffman, 1959), it is perhaps not surprising that one of the elite coaches examined by Jones *et al.* (2004: 139) noted that 'the best coaches would make good actors'. This was further illustrated by Steve Harrison, a professional soccer coach, who stated: 'you've got to think on your feet . . . you've got to get on with it and give the players the impression that you're in control. You've got to be bullet proof, or you've got to portray that you are' (quoted in Jones *et al.*, 2003: 224–225). These coaches demonstrated how they attached importance to presenting the 'right front' (Goffman, 1959) to athletes, including expressing themselves in a confident manner so that the athletes believed they knew what they are talking about. Failure to present such a competent and confident front may lead to a gradual loss of trust and respect from athletes, eventually putting the coach in a rather hopeless position as a leader – a scenario recently portrayed in the work of Purdy *et al.* (2008). Here, elite rowers' initial positive perceptions of their coach were overcome by feelings of frustration and anger, brought about by the way the coach communicated with them, 'missing the whole "social" component of being a good coach' (Purdy *et al.*, 2008: 327). Thus, the athletes' original feeling of being comfortable and safe in the coach's charge (i.e., of being ontologically secure [Giddens, 1990]) was replaced by a growing mistrust: 'I don't even think she cares about this boat, she just wants medals for her CV' (Purdy *et al.*, 2008: 327).

Mutual trust will suffer if the impression management strategies used by the coach are seen by the athletes as calculative, insincere behaviour. Trust, then, in contrast to calculative conduct, can be seen as a normative commitment to a relationship (Blau, 1986), increasing individuals' willingness to work for the continuation of the relationship and to see longer-term outcomes. Trust is also emotional, as opposed to rational, in nature: 'Trust begins where prediction ends' (Lewis & Weigert, 1985: 976). For a relationship to be typically functional, athletes have to *believe* in their coach; his or her performance has to be experienced as genuine and credible if trust is to be facilitated. In the same way, due to the necessity of social reciprocity, each individual or actor in the group has to believe in the others if commitment and ontological security are to develop within the community. Thus, mutual trust should be seen as a joint concern within a team, rather than a result of a coach's performance alone. The development of such trust somewhat echoes that of a collective confidence or, to use Goffman's (1959) term, a 'team performance'. In a recent longitudinal study of an elite sports team, the demonstration of this communal confidence was considered almost an obligation among the players (Ronglan, 2007: 87): 'Handball is a team sport and a martial art, and you have to radiate security to spread security in your team . . . this is the lesson I try to teach the youngsters on the team.' Team confidence did not only refer to perceptions in the minds of players, but was expressed in the 'body work' and interaction among them. Confidence was demonstrated by displaying enthusiasm, will-power and morale, while team rituals were used strategically to express and further develop collective strength. Actively taking part in confidence-building activities and behaviours was regarded as a shared obligation: 'everybody has to contribute' (Ronglan, 2007: 85). This illustrates how the development of trust and confidence among players was seen as a genuine joint concern stemming from the interdependency between the team members.

Coaches' relationships and competencies

Even though the coach–athlete relationship forms the core of the coaching process, coaches also regularly interact with other individuals and groups: for example, with assistant coaches, staff members, administrators, parents and sponsors. Depending on the context, such actors located at the periphery of coaching may have significant impacts on its workings. For example, within professional sport, because economic support may be decisive for a team's existence, the powerful position of the sponsor is a necessary concern for the coach. Alternatively, in youth sport, the presence of 'over-involved' parents is often an issue that cannot be ignored (Strean, 1995). The purpose of this section is to take a closer look at some coaches' social interactions beside those that reside directly within the coach–athlete relationship, and to discuss the competencies needed to negotiate and navigate these sometimes turbulent waters.

Research on coaches' learning indicates that they interact very little with their counterparts who coach similar teams or clubs, because such peers are considered more opponents than collaborators (Cassidy *et al.*, 2006; Lemyre *et al.*, 2007). Perhaps unsurprisingly, due to the competitive world of sports, coaches are often hesitant to share information. Rather, they seem more likely to exchange on a regular basis with assistants and others within their own club (Culver & Trudel, 2008). Such interactions, however, may be more or less collaborative or competitive. For example, the team sport coaches investigated by Lemyre *et al.* (2007: 199) not only asked their assistants for advice but would work together to develop problem-solving strategies: 'the three of us make most of the decisions together'. In contrast, Potrac and colleagues (Potrac *et al.*, 2006; Potrac & Jones, 2009b) tell a very different story. Here, a new head football coach used a number of strategies to persuade the players to 'buy into' his coaching programme in a deliberate attempt to highlight his disloyal assistant's flaws. The story in this latter work positions coaching as a 'micropolitical activity' (Potrac & Jones, 2009b) marked by struggle for positions and the building of alliances rather than frictionless collaboration. Highlighting the contested, negotiated nature of coaching, the study illustrates the need for coaches to develop 'a feel for the game' (Bourdieu, 1990b: 66) in the struggle for field-specific capital, such as trust and respect. This 'feel for the game', or habitus, may include bringing relevant social gifts (Blau, 1986) as well as using intricate strategies and personal resources (Giddens, 1984) to gain the approval of relevant power-brokers within the working context.

Obviously, the coach–assistant relationship can potentially develop both as a fruitful learning association and a well-functioning working partnership. Literature focusing on mentoring in coaching (Cushion, 2006; Jones *et al.*, 2009) and the possibility of developing coaches' communities of practice (Cassidy *et al.*, 2006; Culver & Trudel, 2008) highlight how the coaching environment can be nurtured as a place where professional learning and development takes place. However, when going into, and being part of, a potentially productive coach–assistant relationship, the individuals concerned should be aware of the different interests and motives that might underpin the potential interaction. Clarification of responsibilities and obligations connected to the roles of the head and the assistant coach(es) may, to a certain extent, diminish the space for potential conflict (Lemyre *et al.*, 2007). Further, the ability to take the perspective of the other (Mead, 1934) and read the situation from different points of view could make both parties less naïve and better equipped to contribute to purposeful interaction. By doing so, the coach–assistant relationship does not need to appear only as a place for struggle but as a place for joint development. As a productive social exchange (Blau, 2006), experienced coaches typically might bring wisdom and intuition to the social encounter, while younger assistants potentially bring a willingness to learn, enthusiasm and fresh ideas (Culver & Trudel, 2008).

Besides interacting with athletes, assistants and other staff, coaches, in particular within youth sport, often need to relate to their charges' parents. Smith and Smoll (1996) suggest that regular meetings between coaches and parents create open lines of communication, enabling an uninhibited flow of information exchange. Knowing the child better than anyone, parents obviously can provide the coach with valuable information. This was acknowledged by one of the swimming coaches investigated by Jowett and Timson-Katchis (2005: 279), who stated that 'parents can tell you things that the athlete might not want to tell you or know how to tell you'. Again, from an exchange theoretical point of view (Blau, 1986), access to such 'hidden knowledge' supposes that the coach shares information with parents in return. In the swimming study referred to above, such an invitation 'into' the coaching process was considered a legitimate expectation from the parents' position: 'We want to be informed; she is our child and we have a big part to play in this' (Jowett & Timson-Katchis, 2005: 275). Jowett and Timson-Katchis's study revealed that although both parties valued interaction with each other, parents tended to expect more contact than the coach was able or wiling to provide. Thus, the social exchange was not 'balanced' (Blau, 1986). In particular, coaches found it problematic to interact with parents who were perceived to be over-involved or over-supportive. This tension was even more obvious in the study by Lemyre *et al.* (2007). Few of the investigated team sport coaches here sought advice from parents; some even said they purposely did not make themselves accessible to the parents. The rationale for doing so was the perception of greater subsequent pressure put on both children and coaches; something the latter could really do without.

The above findings illustrate some of the strains placed on coaches, and how such stresses influence the interaction between coach philosophy, coach capacity and context. Given the structural and cultural differences between sports (e.g., between team and individual sports), the extent of individualisation and intensity within coach–parent interactions varies considerably. When coaching a few individual athletes, dyadic coach–athlete relationships and closer coach–parents relations are more likely to develop. Within team sports, marked by more players per coach and a more collectivist culture, a coach's relationship with parents may be weaker. Despite contextual differences, however, both the swimming and team sport coaches mentioned above had mixed and partly problematic experiences with parents. Coaches may restrict their contact with parents for a number of reasons, such as different philosophies, unreasonable complaints, demands that are impossible to meet, or simply lack of time. Coaches also have to prioritise, and there may be good reasons for them not to create complete 'open lines of communication' with parents (even though this is recommended in normative coaching books prescribing 'good practice' guidelines). Such behaviour should not be seen as totally unreasonable, as being honest and truthful in every aspect of interaction can lead only to relationship breakdown, as Goffman (1959) demonstrated. Such a realistic grasp of social interaction gives the lie to the claim often heard in coach education circles that 'honesty' is clean, absolute and unproblematic (Jones, Kingston & Stewart, in press).

Due to the number of different relationships, interests, goals and expectations they have to relate to, it has been suggested that coaches work on or near 'the edge of chaos' (Bowes & Jones, 2006). Rather than looking at coaching as a straightforward enterprise based on identification and control over variables that affect athletes' performances, such a position argues that coaching requires flexible adaption to relationship-imposed constraints. Trying to manage this complexity, the coach is forced to choose among a surplus of possibilities, and 'being forced to select means contingency, and contingency means risk' (Luhmann, 1995: 25). This indicates that each decision could have been different and can always be questioned. By taking account of the limits of coaches' prediction and control over their working context, Jones and Wallace (2005, 2006) concluded that the coach might be better viewed as an 'orchestrator', rather than an all-powerful leader. Orchestration implies steering, as opposed to controlling, a complex interactive process. It is characterised by instigating, organising and coordinating tasks and events 'and coping with the way things are turning out' (Jones & Wallace, 2006: 61). Viewing coaches' interactions with athletes, assistants, parents and the environment through the orchestration metaphor allows coaches to prioritise and not invest as much where efforts are unlikely to bring rewards. In this way, they can make the most of their limited agency.

Athletes' relationships and competencies

Social interaction within the sporting context looks different from the athletes' as opposed to the coaches' point of view. Despite their mutual interdependency, the parties play different roles: athletes are supposed to learn and perform while coaches are supposed to facilitate, teach and orchestrate. The purpose of this section is to discuss athletes' interactions within the coaching context, including an examination of the strategies they can and do employ to cope and develop within it.

Most athletes, within both team and individual sports, are associated or linked to an established group of other athletes, sharing training and competitions. The amount of time spent together as a team or a training squad means that relationships develop, not only between coach and athletes but between team-mates. Recently, authors have begun to clarify and utilise Wenger's general concept of a 'community of practice' (CoP) in relation to sport (Cassidy & Rossi, 2006; Culver & Trudel, 2008); in particular for understanding social interaction and exchange within a team (Galipeau & Trudel, 2004; Miller & Kerr, 2002). Developing his social theory of learning, Wenger defined a CoP as a group of people 'who share a concern, a set of problems, or a passion and who deepen their knowledge and expertise in this area by interacting on an ongoing basis' (Wenger *et al.*, 2002: 4). As a CoP, team members will engage in actions and interact with each other to negotiate the meaning of their participation within the enterprise. Over time, this negotiation process creates routines, stories, a common language and specific ways of doing things. By engaging in the community's practice, members can develop a sense of mutual experience and shared repertoire (Galipeau & Trudel, 2006). In this way, newcomers (or apprentices) learn the culture of practice appropriate to that sport, using veteran athletes or coaches as role models. For example, Light's (2006) study of identity formation within youngsters in an Australian surf club highlighted how joint participation in the club's practices over time provided the participants with resources for understanding the culture.

Applying the notion of CoP offers a perspective from which to view multifaceted social interaction within the community as the key to learning and development. Rather than viewing the coach–athlete dyad as the basic relation, the community is seen as the fundamental unit for negotiation of meanings and the transfer of knowledge. Thus, CoPs have the potential to hold several master–apprentice relations, where players can learn from each other as much as they learn from the coach. For example, in a recent study on peer experiences in youth sport, Holt *et al.* (2008) found that interaction with 'different' types of peer within the football team and dealing constructively with conflicts without involving the coach were important experiences for female athletes. The girls also perceived 'good' peer leaders to be significant: 'helping you with your mistakes and showing you what you're doing right' (Holt *et al.*, 2008: 424). Furthermore, when it came to integrating new members into the peer-group structure, veteran players played an important role. This debunks the notion that a team must include each member of the team equally. Rather, a hierarchy is seen to exist, while newcomers have to be included and actively take part in negotiations and practices to be part of the community. Through 'legitimate peripheral participation' (Lave & Wenger, 1991), newcomers gradually may increase their involvement in the CoP.

A major point that Culver and Trudel (2008) make is that a CoP does not just appear. On the contrary, the role of the individual is paramount to its establishment and maintenance. Similarly, Lave and Wenger (1991) suggested that changing locations, roles and perspectives forms part of individuals' 'learning trajectories' in a community, while 'the most important factor in a community's success is the vitality of its leadership' (Wenger *et al.*, 2002: 159). Thus, the continued involvement of a skilled facilitator is necessary to 'nurture' (Culver & Trudel, 2008) or 'orchestrate' (Jones & Wallace, 2005) the practices of the community. The previously mentioned orchestration metaphor fits well to describe the type of leadership appropriate to initiate and coordinate activities and interactions within a CoP, and so optimise the mutual engagement and knowledge exchange. In addition to coaches, experienced athletes might become influential leaders within a CoP. An example of this was demonstrated in a rowing study conducted by Purdy *et al.* (2009), focusing on athletes' negotiations with their coaches. Some athletes' possession of symbolic and physical capital (Bourdieu, 1986) gave them different status in the group, while the best rower's refusal to comply with the rules encouraged other rowers in the squad to challenge the coaches' authority as well. The story highlighted how negotiations between athletes and coaches were dependent on the distribution of relevant field-specific resources, where coaches' potential social capital ('success') was closely tied to the athletes' existing capital.

As Wenger *et al.* (2002) clearly acknowledged, CoPs are marked not only by collaboration but by contestation and conflict. An important tension specifically characterising social interaction between team players is the inherent doubleness of cooperation and competition: the players are supposed to collaborate to create good team results, while, at the same time, they are also competing for team positions and playing time. Being each other's partners and rivals simultaneously may obviously not be easy to handle, and this seems to be an underexplored aspect of social interaction among team players. Basically, the tension between cooperation and competition is structurally embedded in the team sport context, because there are always more players associated with the team (squad) than there are on the court or the field at any one time. The necessary selection of players and distribution of playing time create an immanent competition between team-mates that can be problematic in many, if not all, sporting contexts: 'I guess it can be difficult sometimes 'cause there's quite a bit of competition between us' (thirteen-year-old footballer quouted in Holt *et al.*, 2008: 421). In elite sport the internal competition may be even harder, although this was alternatively viewed as a mark of quality in a recent study (Ronglan, 2010). One player within this work put it this way: 'Our squad has never been better . . . so the struggle to get on the court has never been tougher.' The internal competition was seen as positive from the perspective of the team, increasing the possibility of winning. On the other hand, it also created greater insecurity for individual players. For some, the situation could be hard to handle. For example, one player stated, 'if I'm not picked, I try to support those who are . . . but it's really frustrating to put in so much hard work, and then not have the chance to participate'. This illustrates how team players have to live and deal with a basic uncertainty created by the internal competition embedded in the context. Such internal competition, however, cannot be 'removed' from the field; it has to be handled.

Although competition is contextually embedded, a coach's agency can influence athletes' perceptions of intra-team contentions. Indeed, a coach's behaviour may intentionally or accidentally increase or decrease rivalry between athletes, as shown by the judo coaches investigated by d'Arripe-Longueville *et al.* (1998). These coaches consciously stimulated interpersonal rivalry by encouraging social comparison and adopting unfair selection processes. They justified their behaviour in terms of mentally 'toughening up' their athletes. Alternatively, coaches may also strive to diminish intra-team competition by reducing social comparison and promoting a mastery-oriented and collaborative learning milieu. This approach is often recommended by the literature. However, no coach behaviour can fully remove the underlying ambiguity and uncertainty created by the competitive context. Thus, athletes often need to find ways to handle such insecurity themselves. For example, the judo players studied by d'Arripe-Longueville *et al.* (1998) adopted interactive strategies, such as showing diplomacy, selecting appropriate feedback from the coaches and utilising others' support, as they negotiated a sometimes hostile environment. The ability to mobilise such social competencies to seek and secure social support also echoes the literature on talent development (Morgan & Giacobbi, 2006). Social support, and the ability to utilise and benefit from such support, has proved to be important for athletes at many competitive levels (Reinboth *et al.*, 2004; Rees & Hardy, 2000). For example, Holt and Dunn (2004) stated that talented athletes used the social support of others to overcome obstacles and cope with adversity during their development. Interestingly, teammates can be important sources in this respect, as shown by Morgan and Giacobbi (2006). The respondents here emphasised how their team-mates were able to 'challenge them', 'bring out the best in them', 'support them' and 'inspire them to work harder' (Morgan and Giacobbi, 2006: 303). Again, the doubleness of cooperation and competition between team-mates becomes obvious.

This section on athletes' social interactions concludes by stating that the relationships within communities of practice are multifaceted, marked by a mixture of competition and collaboration, rivalry and support. Further research is consequently needed to understand better how the inherent tensions are handled in different contexts, and in which ways they influence team dynamics and the functioning of athletic communities.

Contextual influence on interaction

Given that coaching is considered the result of dynamic interaction between coaches, athletes and the socio-cultural context (Cushion *et al.*, 2006), the narrative now focuses on the last of these, the context, and how it might influence the coaching process. Face-to-face interactions between athletes and coaches are always situated in a culture marked by certain norms, values and practices. For example, as illustrated above, the competitive structure of elite sport has a clear impact on team group processes. Rather than looking at 'sport' as one homogeneous culture determining interaction patterns and meaning-making, the text gives a brief insight into the variety of sporting contexts in which coaching processes are embedded and social identities formed. Subsequently, practices and discourses reproduced in specific sports constitute what we might call 'sub-cultures' within the overall field, with identity formation and construction taking place through engagement with these practices.

Cushion and Jones's (2006) study of the coaching culture within youth soccer provides an example of a traditional and pervasive facet of professional coaching. Here, both coaches and players bought into the legitimacy of a working climate marked by strict authoritarian coach actions and compliant players. Aggressive coaching behaviour, coupled with harsh and abusive language, was perceived as 'natural' and in the players' best interests. The dominant values and behavioural schema were uncritically accepted by the coaches, who defended their agency by stating, 'it is the tradition, really' (Cushion and Jones, 2006: 148). Adopting Bourdieu's notions as an analytical framework, the authors demonstrated how dominant structures and values marking the field of professional youth soccer were embodied in the participants' habitus and reproduced by the interaction. Similarly, the study by d'Arripe-Longueville *et al.* (1998) shed light on a coaching setting with some of the same authoritarian characteristics: that is, aggressive coach behaviour and an expectation (and realisation) of athlete compliance. The methods were again legitimised, and thus accepted by the participants, as a 'natural' part of an institutionalised elite judo culture.

In addition to soccer and judo, research within traditional sports like rugby (Light, 2008b; Muir & Seitz, 2004), rowing (Pike & Maguire, 2003; Purdy *et al.*, 2008, 2009), swimming (Jones *et al.*, 2005) and ice hockey (Bloom & Smith, 1996) give support to the argument that specific sports are marked by cultural characteristics. Even though these studies were driven by different questions and theoretical frameworks, they provide insight into aspects of sporting sub-cultures which influence social interaction and identity formation. For example, in heavy contact sports, such as rugby, ice hockey and American football, particular forms of masculinity are expressed and reproduced, marked by strength, toughness and power (Bloom & Smith, 1996; Light, 2008b). The discourses and interaction patterns embedded in these fields differ from those found in competitive swimming. Here, the discourse is often aimed at producing a 'swimming body', a 'slim member of the swimming subculture' (Jones *et al.*, 2005). This is different again from 'lifestyle' sports like windsurfing (Wheaton, 2000) and snowboarding (Thorpe, 2006), where an 'alternative' identity is valued, with insiders developing 'our own language, our own slang' and living 'by our own rules' (Thorpe, 2006: 215). These examples illustrate that sport is far from being a unified context, and that it is necessary to take into account the particularities of the concrete environment when trying to understand the impact on social interaction and individual development.

Skille (2007) analysed adolescents' experiences of participating in two different sporting contexts: a 'conventional' one based on a traditional football club and an 'alternative' one comprising a non-competitive public initiative. The two contexts attracted different participants, produced different experiences, and facilitated different educational opportunities. Among other things, the conventional sport context seemed more based on family socialisation processes and facilitated reproduction to a greater degree. However, given that the two contexts could not be properly understood 'as being either solely reproductive/conventional or purely innovative/alternative' (Skille, 2007: 377), Bourdieu's notion of field was adapted to reflect and illustrate the blurred distinction between the two. Thus, within an overall field (e.g., sport) there might be different sub-fields (e.g., football and windsurfing), again differentiated across continuums between different poles within the sub-field (e.g., conventional/alternative). Viewing the context through such a lens might foster a more nuanced and dynamic understanding of its influence.

To deepen the understanding of cultural diversity in the sporting world, it is worth reflecting upon sociological notions like 'sub-culture' (Giddens), 'sub-field' (Bourdieu) and 'sub-system' (Luhmann). The preceding paragraphs may give the impression that a traditional sport per definition represents a rather holistic and unified sub-culture. However, this may not be the case. Rather than supposing that specific sports, performance levels, social classes and age groups represent clean and distinct sub-cultures, the field of sport can be understood as a complex mix of enabling and constraining discourses intervening in different ways within and across contexts. For example, apparently contradictory discourses like 'authoritarian' (Cushion & Jones, 2006) and 'caring' (Jones, 2009a) may both influence social interaction and practices within a sport or a specific club. Additionally, contextual influence should not be misinterpreted as social determinism; it always takes place through a dynamic interplay between the agential actions and the socio-cultural environment. For instance, studies of female athletes practising male-dominated sports like wrestling (Sisjord & Kristiansen, 2009) and rugby (Chase, 2006), and a study of male athletes practising a female-dominated sport like netball (Tagg, 2008), illustrate how contradictory discourses might collide and challenge dominant understandings of both gender and the sport in question.

Another example of the intricate interplay between context and agents is given by Light (2008b), who explored the masculinities formed in a Japanese high school rugby club. Combining the notions of situated learning (Lave & Wenger, 1991) and Bourdieu's theoretical framework, the analysis demonstrated that the overall culture-specific form of masculinity operating was not simply reproduced through the practices of the club and coaches. Instead, by placing greater emphasis on skill and tactical understanding at the expense of force and power, the hegemonic masculinity was challenged and modified. By striving to play 'thinking rugby' rather than 'old style rugby relying on guts and courage' (Light, 2008b: 171), strategic, tactical and communicative skills were developed. The study highlighted not only diversity in the masculinities constructed through contact sports but how 'particular forms of masculinity are learnt and expressed through ways of playing (game style) and the attendant regimes of training' (Light, 2008b: 163). In other words, it demonstrated that the coaching content and the coach's practices, rather than being pure reflections of tradition and context, also resulted from deliberate agency that held the potential to contribute actively to identity formation. That is, the coach counts.

Conclusion

Social interaction in coaching equates to agency embedded in a specific environment. On the one hand, coaches and athletes are active decision-makers, whose actions reflect their own preferences (Giddens, 1991). On the other, they are situated in cultural contexts, and their choices are made in relation to their perceptions of external opportunities and internal dispositions (Bourdieu, 1986). The coaching process, then, should be viewed as socially and culturally embedded, but not determined; similarly, coaching situations are considered as created by actors, but not detached from social expectations and norms. When trying to understand social interaction in coaching from one side or another, we have to pay attention to this doubleness. The strength of a sociological view on interaction in coaching should be that it allows looking for agency *within* structure. As such, the sociological view can further our understanding of the interactional behaviours that coaches and athletes utilise when in the presence of the different individuals and groups that form the various parts of the coaching environment. The value of such enquiry lies in its ability to enhance our sociological sensitivities by going beyond the veneer of coaching and coaching personas to illustrate how coaches and athletes understand and deal with the issues and dilemmas that arise. Such a recognition of the social and emotional nature of coaching is necessary if we are adequately to theorise and develop educational interventions that reflect the complex reality of coaching practice.

13 Coach and athlete learning

A social approach

Chris Cushion

Introduction

Sociological research and theory have much to contribute to the understanding of coach education, and coach and athlete learning. This potential has, to date, been largely ignored, as current trends in coach learning, research and practice have been towards 'what works', seemingly content to fulfil instrumental ends. Despite Cassidy *et al.*'s (2009) emphasis on the ambiguous nature of coach learning, the tendency, then, has been to treat complex educational issues (knowledge, delivery, curriculum) as solvable by quick-fix data, with learning assumed as a generic, identifiable phenomenon. Much coach development is still restricted and designed by a 'train and certify' approach (Trudel & Gilbert, 2006; Gilbert *et al.*, 2009), where coaches are assumed to 'acquire' concepts, skills and behaviours (Sfard, 1998; Fenwick, 2008) that are seamlessly assimilated and transferred (Gilbert *et al.*, 2009). There is nothing to support the legitimacy of this approach (Cushion *et al.*, 2010; Gilbert *et al.*, 2009). What we have, then, is a paradox: a body of coaches not influenced to any significant degree by formal coach education and yet deemed 'competent' practitioners. Consequently, coaching, inclusive of values, beliefs and practice, remains largely unchanged as coach education remains utilitarian, technocratic, lacking a micro-political consciousness and a social criticality (Cushion *et al.*, 2003; Fernandez-Balboa, 2000).

The current crop of coach learning studies is largely descriptive in nature. They can list learning perceptions and preferences (e.g., Erickson *et al.*, 2008; Fleurance & Cotteaux, 1999; Lemyre *et al.*, 2007; Reade *et al.*, 2008; Schempp *et al.*, 2007; Wright *et al.*, 2007), but offer little in the way of *why* these may be so, while having even less to say about the complex influence of coaching, coaches, athletes or contexts. A sociological perspective to coach learning can address this gap as it considers both issues and explanations (Moore, 2004). It also ensures that there is a place for critical theory in the wider practices of coaching and coach education: that is, 'those sets of ideas which endeavour to explain the nature of relationships in the social world . . . and which, in so doing, generate opportunities not just for further reflective action but also social amelioration and change' (Evans & Davies, 2002: 18). For example, using interpretive social theory to deconstruct coaching compels us to problematise conventional or common-sense ways of thinking. This could be specifically in relation to hierarchies of content (e.g. 'appropriate' for level 1), taken-for-granted notions such as 'skills', 'competencies' and 'good coaching', and disciplinary discourses (e.g., sport sciences), which are routinely employed to organise and constrain social reality (Evans & Davies, 2002).

This chapter considers learning in coaching (from the locations of coach, athlete and context) from a sociological standpoint. Drawing on many of the concepts and thinkers outlined in Part II of this book, the chapter tracks across the field looking at how different perspectives approach particular issues. The organisation and content of the chapter considers: the nature of learning; social approaches to learning; coaches' and athletes' learning, including learning as becoming; and the influence of context. Finally, a conclusion pulls together the main arguments.

The nature of learning

What is learning? There are different ways of understanding learning (Hodkinson *et al.*, 2008). Any understanding relates to how the person is perceived, the nature of reality, and the nature of knowledge. In other words, there is an underlying philosophy that informs that understanding (Cushion *et al.*, 2010), and this frames theories, theoretical models and subsequent practice (Light, 2008a; Brockbank & Magill, 2007). Seen as such, theory is not value free and cannot be divorced from the wider world of ideology and belief (Jarvis, 2004). All theories of learning, then, are based on assumptions and beliefs concerning the individual, the world and the relationship between the two.

An examination of the literature illustrates something of the variation that exists here. Merriam and Caffarella (1999) typified the variety of learning theories as behavioural, cognitive, humanist and social; while Brockbank and Magill (2007) collapsed humanist and social theories, seeing them simply as 'constructivist'. Alternatively, Anderson *et al.* (1996) and Greeno (1997) classified learning theories as cognitive or situational. Sfard (1998), meanwhile, takes a similar stance and examines contrasting root metaphors for learning: as acquisition and as participation.

Traditionally, coaching has been led by behavioural educational practices and psychological conceptions of learning that have developed 'punish-and-reward' systems. Allied to quantifiable methods of evaluation, these have contributed to a 'factory model' of learning (Toffler, 1990). From this perspective, 'knowledge is unchanged and transitive' (Brown & Duguid, 1996: 49): once grasped, it is easily transported from a particular learning situation to different contexts in which that knowledge can be put to work (Brown *et al.*, 1989). A picture of the coach and athlete is painted as primarily cognitive entities promoting a non-personal and objective view of knowledge, skills, tasks and activities (Lave & Wenger, 1996). Any resulting theoretical analysis and subsequent 'instruction' is driven by knowledge rather than practice, while being constrained by an understanding of learning mechanisms as acquisition and assimilation (Lave & Wenger, 1996). While cognitive/behavioural approaches have tended to underpin much coach learning and practice, increasingly more 'social' approaches to learning are being advocated in the literature. Indeed, some principles from adult learning (e.g., reflection, problem-based learning, experiential learning) are emerging in coach education programmes (Cushion *et al.*, 2010). It is to social approaches to learning that this chapter now turns.

Social approaches to learning: constructivism

A constructivist perspective suggests that 'cognitive' approaches ignore the social aspect of learning. Constructivism, however, is not strictly a theory but a description that encompasses a range of approaches to learning. Under this umbrella term, these approaches share a common epistemological or philosophical explanation about the nature of learning (Simpson, 2002: Schunk, 2009). Constructivist approaches are concerned with how learners build their own mental structures through interaction with their environment. These theories have an historical and cultural aspect with respect to individual experience (Brockbank & Magill, 2007). With constructivism, understanding and experience are in constant interaction and, through participation, persons, action and the world, are connected in all knowing and learning (Lave & Wenger, 1996). The constructivist approach also stresses the developmental nature of learning and how differing progressive phases are engaged with over time (Cushion, 2006). There are several social theories of how individuals construct knowledge. The common thread running through them suggests that learning is most effective when new knowledge and skills are used, and individuals construct meanings for themselves within the context of interaction with others (Cushion, 2006; Kerka, 1998).

As Merriam and Caffarella (1999: 22) contend, 'learning does not occur in a vacuum'. In contrast to cognitive-behavioural understandings, a social-constructivist approach posits that learning is not something that happens but is, instead, shaped by the environment, culture and tools in the immediate situation. It is founded on the belief that all human activities are influenced by various levels of interaction, shared values, knowledge, skills, structured relationships and symbolic systems (Wertch *et al.*, 1995). Such a perspective is seen as rooted in the thinking of Dewey (1916: 26), who asserted:

> the social environment . . . is truly educative in the degree in which an individual shares or participates in some conjoint activity. By doing his [*sic*] share in the associated activity, the individual appropriates the purpose which actuates it, becomes familiar with its methods and subject matters, acquires needed skills, and is saturated with its emotional spirit.

The evidence suggests that learning within coaching happens over time and is mediated by the experiences both in and out of coaching sessions (e.g. Cushion *et al.*, 2003; Trudel & Gilbert, 2006; Hansman, 2001). Learning is shaped by interaction between coaches and athletes, discussing with and observing others, trying different ways, reflecting on practice, and negotiating the rules and guidelines set by the sport (Cushion *et al.*, 2003, 2010). A social perspective demonstrates that authentic learning in and about coaching consists of more than formal engagement; it is also in the unplanned intersection of people, culture, tools and context (Hansman, 2001). Coach and athlete learning, coaching and learning to coach, then, are complex practices in a social world. A social approach to learning, in this sense, reminds us that there is no such thing as one kind of learner, one learning goal, one way to learn, nor one setting in which learning takes place (Kilgore, 2001). Indeed, while the 'principles of coaching' may remain the same, different contexts place different demands on the coach and athlete and, therefore, impact upon learning. These demands may be ideological, institutional, cultural or social in nature, in addition to being rooted in the age or experience of those taking part.

Recent research has indicated that the experiences of both coach and athletes(s) within coaching, and therefore the nature of the learning undertaken, will vary according to a range of mediating contextual factors. Such factors include the position of the coach in the club 'hierarchy', the relational status of coach and athlete, the genders of both, if the athlete is a 'starter' or 'non-starter', if he or she has high or low expectancy (favourite or reject), skill levels, age, the aim or philosophy of the programme, and the stage of the season (Cushion & Jones, 2006; Potrac *et al.*, 2007; Purdy *et al.*, 2009; Norman, 2008). From this perspective, learning and development are inherently social phenomena, with the construction of knowledge and meaning being situated within a constructed context (Doherty *et al.*, 2002). Knowledge, action and learning can be seen as both the product and manifestation of a personally experienced involvement with the coaching process (Cushion, 2006). They are linked to an individual's history and are attributable to how they were learned. The implications of this for coaching lie in understanding how knowledge and experience are constructed, passed on and become translated within the coaching process (Cushion, 2006).

Coach and athlete learning

So far the case has been presented that coaching practice is socially constructed and deeply embedded within social and cultural contexts; it involves the relationship between the coach, the athlete and the environment (Cushion, 2010a, 2010b). This relationship is crucial as no party/force has the capacity to determine action unilaterally. Wenger (1998) would express this relationship in terms of membership of a community of practice (CoP). This means that learning becomes shaped by what Billet and Somerville (2004) have called the 'social press' (by historical, social, cultural, institutional factors) but is still determined by individual coaches and athletes. Therefore, engagement with a community may not lead inevitably to learning as it has a relational basis, founded on the intensity of individual agency on the one hand, and the social on the other, within the given situation (Billet & Somerville, 2004). Consequently, while this section considers coach and athlete learning, it necessarily attempts to locate both in relation to one another and to context.

Coaches

How do coaches learn? The literature suggests that they are subjected to a standardised 'curriculum' that privileges a technocratic rationality through a 'tool box' of professional knowledge (Abraham & Collins, 1998; Cushion *et al.*, 2003, 2010). In a state of passive alertness, ideas and seemingly abstract concepts about coaching and sport science are, hence, 'delivered'. The obvious assumption held by the planners of these programmes is that the knowledge given will be transferred unproblematically into coaches' practice and, by similar means, into athlete learning. By the end of delivered courses, coaches are usually declared 'competent' and therefore ready to coach.

This approach aims to develop a requisite 'standardised' coaching knowledge base, together with a battery of strategies to overcome what are perceived as 'typical' coaching dilemmas (Cushion *et al.*, 2010; Chesterfield *et al.*, in press). Such formal coach learning defines what knowledge is necessary for coaches to practise, and how that knowledge can 'best' be transmitted. Certification requires coaches to structure sessions, deliver information and provide feedback in a prescribed manner in order to be deemed competent (Abraham & Collins, 1998; Cushion *et al.*, 2003; Chesterfield *et al.*, in press). This competence is measured by predetermined parameters that focus largely on the technical aspects of coaching rather than on the particular needs of athletes or athlete learning.

This approach is problematic in three key ways. First, coach education packaged as a series of courses or workshops incorporating lecture-style classes can be described as indoctrination (Cushion *et al.*, 2010; Nelson *et al.*, 2006): that is, 'activities that set out to convince us that there is a "right" way of thinking and feeling and behaving' (Rogers, 2002: 53). Indoctrination denies coaches choice, instead exposing them to a single set of values and attitudes that they are expected to acquire and abide by (Cushion *et al.*, 2010). Examples of this might include a prescribed method of delivery, feedback sequence, coaching philosophy, tactical and technical approaches (Jones *et al.*, 2003).

Second, the coaches who progress through the 'system' learn to value certain types of knowledge over others and, in turn, will perpetuate these perspectives (Cushion *et al.*, 2003). Cushion and Jones (2006) examined this process through Bourdieu's lens of symbolic violence: the imposition of systems of symbolism and meanings upon groups 'in such a way that they are experienced as legitimate' (Jenkins, 2002: 104). Symbolic violence is 'violence which is exercised upon a social agent with his or her complicity' (Bourdieu & Wacquant, 1992: 167). In other words, there is acceptance of the dominant values and the behavioural schema in use (Kim, 2004). It is this legitimacy that obscures the existing power relations, often making them unrecognisable to, and misrecognised by, agents (Kim, 2004). Of particular importance here (when considering coach and athlete learning) is the contextual discourse used, with the imposition and enforcement of a 'correct way' at the expense of limitless others being at the heart of the phenomenon (Schubert, 2002). Cushion and Jones (2006) argued that the discourse used in professional coaching helps create and recreate the coaching field, giving current practice an entrenched legitimacy. In this respect, coach education and learning, despite frequent rhetoric to the contrary, can be viewed as professional disempowerment (Macdonald & Tinning, 1995).

Lastly, this rationalistic approach to coach education suggests a striving for a generic coach learner who acquires knowledge through one of a few predictable ways (Kilgore, 2001). The assumption is that where there is agreement about which knowledge is worth acquiring, 'models' of coach and athlete learning can be guides to successful outcomes: the process is linear and largely problem free.

This critical analysis reveals a second general paradox around learning in coaching: namely, the existence of an indoctrinating approach to 'necessary knowledge' while the formal learning associated with it has a low impact on coaches' practice. Bourdieu's habitus is helpful in offering an explanation in this case. As an example, an established coach arrives at a professional development course with a long-standing and deep-rooted habitus, a set of beliefs and dispositions tempered by years of experience in the sport (Cushion *et al.*, 2003, 2006). The course's format and discourse, however, assume that he or she is an empty vessel to be filled with the 'professional dogma' of coaching theory (Schempp & Graber, 1992). Such courses, with their 'parcelled' and specific ways of knowing and communicating (Cushion *et al.*, 2003; Saury & Durand, 1998) are unable to compete with an established habitus conceived from practical know-how. As a result, with his experience acting as a filter, our experienced coach either directly or indirectly contests some of the principles the coach education programme attempts to instil (Cushion *et al.*, 2003). However, due to the power of the coach educator, and the governing body, through their responsibility for certification and position in the sport, our coach has much to lose by directly challenging the programme. The critical scrutiny necessary to do things better, and to create the possibility of changing practice as and when the need arises, is consequently driven underground as the coach gives an outward appearance of acceptance while harbouring and restricting disagreement with the official coaching orientation (Cushion *et al.*, 2003). So, while coach education may give the appearance of being subject to a so-called 'wash-out' effect (i.e., it is not retained in practice; Zeichner & Tabaachnick, 1981), evidence suggests that many coaches never accept or appropriate the programme behaviours and beliefs in the first place but, out of necessity, merely appear to do so (Cushion *et al.*, 2003).

This was well illustrated by Chesterfield *et al.* (in press), who found that coaches used 'front' and 'impression management' (Goffman, 1959) to create a convincing impression for coach educators that they were acting in a manner deemed appropriate to achieve the goal of passing the course. Upon successfully 'passing', the coaches reverted to their preferred coaching methods and behaviours, which were largely implicit and learned from experience (see also Cushion *et al.*, 2010).

Informal learning through practice and engaging with other coaches is currently the dominant mode of learning by coaches. This is due to the limitations of current formal provision, the lack of an overarching structure, and issues around volunteerism, which combine to encourage a negotiated and individual learning curriculum (Cushion *et al.*, 2010). As Cushion *et al.* argue, this curriculum is problematic, often inclusive of underlying power relations, while promoting and reinforcing certain ideological interpretations of knowledge and practice.

Athletes

Discourses are shaped by 'beliefs and commitments, explicit ideologies, tacit world views, linguistics and cultural systems, politics and economics, and power arrangements' (Cherryholmes, 1988: 106). They are the prevailing 'set of meanings, metaphors, representations, images, stories [and] statements that, in some way, together produce a particular version' of coaching (Burr, 1995: 48). Cassidy *et al.* (2009) argue that the language of sports coaching is a performance 'discourse of expertise'. Here, learning is focused on the individual and is positioned as the development of proficiency, where athletes and coaches are empowered by their goal orientation and the self-chosen means to achieve it (Johns & Johns, 2000).

The expertise literature pertaining to coaching assumes a novice–expert continuum and a predominantly cognitive/behavioural approach to learning within an acquisition metaphor (Cushion *et al.*, 2010). That is, 'the language of knowledge acquisition and concept development makes us think about the human mind as a container to be filled with certain materials, and about the learner as becoming owner of these materials' (Sfard, 1998: 5). In other words, there is a body of coaching knowledge, and coaches and athletes will accumulate this as they progress along the continuum (Cushion *et al.*, 2010; Trudel & Gilbert, 2006).

This performance pedagogy, associated with the ascendency of modern sport, is based on scientific functionalism (Johns & Johns, 2000; Cassidy *et al.*, 2009). Within it, coaches construct the learning environment for their athletes based on knowledge gained from 'professional' bio-scientific sport science disciplines. This knowledge is then packaged into a curriculum and disseminated in the hope that it will be acquired and transferred through coaches to athletes (Trudel & Gilbert, 2006). The curriculum relies on technical procedure and given 'facts' to provide sequence and direction, with the athlete being viewed as a biological object and docile body (Johns & Johns, 2000). Through this discourse, coaches determine the nature of athlete learning through shaping the athletic experience (Johns & Johns, 2000; Cushion & Jones, 2006). Guilianotti (1999) has likened this relationship to Foucault's notions of body subjugation and discipline. Here, the body is developed through intense and rigid training, with the learning linked to ways valued in the social field to acquire status and distinction. Cushion and Jones (2006) and Cushion (2010a), however, illustrate that athletes are not helpless and totally at the mercy of social forces in this regard. Rather, through pursuing their own goals, athletes also engage in impression management, presenting themselves as submissive and compliant learners while engaging in peer-group resistance which, in turn, impacts upon the nature of their learning (Cushion & Jones, 2006).

An expertise/acquisition approach to learning avoids any critical analysis of knowledge, politics or even micro-politics; power is viewed as benign, and considered around mobilising individuals' motivation. This assumed linear approach fails to consider what constitutes knowledge, how coaches and athletes are tied to one another and their environments, or how action and reflection are connected (Fenwick, 2008). Importantly, these issues constitute how learning can be understood, in addition to what coaches and athletes actually learn.

In considering developing knowledge as part of coach and athlete learning, we should be mindful of the postmodern view of Foucault, who regarded knowledge itself as discourse and, therefore, ideological. As a system of ideas, beliefs, values, commitments, patterns of thought and social practices, ideology operates dialectically between individuals and structures to reproduce and maintain social characteristics (Devis-Devis, 2006). Ideology is twofold. First, it functions as a necessary shared system of symbols and social practice that would make any social situation incomprehensible without it. Second, it operates as a system embedded in power relationships and sedimented forms of thought of everyday life that can distort communication and understanding (Devis-Devis, 2006). What coaches and athletes learn, and the process of their learning, is a social system of beliefs, structures and practices, and, as an ideology, is a systemised influence on the social construction of knowledge. In these terms, learning and coaching are historical products that are shaped by ever-changing social, political-economical, cultural and educational forces.

This was well illustrated by Cushion and Jones (2006) and Cushion (2010b), who demonstrated coaching as ideologically laden, where athletes were not merely learning technical and tactical lessons but developing attitudes, values and beliefs. The coaching process, in this respect, was used to impose learning related to language, meanings and symbolic systems with the athletes 'misrecognising' the arbitrary nature of the culture. Similarly, Johns and Johns (2000) described how coaches drew on their claims to expertise and technical knowledge to set workloads and establish ways and conditions related to athlete behaviour. The coaches' authority here was backed by institutional forces emanating from both their coaching qualifications and the governing bodies, which, in turn, legitimised certain knowledge and learning (Johns & Johns, 2000). The practices, and learning therein, became normalised, with a 'regime of truth' being established through the coaching discourse (Chapman, 1997: 206).

Critical theorists challenge what we think we know is true by demonstrating how it serves the interests of certain groups at the expense of others. Such thinking is explicitly political, and includes 'the relentless criticism of all existing conditions' (Marx, 1983: 93). Habermas (1971) has been particularly influential in his criticism of learning. In this respect, he described three human interests for which knowledge is developed. First, technical interest, which guides the control of the material environment. Technical knowledge is developed to organise and maintain economic and political systems. Second, practical interests, which stem from our need to know one another. This knowledge is related to shared meanings in the everyday world of human interaction, the lifeworld. And third, emancipatory interests, which form the desire to be free of oppression. These are concerned with understanding the difference between what we know is true or best and how this knowledge can be oppressive when put into practice (Usher *et al.*, 1997). Taking this perspective means that an emancipatory approach would enable athletes and coaches to examine their social world critically and consider the political interests and structures being served, and how their own actions might be perpetuating a dominant discourse (Edgar, 2006).

Importantly, as Habermas notes, inequalities of power relations, structures of privilege and oppression are often reinforced through practice, because the logic that maintains them becomes a common-sense lens through which people view and interpret their everyday experiences. Learning socialises coaches and athletes into accepting inequalities as part of everyday life. This reinforcing logic or hegemony concerns the success of dominant groups in presenting their definition of reality in such a way that it is accepted by other groups although it serves the interests of the dominant group alone (Giroux, 1997). In terms of coach and athlete learning, a hegemonic technocracy 'closes off rather than opens the mind, depoliticises rather than politicises, and disempowers rather than empowers' (McKay et al., 1990: 57). It is important for athletes and coaches to consider the knowledge they acquire, as it cannot be treated as if it were neutral or value free. Indeed, Cushion (2010b) and Cushion and Jones (2006) demonstrated that coaching practice, and subsequent athletes' learning, was imbued with powerful cultural messages. This work demonstrated that knowledge is produced within distinct socio-cultural contexts, serves particular interests and carries certain values (in this case those related to winning, conformity and obedience). Knowledge, then, was positioned as socially constituted, socially mediated and open ended, with 'its meaning to given actors, its furnishings, and the relations of humans within it, [being] produced, reproduced, and changed in the course of activity' (Lave & Wenger, 1991: 51).

The process of selecting, organising and distributing coaching knowledge through learning is part of, and at the same time contributes to, power production (Kirk, 1992). What (and how) athletes (and coaches) learn is not purely a technical exercise but involves a complex set of interests at work. For example, the act of planning sessions or programmes can be considered an exercise of power, as it entails the imposition of an idea, or set of ideas (St Clair, 2004). Crucially, this implies a choice between different views of what knowledge is essential for practice (Cushion et al., 2003; Tinning, 1997). It is a form of social editing or 'gatekeeping', where some themes are eliminated and others are promoted (Lawson, 1993). The process of what athletes learn, therefore, becomes a political act intimately linked with power and control regarding what constitutes legitimate knowledge, and who holds that knowledge in the culture and profession (Cushion et al., 2003). Arguably, through this control, the sport's governing body, coach educators (i.e., the 'gatekeepers') and coaches seek to maintain the dominance of a body of knowledge in order to sustain and improve their own positions.

Coach and athlete learning: learning as becoming

Postmodernist thinking is useful for questioning the belief that there is a coherent, autonomous, rational, unitary self (Hill, 2008). Such a conviction presents a static view of learning, where individual values or goals are critical determinants for success. Understanding the coach and athlete as 'decentred' or 'emergent' (Rosenau, 1992), however, means that the learner is no longer a stable individual exploring potential and self-actualisation (Kilgore, 2004). This suggests a strong relationship between learning and identity. Seen as such, the learner is always becoming (i.e., their identity is being developed, transformed) and is always situated in a context that is becoming (i.e., changing situations) (Kilgore, 2004: Colley *et al.*, 2003).

This broadens learning as a concept to one that involves the whole person, and only partly implies becoming able in new tasks or understandings. This is because task functions and understandings do not exist in isolation; they are part of a broader system of relations in which they have meaning. The person is subsequently defined by and defines these relations; learning, then, involves the construction of identity (Lave & Wenger, 1996). From such a perspective, learning is also understood as social and embodied (practical, physical and emotional as well as cognitive), and as coaches or athletes construct or reconstruct knowledge or skills, they are also reconstructing themselves (Hager & Hodkinson, 2009). This personal reconstruction can be a process that is sometimes explicit and agentic. Giddens (1979), for example, argues for a view of decentring that avoids the pitfalls of structural determination by considering intentionality as an ongoing flow of reflective moments in the context of practical engagement. Nevertheless, coach and athlete learning, while co-constructed by and with others (e.g., coach, coach educator, mentor, athlete), remains in part determined by the dominant structures of thought that prevail in particular sports and particular levels within sports. For example, in Cushion and Jones (2006), Cushion (2010b) and Wilson *et al.*'s (2006) studies, coaches adapted their pedagogy to the habitus of the athletes (not based on athletic ability alone), while at the same time the athletes were informed by sporting notions (e.g., what it means to be a 'pro' – professional athlete) that influenced the coaching discourse. In Cushion and Jones's (2006) work, in particular, those athletes' whose dispositions (habitus) did not align or develop became increasingly isolated and excluded (characterised perhaps as having a 'poor attitude'). The 'successful' players learned to fit; becoming a 'pro' was right for them, while they were becoming right to be a 'pro'. This involved a constant reconstruction of identity, what Bourdieu (1986) calls the 'choice of the necessary'.

Identity has been explored in social theory as a way of placing the person in the context of mutual constitution between individuals and groups (Giddens, 1991). Identity theory assumes that identity is created through the interrelationship between the context and the self (Stroot & Ko, 2006). Giddens (1991) described the changing nature of self-identity, recognising that it is not a set of traits possessed by an individual. Rather, a person actively constructs and revises a story of self that provides a basis for self-identity. Identity theory is changed through the concepts of personal and social transformation (Stroot & Ko, 2006). Giddens (1991: 53) stated that 'the self is reflexively understood by the person in terms of their biography'. Hence, it can be conceived that coaches and athletes are active in trying to make sense of their positions and, in this respect, are constantly in a process of identity development (Mead, 1934). A learner's identity will thus be influenced by contextual factors (developed in detail in the next section) that need to be foregrounded to understand the nature of the learning taking place. For example, in work by Parker (1996) and Cushion (2010a), issues within a 'hidden curriculum', such as conformity and submission to hierarchical relationships, were evident and impacted upon the athlete.

How the person is defined as well as how he or she defines relations within a context arguably moves beyond the ideas conveyed by the simple notion of 'identity'. Bourdieu's work is helpful in this respect in incorporating subjective dispositions and collective structural predispositions (Colley *et al.*, 2003). Bourdieu argued that the body is a site of social memory involving the individual culturally learning and evoking dispositions to act (Jarvie & Maguire, 1994), a phenomenon known as habitus. These deep-seated orientations develop through coaches' and athletes' lives. Their habitus is acquired as a result of past experiences through adjustment and readjustment following interaction with specific coaching contexts. Given the interconnectedness of coaching, the body and culture, coaches' and athletes' practice takes on enormous significance in the process of cultural production and reproduction (Kirk & Tinning, 1990). Therefore, the acquisition and development of habitus have serious implications for both coaching practice and learning.

We return, therefore, to the idea of an athlete and/or a coach's becoming, which helps guard against a literal or compressed concept of learning that confines our interest to short-term cause and possible effect: for example, training sessions and courses (though these have a place) (Colley *et al.*, 2003). Instead, learning is seen as part of a lifelong habitus formation that has no clear endpoint, even though the learner or others may be explicitly interested in one (Hager & Hodkinson, 2009). The ways in which people learn and are willing to learn will depend on their prior positions, experiences and dispositions. Viewed as such, learning as becoming is well under way before the course or session begins, and it continues after it has finished (Hager & Hodkinson, 2009). This helps explain the relatively low impact of short, isolated coach education episodic workshops (Cushion *et al.*, 2003), and suggests the need to consider coach learning as a more long-term endeavour.

Context

The notion of practice involves a way to address the constitution of culture and local activities (Wenger, 1998). In theories of social practice (e.g., Bourdieu, 1977; Giddens, 1979), the emphasis is on the relational interdependency of not just the individual and social world, but activity, meaning, cognition, learning and knowing (Lave & Wenger, 1996). By situating learning within social and cultural contexts, the individual is less involved with objective knowledge acquisition but is constructing knowledge through direct experience of social practice.

A social practice focus on learning shifts the attention away from the individual coach or athlete to their interaction with the context within which the learning takes place, and brings power issues into clearer focus. This is an important issue as, although it can certainly facilitate learning, context can also constrain; it can set up boundaries, parameters and criteria for membership, thus engendering exclusionary practice. Indeed, the tendency to conceptualise the learning context or community simplistically and functionally disregards the influence of power in pedagogy (Alfred, 2002). It must be recognised that the social context is a power-ridden one, where members take on the values and mores of a dominant group, regarding them as normal. Similarly, values and behaviours that do not mirror those of the majority are viewed as deviant or wrong (Alfred, 2002). As Nieto (2000: 140) argues, 'the difference in perception is due more to the power of these groups than to any inherent goodness or rightness in values themselves'. This was demonstrated by Cushion and Jones (2006) and Purdy *et al.* (2009), who found that non-conforming athletes were arbitrarily perceived as dysfunctional and were often rejected.

According to Alfred (2002), context is defined by the interactional experiences of members of a social group, through communicative processes and the activities in which they engage. Socio-cultural contexts, therefore, make up the total life space in which individual development takes place. The idea of social context as central to learning has increasingly gained importance (Hansman, 2001). Indeed, Wilson (1993: 73) argues:

> learning is an everyday event that is social in nature because it occurs with other people; it is 'tool dependent' because it provides mechanisms that aid, and more importantly, structure the cognitive process; and finally, it is the interaction with the setting itself in relation to its social and tool dependent nature that determines the learning.

In other words, learning in context results from the interaction between and intersection among people, tools and context.

As Alfred (2002) argues, there is a tendency to view the learning context in terms of physical location. Similarly, Lave and Wenger (1991) argue that context is often seen as the container into which the individual is dropped: for example, the classroom, gym or pitch. Other contextual factors (some of which have already been discussed in the chapter), however, could include the histories, cultures, races, genders and physical abilities of the coaches and athletes; their roles and responsibilities; their prior knowledge and their experiences; the course or programme design, the curriculum, the learning activities; in addition to the history, culture and structure of the sport (Alfred, 2002). Alfred believes that the interaction of these contextual factors will influence the meaning that coaches and athletes make of the learning process. Contextual factors can impact upon the learning environment in overt and covert ways, and, as has been suggested, can be powerful in terms of a 'hidden curriculum'. Such factors are invariably influenced by inherent power relationships (Cushion, 2008), which are stratified through complex social divisions organised along both social and cultural lines (Cushion, 2008; Cushion & Jones, 2006). It is this power that sets and relocates boundaries which extend or deny opportunities for learning. A social (community of) practice perspective as applied to context identifies something of the complexity of learning within coaching, and allows a grasp of the contradictions and struggles inherent in the activity. In this way, it is able to engage with questions of politics and power, to address some fundamental questions. Who is excluded from the construction of knowledge? What dysfunctional or exploitative practices are perpetuated? And what hierarchical relations are reproduced? (Fenwick, 2008).

Conclusion

A sociological approach to coach and athlete learning, alongside the impact of context, provides an opportunity to think about the process of learning more broadly than current accounts allow (Cushion *et al.*, 2010; Colley *et al.*, 2003). This chapter has gone some way to highlighting the need to move beyond explanations of prescribed curricula, the acquisition of technical skills of athletes, or coach expertise and knowledge and, instead, to consider the social, historical and cultural aspects of learning. Importantly, this approach begins to recognise that learning is not simply the 'transfer' of knowledge but is part of situations, practice and context. Moreover, learning is impacted by individual biography as well as by contextual factors, and is as much about 'becoming', a transitional process across boundaries (Hager & Hodkinson, 2009). Viewing learning through this sociological lens allows those involved with coach and athlete development to create or enhance contexts for learning and to discover, discuss and make explicit discourse and/or any overarching hegemonic frame (Kilgore, 2004).

   This, of course, is not an easy task, as transcending these issues while suspended within them presents a considerable challenge. However, it is a challenge worth accepting as it holds the potential to create sites for 'intervention and change' (Tierney, 2001: 362).

14 Concluding thoughts and ways forward

Robyn L. Jones, Lars Tore Ronglan,
Paul Potrac and Chris Cushion

A broad summary

A principal purpose of this text was to provide an insight into the social nature of coaching, inclusive of such notions as power, interaction, structure and agency. A base point to highlight was that what we need to know about coaching is rich, complex and diverse. A second aim was to encourage a healthy suspicion of rather simplified a-theoretical explanations of coaching that do not take heed of such social complexity. Echoing Stones (1998a), the more one looks at the varied insights offered by thinkers such as Goffman, Foucault, Bourdieu and others, the more one realises that there is much to know about coaching that cannot be contained in sound bites and 'chat-show' logic. We should not (and in any real sense cannot) forcibly simplify the complexity: for example, by assuming functional relations exist (or should exist) among various groups or individuals (Guilianotti, 2005), or skipping over such notions as 'social skills' and 'communication' as if they are self-explanatory. Similarly, just developing a literal grasp of the theories presented is not enough. The point here is not to make 'accuracy a virtue' (Housman, 1937). That would be like 'praising an architect for using well-seasoned timber or properly mixed concrete in his [*sic*] building. It is a necessary condition of his work, but not his essential function' (Carr, 1961: 11). In coaching terms, such a perspective would privilege the precision of communicative behaviours over the quality of communicative interaction (Pineau, 1994). Alternatively, through this book, we advocate a critical understanding of coaching that challenges instrumental reasoning.

Like Guilianotti (2005), we believe that more of what is worth knowing is contained in the interrelated writings of numerous major thinkers as opposed to a single school of thought. This is not to decry the value of a lucid body of sociological work through which a certain argumentative criteria can be developed in significant detail (Inglis & Howson, 2002). Nor is it a licence to 'cherry-pick' convenient theoretical aspects, which only results in a loose patchwork of assumed related notions on a particular topic – what Turner (2000) derided as 'decorative' theorising, and Everett (2002) as 'theoretical tinsel'. On the contrary, it is a call for theorists to be deployed selectively and imaginatively; to encourage engagement with 'a plurality of [academic] torch holders', resulting in 'more creative, rigorous and systematic sociological thought' (Stones, 1998a: 292). Such an approach holds the potential not only to shed new light on enduring coaching issues but to generate new questions through a commitment to critical thinking and the 'ideal of doubt' (Evans & Davies, 2002).

We began this book with a lament about the value of a sociology of coaching not being acknowledged. During the course of the book's development, however, things have started to change (we hope this is not false consciousness). This has been evidenced by invitations to present a symposium at the European College of Sport Science Conference in Oslo, a keynote address at the Gaelic Athletic Association Coach Development Conference in Dublin, both in 2009, and, perhaps more significantly, a similar lecture at the Sports Coach UK Research Forum in Cardiff in 2010. Hopefully, then, our message is beginning to be heard. Despite such positive signs, we are fully aware that the agenda has a long way to go to attain the status and recognition we seek for it. This is because we are trying to develop a strategic current of thought – a process to change events, actions and perceptions – so that new ideas are generated (McCarthy, 1996). Obviously, this is not an easy task.

Structure and/or agency: the enduring debate in understanding coaching

As highlighted throughout this book, but perhaps most obviously in the later 'theme' chapters, there can be no real escape from issues of structure and agency in the quest to understand coaching. As nobody would realistically argue that structure controls us completely or that we are totally free to do what we will, the issues to be investigated here revolve around intent, consciousness and consequences. In simplistic terms, agency puts a greater onus on individual reflexivity while structuralists focus on the constraints and structures within which such individuals exist. Indeed, these are the core debates we have among ourselves and with our students: more macro or micro? More Foucault or Goffman? Or maybe something (or someone) in the middle, representing an attempt at synthesis, like Giddens or Bourdieu? Without reflecting individual leanings, when we scrutinised and perused the book as part of the final editing process, it became increasingly obvious that the emphasis was placed on what social structures allow coaches to do: Lemert's (1997: 152) 'far peaks' that 'define the dark valleys or pleasant streams below, where people live'. This certainly was not intentional on our part, but perhaps it reveals one of the unique features of the book in terms of what has gone before: that is, a greater credence given to social forces in determining coaches' behaviour as opposed to their frequent portrayal as 'free floating heroes or villains' (Stones,1998b: 3).

To give a concrete example of how this shadow of structure, essentially ignored in previous texts, looms larger in this one, let us look at recent coaching 'policy' in the UK. For many of us, as hinted at earlier, how coaching is perceived both practically and academically, in addition to how it is taught, seems to be at a crossroads. Rather than merely attributing this to a few unrelenting 'transformational' voices who, over the past decade or so, have constantly proclaimed the need for coaching's reconceptualistion, perhaps what created the situation was more akin to the mobilisation of structural resources for change (e.g., Tilly, 1978). Here, the obvious dissatisfaction of coaches with content taught (e.g., Chesterfield *et al.*, in press), the opposition of some sports' governing bodies to adopting given guidelines from central coach education organisations, and the similar antagonism felt by universities when requested to bring coaching-related degrees into line with a more 'competency-based' approach were symptoms and signs of larger structural weaknesses within the coaching (sports) policy-making system. It is likely that the resulting shift in power arrangements reflects a realignment of the structural aspects of coaching policy-making, governance and conceptualisation as opposed to the unfettered activities of a fervent few. This is not to underplay the actions of individuals as agents of change, but to place their conduct and deeds within the context of structured social positions.

Like Lemert (1997:156), however, we increasingly feel that practical socio-logical thought should extend to more than a question of causes. Rather, it should follow up explorations and explanations with such driving questions as: 'what must I know, feel and believe in order to act in ways that will make life (or coaching) better for me and mine, and more just for all?' Coaches, then, despite being aware of governing dictates, social norms and sub-cultures will always need to find a way 'to get the job done' as best they can. To practise sociologically is to adhere to the rules of social participation, never exactly as they are passed down but with a flourish of independence (Lemert, 1997). This is where coach education should venture in future, and in some instances *is* venturing now (Jones, Morgan & Harris, in press). It should be grounded not only *in situ* but in the dance of agency located within an acknowledged 'social press' of structural choreography (Billet & Somerville, 2004). It should be considered, to borrow a phrase from Bourdieu, as 'structured improvisation'. That way, it is based on both an acceptance of the hand dealt, of what comes across one's path, and, crucially, the promise of future possibilities – to see what can be. This is a position which echoes Jones and Wallace's (2005, 2006) conceptualisation of coaching as orchestration in terms of investing effort where it can have the most impact. Selecting and realising such possibilities is often not very neat and pretty, however; indeed, 'more times than not, the sociological life makes of the dreamer a rude, improper guest' disrupting a shiny, well-planned party (Lemert, 1997: 190). Such a perspective is the anathema of unproblematic, enthusiastic, 'song-and-dance' pedagogy and management. Rather, coaching is seen as messy, challenging, personal and often frustrating; a social practice arising in, with and from the socially and culturally structured world (Lave & Wenger, 1996). Yet, we believe coaches who are educated in and subsequently practise sociologically are somewhat liberated, with freer rein given to both creativity and imagination – the places where excellence and exceptionality can exist.

Potential ways forward

So, what of the road ahead? Where can the sociology of coaching lead us next? No doubt, the theorists in this book have not been exhausted in terms of what their thinking has to offer coaching. There is much left to mine and explore here. Alternatively, new areas of investigation are coming to light which could prove equally valuable and fruitful in the quest for an understanding of the dynamics that underpin coaching. One of these has been hinted at quite strongly through the work of Arlie Hochschild (see Chapter 5): that related to the sociology of emotions.

Recent work (e.g., Jones, 2006a, 2009a; Purdy *et al.*, 2008) has suggested that coaches and athletes experience a variety of strong emotions as they strive to navigate the challenges and opportunities of their dynamic coaching worlds. This would appear quite obvious, yet it remains very under-researched. The relative invisibility of emotions in coaching research and coach education provision could, in part, be attributed to the wider societal view that reason and emotion have been regarded as being at opposite ends of a continuum, with cognition and rationality at one pole and emotions and irrationality at the other (Turner & Stets, 2005). However, if we are to produce accounts of coaching that more accurately recognise its intensive personal demands, then it would seem prudent to explore not only the emotions experienced by coaches but the relationship between emotion and coaches' decision-making (Hargreaves, 2005; Nias, 1996). This view is supported by Barbalet (2001, 2002), who believed that reason has its background in emotion, as without the accompanying feelings of calmness, security and confidence, reason turns to its opposite. Denzin (2007: 1), meanwhile, has gone so far as to assert that 'people are their emotions. To understand who a person is, it is necessary to understand emotion.' Emotions are thus increasingly being understood not as solely biological phenomena, but as socio-cultural, political and institutional forces that continuously shape and reshape the terrain of identity and practice (see also Hargreaves, 1998). They are considered 'temporarily embodied, situated self-feelings that are highly dependent on our perceptions of others and their (imagined) perceptions of us' (May & Powell, 2008: 245). While developing this recognition has not been easy, sociologists have since made up for lost time with the study of emotion being at the forefront of micro-sociology, as well as providing an important link between micro- and macro-levels of social understanding (Barbalet, 2002; Stets, 2003; Turner, 2002; Turner & Stets, 2005; Zembylas, 2005). In addition, Turner and Stets (2005: 1) have argued that a sociologically orientated approach to the study of emotion can potentially explain the relationship between the physical body, cognitive processes and cultural constructions: 'Emotions are the glue that bind people together, and generate commitments to large-scale social and cultural structures; in fact, emotions are what make social systems of cultural symbols viable. Conversely, emotions can also drive people apart and push them to tear down cultural tradition.'

The emotional nature of teachers' work is being increasingly uncovered (e.g., Hargreaves, 2000, 2005; Kelchtermans, 2005; Kelchtermans & Ballet, 2002a, 2002b). For example, Zembylas (2005) explored how excitement, anger, nervousness and embarrassment were produced in teachers' interactions with significant others within the socio-political milieu of the school. It has also been suggested that emotions are embodied: they do not exist solely in the mind (Layder, 2006). For example, being embarrassed or shy may lead us to blush, shake or avoid eye contact when with others (May & Powell, 2008). Although such work has highlighted how emotion is a central concern for educational researchers, emotions within coaching have been treated as little more than extraneous variables that need to be managed appropriately if coaches (and athletes) are to focus on the technical and cognitive components of their role (Hargreaves, 1998). However, unless we better recognise and theorise some of the muddled realities of personal feeling, it is highly unlikely that we will be able to prepare coaches in the best way for the complex realities they face daily. For example, we need to understand how the emotions coaches experience in their everyday coaching lives (e.g., shame, anger and confidence) become embodied in their practice. We need to examine how we coach in terms of how we feel and how we make athletes feel.

A second area of potential fruitful investigation is that of trust. As touched upon in Chapter 12, the sociology of trust is highly relevant to coaching. This is particularly because of coaching's fluid, ambiguous nature (Jones & Wallace, 2005, 2006). In this respect, coaching mirrors wider society in late modernity – a contextual system characterised by increasing complexity and, therefore, uncertainty. Following Ulrich Beck's classical book *Risk Society* (1992), which focused on everyday strategies for managing risk and uncertainty, trust has gained increased emphasis in social research over the last two decades (e.g., Tulloch & Lupton, 2003; Zinn, 2008). A particularly interesting aspect of this work is the importance it places on social beings' handling of complex situations, much of which is guided by trust. According to Zinn (2008: 443), the strength of trust in 'managing uncertainty . . . appears to lie in its combination of experience-based knowledge with intuition and emotions'. Zinn labels trust, intuition and emotion as 'in-between-strategies': strategies lying between the rational and non-rational. Because individuals (and, one could argue, particularly coaches) often have to make important or 'fateful' decisions without enough time or available knowledge, such strategies form an important basis for judgement and action.

A related important dimension of trust is its precondition when forming any kind of social interaction. Even to compete in a mutually non-destructive way 'one needs at some level to trust one's competitor to comply with certain rules' (Gambetta, 1988: 215). As a multi-layered concept, trust consists of a cognitive element grounded in rational judgements, and an affective dimension developed in social relationships accompanied by emotive social bonds, including empathy and identification with others (Lewis & Weigert, 1985). McNamee (1998) focused on this affective dimension when he discussed the basic trust underlying coach–young-athlete relationships. Comparing an economic and a moral conception of trust, he argued that such (often close) relationships are 'not best characterized by a contractual mindset' (McNamee, 1998: 167). Rather, that the mutual trust underlying long-term coach–athlete relations are based on 'partially shared identities' and 'the qualities of character' that the participants display over time (McNamee, 1998: 171). This highlights trust's close relation to vulnerability: that is, 'as trust develops in social relationships an individual becomes even more "unprepared" for ethical attacks' (McDonagh, 1982: 672). Hence, with an increase in trust comes the possibility to exploit that trust; to transcend personal boundaries or otherwise abuse the power arising from the other's given trust. Consequently, we need to examine further the social dynamics of trust, mistrust and possible abuse of trust within different coaching contexts. We also need to know more about coaches' awareness of trust; about how they view the trusting relations they engender, their ethical conduct in the creation of such relations, and their recognition of the legacy of action.

A third area for a future social investigation of coaches' practice which we believe holds much promise is that of humour. Indeed, this is alluded to by a few of the coaches featured in this book. The use of humour within social interaction, of course, has long been researched, with many definitions and theoretical perspectives emerging (Romero & Pescosolido, 2008). Its use within the coaching context, however, has been relatively free of investigation, particularly from a sociological perspective. Nevertheless, according to some (Romero & Pescosolido, 2008; Romero, 2005), humour has the potential to keep groups intact, serving as a social lubricant. The same authors have claimed that it can generate group innovation and synergy, creating an attractive working environment. Although in their work (as with most), humour is portrayed as having a generally positive, even charismatic effect, Romero and Pescosolido (2008) acknowledge that it can be a 'double-edged sword', as what may be amusing to one might not be, or might even be offensive, to another.

It has been argued that humour makes communication easier, with self-depreciation or irony being particularly useful for increasing persuasiveness (Lyttle, 2001). This can highlight a shared commonality, a feeling that 'we're all human', tightening social bonds. In this regard, it echoes Goffman's notions of role distance, 'face work' and the (idealistic) impressions we give to others to garner their respect (see Chapter 2). Similarly, laughter, particularly through ridicule, can serve as a means of social control, through reaffirming group norms (Billig, 2005). Seen in this way, humour can be disciplinary. Indeed, according to Billig, humour can be enlisted in the service of both conservatism and radicalism, highlighting its contextual complexity. Recent work (e.g., Billig, 2005), then, has tended to provide more of a social critique of humour. This has been particularly in terms of how we use humour within power relations to ensure compliance and, acknowledging its polysemic nature, how it is perceived by those who are subject to it (i.e., its outcome). Finally, here, humour has also been viewed as a coping mechanism, a symbolic resource to relieve (personal) anxiety and fear (Sanders, 2004). In this regard, it is used in stressful environments to manage perceived difficult relationships and conditions. This strategy was mentioned in Chapter 11 by the Australian coach Bob Dwyer, who deliberately uses quirky expressions in his delivery, primarily to lift tension (Jones *et al.*, 2004). It was also hinted at by the coach in Potrac and Jones's (2009a) study of micro-political coaching actions, where Gavin (the coach in question) stated that he tried to 'laugh things off' and 'not take things too personally'. Such actions echo those of 'managing emotions' (Hochschild, 2000 [1983]; see Chapter 5) to the act of shaping as well as suppressing feelings in oneself. Often, then, humour appears to be no laughing matter (Sanders, 2004). Nevertheless, taking account of its vibrant sociality, we believe that researching the multi-functional use of humour, its intent, manifestation and effect within the often emotionally charged world of coaching holds very interesting possibilities.

Final thoughts

The theorists presented in this book, with their various perspectives of social practice and connections, provide us with many resources to consider questions of coaching possibilities. They supply the means for us to think adequately and responsibly about how we live, how we coach and the 'social issues which affect every one of us and which we usually have an opinion about' (Stones, 1998a: 305). Engaging with these theorists and their thinking can make us work hard at those opinions. Echoing the developing concept of the coach as social orchestrator (Jones & Wallace, 2005, 2006), such consideration can help us work out which parts of structure and context are malleable enough to influence; where to invest efforts to get the most rewards. As Stones (1998a: 305) reminds us, however, 'there is no royal road to good thought'. Indeed, the intention within this book was not to write a 'recipe' or a 'how-to' manual. Considerable thought still needs to be given to the concepts that have been presented, and they need to be contemplated with imagination, not just taken as *a priori* knowledge.

We have also tried to be sociologically discursive about coaching, so that a real exploration of the 'not (yet) quite conscious understandings' of the activity can begin, with coaching brought out of 'the dusky realm of secrets everyone knows' but rarely discusses (Lemert, 1997: 32). The purpose is to get coaching scholars and students to talk about complexity, power, structure and knowledge, both professionally and practically: that is, to engage with coaching in a more 'grown-up way'. We conclude this book paraphrasing Stones (1998a) in the hope that this collection of insightful thinkers, and the attempt to relate them to our field of study, has imbued readers with an enthusiasm to engage with the sociology of sports coaching. There are certainly many avenues, some of which we have mentioned, that are currently ripe for exploration, not only in terms of describing the restrictive social norms which confine coaches' behaviours but to examine how coaches contribute to these patterns and what they can do 'to exercise some control over them' (O'Brien & Kollock, 1991: 141).

This is not to say that all social norms need changing; indeed, as humans, we depend on an 'ordered' environment and one another's expectations within it to make social situations (such as coaching) work. Similarly, a shared mutual interpretation holds the potential to provide a meaningful and coherent sense of reality to preserve identity and legitimate action (McCarthy, 1996). Nevertheless, through a sensitivity to how culture and language contribute to the emergence of behavioural patterns, coaches, if they so desire, should be able to imagine different combinations of such norms, thereby envisioning 'possibilities for change' (McCarthy, 1996: 144). The result might be an increase in personal creativity, with 'cultural entrepreneurship' stemming from a better understanding of the potential outcomes of anticipated behaviour. This would also place coaching firmly within the bounds of social enquiry which is inherently revisionist, thus contributing to a field of research 'which achieves its present through continual reassessment of its past' (McCarthy, 1996: 106).

As sociologists, then, we are not in the business of 'offering timeless truths' (McCarthy, 1996: 8). Rather, through this book, we hope to have pressed the case for situational diagnoses of coaching, so we can better understand what coaches do and why they do it.

References

Abraham, A. & Collins, D. (1998). Examining and extending research in coach development. *Quest*, 50: 59–79.

Alfred, M.V. (2002). The promise of sociocultural theory in democratizing adult education. *New Directions for Adult and Continuing Education*, 96: 3–13.

Allee, V. (2000). Knowledge networks and communities of practice. *Journal of Organisational Development Network*, 32(4). Retrieved from: http://www.odnetwork.org/odponline/vol32n4/knowldegenets.html.

Allen, D. & Pilnick, A. (2007). Making connections: Healthcare as a case study in the social organization of work. *Sociology of Health and Illness*, 27(6): 683–700.

Andersen, N.Å. (2003). *Discursive analytical strategies: Understanding Foucault, Koselleck, Laclau, Luhmann*. Bristol: Polity Press.

Anderson, G. & Herr, K. (1999). The new paradigm wars: Is there room for rigorous practitioner knowledge in schools and universities? *Educational Researcher*, 28(5): 12–21, 40.

Anderson, J.R., Reder, L.M. & Simon, H.A. (1996). Situated learning and education. *Educational Researcher*, 25(4): 5–11.

Apple, M. (1999). *Ideology and curriculum*. New York: Routledge.

Armour, K.M. & Jones, R.L. (2000). The practical heart within: The value of the sociology of sport. In R.L. Jones & K.M. Armour (eds), *Sociology of sport: Theory and practice* (pp. 1–10). London: Addison-Wesley Longman.

Arnoldi, J. (2001). Niklas Luhmann: An introduction. *Theory, Culture & Society*, 18(1): 1–13.

Augestad, P., Bergsgard N.A. & Hansen, A.Ø. (2006). The institutionalisation of an elite sport organisation in Norway: The case of 'Olympiatoppen'. *Sociology of Sport Journal*, 23(3): 293–313.

Baecker, D. (2001). Why systems? *Theory, Culture & Society*, 18(1): 59–74.

Ball, S.J. (1987). *The micro-politics of the school: Towards a theory of school organization*. London: Methuen.

Ball, S. J. (1991). Power, conflict, micropolitics and all that. In G. Walford (ed.), *Doing educational research* (pp. 166–192). London: Routledge.

Bandura, A. (1977). *Social learning theory*. Englewood Cliffs, NJ: Prentice-Hall.

Barab, S.A. & Duffy, T.M. (2000) From practice fields to communities of practice. In D.H. Jonassen and S.M. Land (eds), *Theoretical foundations of learning environments* (pp. 25–44). Mahweh, NJ: Lawrence Erlbaum Associates.

Baraldi, C., Corsi, G. & Esposito, E. (1997). *Glossar zu Niklas Luhmanns Theorie sozialer Systeme*. Frankfurt am Main: Suhrkamp.

Barbalet, J. (2001). *Emotion, social theory, and social structure: A macrosociological approach*. Cambridge: Cambridge University Press.

Barbalet, J. (2002). *Emotions and sociology*. Oxford: Blackwell.

Bateson, G. (1972). *Steps to an ecology of mind*. London: University of Chicago Press.

Beck, U. (1992). *Risk society: Towards a new modernity*. London: Sage.

Becker, H.S. (1963) *Outsiders: Studies in the sociology of deviance*. New York: Free Press.

Beckmann, G. & Stehr, N. (2002). The legacy of Niklas Luhmann. *Society*, 39(2): 67–75.

Biddle, B.J. (1986). Recent developments in role theory. *Annual Review of Sociology*, 12: 67–92.

Billet, S. & Somerville, M. (2004). Transformations at work: Identity and learning. *Studies in Continuing Education*, 26(2): 309–326.

Billig, M. (2005). *Laughter and ridicule: Towards a social critique of humour*. London: Sage.

Birrell, S. & Donnelly, P. (2004). Reclaiming Goffman: Erving Goffman's influence on the sociology of sport. In R. Guilianotti (ed.), *Sport and modern social theorists* (pp. 49–64). Basingstoke: Palgrave Macmillan.

Blau, P.M. (1960). A theory of social integration. *American Journal of Sociology*, 65, 545–556.

Blau, P.M. (1964). *Exchange and power in social life*. New York: John Wiley & Sons.

Blau, P. (1986). *Exchange and power in social life* (2nd edn). New Brunswick, NJ: Transaction.

Bloom, G.A. & Smith, M.D. (1996). Hockey violence: A test of cultural spillover theory. *Sociology of Sport Journal*, 13: 65–77.

Bolton, S. (2005). *Emotion management in the workplace*. Basingstoke: Palgrave Macmillan.

Bompa, T.O. (1994). *Theory and methodology of training: The key to athletic performance* (3rd edn). Dubuque, IA: Kendall/Hunt.

Bottero, W. (2009). Relationality and social interaction. *The British Journal of Sociology*, 60(2): 399–420.

Boucaut, R. (2001). Understanding workplace bullying: A practical application of Giddens' structuration theory. *International Education Journal*, 2(4): 65–73.

Bourdieu, P. (1962). *The Algerians*. Boston, MA: Beacon.

Bourdieu, P. (1977). *Outline of a theory of practice*. London: Cambridge University Press.

Bourdieu, P. (1984). *Distinction: A social critique of the judgement of taste*. Cambridge, MA: Harvard University Press.

Bourdieu, P. (1986). *Distinction: A social critique of the judgement of taste*. London: Routledge.

Bourdieu, P. (1987). *Chose dites*. Paris: Editions de Minuit.

Bourdieu, P. (1988). *Homo academicus*. Stanford, CA: Stanford University Press.

Bourdieu, P. (1989). Social space and symbolic power. *Sociological Theory*, 7: 14–25.

Bourdieu, P. (1990a). *In other words: Essays towards a reflexive sociology*. Cambridge: Polity Press.

Bourdieu, P. (1990b). *The logic of practice*. Cambridge: Polity Press.

Bourdieu, P. (1998). *Practical reason*. Stanford, CA: Stanford University Press.

Bourdieu, P. (2000). *Pascalian meditations*. Stanford, CA: Stanford University Press.

Bourdieu, P. & Passeron, J. (1996 [1977]). *Reproduction in education, society and culture*. London: Sage.

Bourdieu, P. & Wacquant, L.J.D. (eds) (1992). *An invitation to reflexive sociology*. Chicago, IL: University of Chicago Press.

Bowes, I. & Jones, R.L. (2006). Working at the edge of chaos: Understanding coaching as a complex, interpersonal system. *The Sport Psychologist*, 20: 235–245.

Branaman, A. (1997). Goffman's social theory. In C. Lemert & A. Branaman (eds), *The Goffman reader* (pp. xlv–lxxxii). Oxford: Blackwell.

Brockbank, A. & Magill, I. (2007). *Facilitating reflective learning in higher education* (2nd edn). London: Open University Press.

Brook, P. (2009). In critical defence of 'emotional labour': Refuting Bolton's critique of Hochschild's concept. *Work, Employment and Society*, 23(3): 531–548.

Brown, D. (2005). An economy of gendered practices? Learning to teach physical education from the perspective of Pierre Bourdieu's embodied sociology. *Sport Education and Society*, 10(1): 3–23.

Brown, J., Collins, A. & Duguid, P. (1989). Situated cognition and the culture of learning. *Educational Researcher*, 18(1): 32–42.

Brown, J. & Duguid, P. (1996). Stolen knowledge. In H. McLellen (ed.), *Situated learning perspectives* (pp. 47–56). Englewood Cliffs, NJ: Educational Technology Publications.

Brubaker, R. (1995). Social theory as habitus. In C. Calhoun, E. LiPuma & M. Postone (eds), *Bourdieu: Critical perspectives* (pp. 212–234). Oxford: Blackwell.

Burr, V. (1995). *An introduction to social constructionism*. London: Routledge.

Burr, V. (2003). *Social construtionism* (2nd edn). London: Routledge.

Buysse, V., Sparkman, K.L. & Wesley, P.W. (2003). Communities of practice: Connecting what we know with what we do. *Exceptional Children*, 69(3): 263–278.

Calhoun, C. (1995). Habitus, field and capital: The question of historical specificity. In C. Calhoun, E. LiPuma & M. Postone (eds), *Bourdieu: Critical perspectives* (pp. 61–88). Oxford: Blackwell.

Calhoun, C., LiPuma, E. & Postone, M. (1995). Bourdieu and social theory. In C. Calhoun, E. LiPuma & M. Postone (eds), *Bourdieu: Critical perspectives* (pp. 1–13). Oxford: Blackwell.

Callero, P. (1994). From role-playing to role using: Understanding role as a resource. *Social Psychology Quarterly*, 57(3): 228–243.

Carr, E.H. (1961). *What is history?* London: Pelican.

Casell, P. (1993). *The Giddens reader*. London: Macmillan.

Cashay, K. (1988). *Sport und Gesellschaft. Zur Ausdifferensierung einer Funktion und ihrer Folgen*. Schorndorf: Verlag Karl Hofmann.

Cassidy, T., Jones, R.L. & Potrac, P. (2009). *Understanding sports coaching: The social, cultural and pedagogical foundations of coaching practice* (2nd edn). London: Routledge.

Cassidy, T., Potrac, P. & McKenzie, A. (2006). Evaluating and reflecting upon a coach education initiative: The code of rugby. *The Sport Psychologist*, 20: 145–161.

Cassidy, T. & Rossi, T. (2006). Situated learning: (Re)examining the notion of apprenticeship in coach education. *International Journal of Sports Science and Coaching*, 1/3: 235–246.

Chaitin, J. (2004). My story, my life, my identity. *International Journal of Qualitative Methods*, 3(4): Article 1. Retrieved from: http://www.iiqm.ualberta.ca/Journals.cfm.

Chapman, G. (1997). Making weight: Lightweight rowing, technologies of power, and technologies of the self. *Sociology of Sport Journal*, 14: 205–223.

Chase, L.F. (2006). (Un)disciplined bodies: A Foucauldian analysis of women's rugby. *Sociology of Sport Journal*, 23: 229–247.

Cherryholmes, C. (1988). *Power and criticism: Post-structural investigations in education.* New York: Teachers College Press.

Chesterfield, G., Potrac, P. & Jones, R.L. (in press). 'Studentship' and 'impression management': Coaches' experiences of an advanced soccer coach education award. *Sport, Education and Society.*

Clegg, S., Courpasson, D. & Phillips, N. (2006). *Power and organisations.* London: Sage.

Coakley, J.J. (1982). *Sport and society: Issues and controversies* (2nd edn). St Louis, MO: C.V. Mosby.

Coakley, J.J. (1986). *Sport in society: Issues and controversies* (3rd edn). St Louis, MO: C.V. Mosby.

Coakley, J.J. (1994). *Sport and society: Issues and controversies* (7th edn). St Louis, MO: C.V. Mosby.

Colley, H., James, D., Tedder, M. & Diment, K. (2003). Learning as becoming in vocational education and training: Class, gender and the role of vocational habitus. *Journal of Vocational Education and Training,* 55(4): 471–496.

Collinson, D. (1988). Engineering humour: Masculinity, joking and conflict in shopfloor relations. *Organization Studies,* 9(2): 181–199.

Cook, D. & Emerson, R. (1978). Power and equity and commitment in exchange networks. *American Sociological Review,* 43: 721–739.

Côté, J. & Sedgwick, W.A. (2003). Effective behaviours of expert rowing coaches: A qualitative investigation of Canadian athletes and coaches. *International Sports Journal,* 7(1): 62–77.

Cudd, A. (2006). *Analyzing oppression.* Oxford: Oxford University Press.

Culver, D.M. & Trudel, P. (2006). Cultivating coaches' communities of practice: Developing the potential for learning through interactions. In R.L. Jones (ed.), *The sports coach as educator: Re-conceptualising sports coaching* (pp. 97–112). London: Routledge.

Culver, D. & Trudel, P. (2008). Clarifying the concept of communities of practice in sport. *International Journal of Sports Science & Coaching,* 3(1): 1–10.

Culver, D., Trudel, P. & Werthner, P. (2009). A sport leader's attempt to foster a coaches' community of practice. *International Journal of Sport Science and Coaching,* 4: 365–383.

Cushion, C. (2001). The coaching process in professional youth football: An ethnography of practice. Unpublished Ph.D. dissertation, Brunel University.

Cushion, C. (2006). Mentoring: Harnessing the power of experience, in R.L. Jones (ed.), *The sports coach as educator. Re-conceptualising sports coaching* (pp. 128–144). London: Routledge.

Cushion, C. (2007). Modelling the complexities of the coaching process. *International Journal of Sports Science and Coaching,* 2(4): 395–401.

Cushion, C.J. (2008). Clarifying the concept of communities of practice in sport: A commentary. *International Journal of Sport Science and Coaching,* 3(1): 15–17.

Cushion, C.J. (2010a). The coaching process in elite youth soccer: The players' experiences. In B. Drust, T. Reilly & M. Williams (eds), *International research in science and soccer: The proceedings of the First World Conference on Science and Soccer* (pp. 207–213). Abingdon: Routledge.

Cushion, C.J. (2010b). Understanding the coaching process in elite youth soccer. In B. Drust, T. Reilly & M. Williams (eds), *International research in science and soccer: The proceedings of the First World Conference on Science and Soccer* (pp. 213–220). Abingdon: Routledge.

Cushion, C.J., Armour, K.M. & Jones, R. L. (2003). Coach education and continuing professional development: Experience and learning to coach. *Quest*, 55: 215–230.

Cushion, C.J., Armour, K.M. & Jones, R.L. (2006). Locating the coaching process in practice: Models 'for' and 'of' coaching. *Physical Education and Sport Pedagogy*, 11(1): 83–89.

Cushion, C.J. & Jones, R.L. (2006). Power, discourse and symbolic violence in professional youth soccer: The case of Albion FC. *Sociology of Sport Journal*, 23(2): 142–161.

Cushion, C.J. & Lyle, J. (2010). Conceptual development in sports coaching. In J. Lyle & C.J. Cushion (eds), *Sports coaching professionalisation and practice*. London: Elsevier.

Cushion, C.J., Nelson, L., Armour, K.M., Lyle, J., Jones, R., Sandford, R. & O'Callaghan, C. (2010). *Coach learning and development: A review of literature*. Leeds: Sportscoach UK.

Damasio, A. (1994). *Descartes' 'error': Emotion, reason and the human brain*. New York: Grosset-Putman.

d'Arripe-Longueville, R., Fournier, J.F. & Dubois, A. (1998). The perceived effectiveness of interactions between expert French judo coaches and elite female athletes. *The Sport Psychologist*, 12: 317–332.

Delanty, G. (1999). *Social theory in a changing world*. Cambridge: Polity Press.

Denison, J. (2007). Social theory for coaches: A Foucauldian reading of one athlete's poor performance. *International Journal of Sports Science & Coaching*, 2: 369–383.

Denison, J. (in press). Planning, practice and performance: The discursive construction of coaches' knowledge. *Sport, Education & Society*.

Denison, J. & Winslade, J. (2006). Understanding problematic sporting stories: Narrative therapy and applied sport psychology. *Junctures*, 6: 99–105.

Dennis, A. & Martin, P.J. (2005). Symbolic interaction and the concept of power. *The British Journal of Sociology*, 56(2): 191–213.

Denzin, N.K. (2007). *On understanding emotion*. New Brunswick, NJ: Transaction.

Devis-Devis, J. (2006). Socially critical research perspectives in physical education. In D. Kirk, D. Macdonald & M. O'Sullivan (eds), *Handbook of research in physical education* (pp. 37–58). London: Sage.

Dewey, J. (1916). *Democracy and education: An Introduction to the philosophy of education*. New York: Macmillan.

Dillon, M. (2010). *Introduction to sociological theory: Theorists, concepts, and their applicability to the 21st century*. Oxford: Wiley-Blackwell.

DiPardo, A. (1993). When teachers become graduate students. *English Education*, 25(4): 197–212.

Doherty, R.W., Hillberg, R.S., Epaloose, G. & Tharp, R.G. (2002). Standards performance continuum: Development and validation of a measure of effective pedagogy. *The Journal of Educational Research*, 96(2): 78–91.

Edgar, A. (2006). *Habermas: The key concepts*. London: Routledge.

Egan, T. & Jaye, C. (2009). Communities of clinical practice: The social organisation of clinical learning. *Health*, 13(10): 107–125.

Eisner, E. (1993). Foreword. In D.J. Flinders and G.E. Mills (eds), *Theory and concepts in qualitative research*. New York: Teachers College Press.

Ely, M., Vinz, R., Downing, M. & Anzul, M. (1997). *On writing qualitative research: Living by words*. London: Falmer.

Emerson, R. (1962). Power–dependence relations. *American Sociological Review*, 27(1): 31–41.

Emerson, R. (1976). Social exchange theory. *Annual Review of Sociology*, 2: 335–362.

Eraut, M. (2000). Non formal learning and tacit knowledge in professional work. *British Journal of Educational Psychology*, 70: 113–136.

Erickson, K., Bruner, M., MacDonald, D. & Côté, J. (2008). Gaining insight into actual and preferred sources of coaching knowledge. *International Journal of Sport Science and Coaching*, 3(4): 527–538.

Eskes, T.B., Duncan, M.C. & Miller, E.M. (1998). The discourse of empowerment: Foucault, Marcuse and women's fitness texts. *Journal of Sport & Social Issues*, 22: 317–344.

Evans, J. & Davies, B. (2002). Theoretical background. In A. Laker (ed.), *The sociology of sport and physical education* (pp. 15–35). London: Routledge.

Everett, J. (2002). Organisational research and the praxeology of Pierre Bourdieu. *Organisational Research Methods*, 5(1): 56–80.

Fenwick, T. (2000). Expanding conceptions of experiential learning: A review of the five contemporary perspectives of cognition. *Adult Education Quarterly*, 50(4): 248–272.

Fenwick, T. (2008). Workplace learning: Emerging trends and new perspectives. *New Directions for Adult and Continuing Education*, 119: 17–26.

Fernandez-Balboa, J.-M. (2000). Prospective physical educators' perspectives on school micropolitics. *Journal of Sport Pedagogy*, 6(2): 1–33.

Fineman, S. (1993). *Emotions in organizations*. London: Sage.

Finlayson, J. (2005). *Habermas: A very short introduction*. Oxford: Oxford University Press.

Fleurance, P. & Cotteaux, V. (1999). Construction de l'expertise chez les etraîneurs sportifs d'athlètes de haut–niveau Français. *Avante*, 5(2): 54–68.

Foucault, M. (1972). *The archaeology of knowledge and discourse on language*. New York: Pantheon.

Foucault, M. (1977). Intellectuals and power. In D.F. Bouchard (ed.), *Language, counter-memory, practice: Selected essays and interview by Michel Foucault* (pp. 120–142). Ithaca, NY: Cornell University Press.

Foucault, M. (1978). *The history of sexuality, Volume 1: An introduction* (trans. R. Hurley). New York: Pantheon.

Foucault, M. (1979). *Discipline and punish: The birth of the prison*. New York: Vintage.

Foucault, M. (1980). *Power/knowledge: Selected interviews and other writings*. New York: Pantheon.

Foucault, M. (1982). Afterword: The subject and power. In H.L. Dreyfus & P. Rabinow (eds), *Michel Foucault: Beyond structuralism and hermeneutics* (pp. 208–226), Chicago, IL: University of Chicago Press.

Foucault, M. (1983). The subject and power. In H. L. Dreyfus & P. Rabinow (eds), *Michel Foucault: Beyond structuralism and hermeneutics* (2nd edn) (pp. 58–72). Chicago, IL: University of Chicago Press.

Foucault, M. (1988). Technologies of the self. In L.H. Martin, H. Gutman & P.H. Hutton (eds), *Technologies of the self: A seminar with Michel Foucault* (pp. 8–23). Amherst: University of Massachusetts Press.

Foucault, M. (1991). *Discipline and punish: The birth of the prison* (paperback edn). London: Penguin.

French, J.R.P., Jr. & Raven, B. (1959). The bases of social power. In D. Cartwright (ed.) *Studies in social power* (pp. 150–167). Ann Arbor: University of Michigan Press.

Fuchs, S. (1999). Niklas Luhmann. *Sociological Theory*, 17(1): 117–119.

Fuller, A., Hodkinson, H., Hodkinson, P. & Unwin, L. (2005). Learning as peripheral participation in communities of practice: A reassessment of key concepts in workplace learning. *British Educational Research Journal*, 31(1): 49–68.

Gair, M. & Mullins, G. (2001). Hiding in plain sight. In E. Margolis (ed.), *The hidden curriculum in higher education* (pp. 21–24). New York: Routledge.

Galipeau, J. & Trudel, P. (2004). The experiences of newcomers on a varsity sport team. *Applied Research in Coaching and Athletics Annual*, 19: 166–188.

Galipeau, J. & Trudel, P. (2005). The role of athletic, academic and social development of student-athletes in two varisty sport teams. *Applied Research in Coaching and Athletics Annual*, 20: 27–49.

Galipeau, J. & Trudel, P. (2006). Athlete learning in a community of practice: Is there a role for a coach? In R.L. Jones (ed.), *The sports coach as educator: Re-conceptualising sports coaching* (pp. 77–94). London: Routledege.

Gambetta, D. (ed.) (1988). *Trust: Making and breaking cooperative relations*. Oxford: Basil Blackwell.

Gardiner, M.E. (2000). *Critiques of everyday life*. London: Routledge.

Giddens, A. (1979). *Central problems in social theory: Action, structure and contradiction in social analysis*. London: Macmillian.

Giddens, A. (1984). *The constitution of society*. San Fransisco: University of California Press.

Giddens, A. (1990). *The consequences of modernity*. Cambridge: Polity Press.

Giddens, A. (1991). *Modernity and self-identity. Self and society in late modern age*. Cambridge: Polity Press.

Gilbert, W.D., Côté, J. & Mallett, C. (2006). Developmental paths and activities of successful sport coaches. *International Journal of Sport Sciences and Coaching*, 1(1): 69–76.

Gilbert, W., Gallimore, R. & Trudel, P. (2009). A learning community approach to coach development in youth sport. *Journal of Coaching Education*, 2(2): 1–21.

Gilbert, W. & Trudel, P. (2001). Learning to coach through experience: Reflection in model youth sport coaches. *Journal of Teaching in Physical Education*, 21: 16–34.

Gilbert, W. & Trudel, P. (2006). The coach as a reflective practitioner. In R.L. Jones (ed.), *The sports coach as educator: Re-conceptualising sports coaching* (pp. 113–127). London: Routledge.

Giroux, H.A. (1997). *Pedagogy and politics of hope: Theory, culture and schooling*. Boulder, CO: Westview Press.

Goffman, E. (1959). *The presentation of self in everyday life*. Reading: Penguin.

Goffman. E. (1961a). *Encounters: Two studies in the sociology of interaction – Fun in games & role distance*. Indianapolis, IN: Bobbs-Merrill.

Goffman, E. (1961b). *Asylums*. Garden City, NY: Doubleday.

Goffman, E. (1963). *Stigma: Notes on the management of spoiled identity*. Englewood Cliffs NJ: Prentice-Hall.

Goffman. E. (1967). *Interaction ritual: Essays on face-to-face behaviour*. Garden City, NY: Doubleday, Anchor Books.

Goffman, E. (1969a). *Strategic interaction*. Philadelphia: University of Pennsylvania Press.

Goffman, E. (1969b). *Where the action is*. London: Penguin.

Goffman, E. (1971). *Relations in public: Microstudies of the public order*. New York: Basic Books.

Goffman, E. (1974). *Frame analysis: An essay on the organization of experience*. New York: Harper and Row.

Goffman, E. (1983). The interaction order. *American Sociological Review*, 48: 1–17.

Goldstein, L. (2002). *Reclaiming caring in teaching and teacher education.* New York: Peter Lang.

Goodwin, D., Pope, C., Mort, M. & Smith, A. (2005). Access, boundaries and their effects: Legitimate participation in anaesthesis. *Sociology of Health and Illness*, 27(6): 855–871.

Gouldner, A.W. (1970). *The coming crisis of Western sociology.* London: Heinemann.

Greeno, J.G. (1997). On claims that answer the wrong questions. *Educational Researcher*, 26(1): 5–17.

Guilianotti, R. (1999). *Football: A sociology of the global game.* Cambridge: Polity.

Guilianotti, R. (ed.) (2004). *Sport and modern social theorists.* London: Macmillan.

Guilianotti, R. (2005). *Sport: A critical sociology.* Cambridge: Polity.

Gumbrecht, H.U. (2001). How is our future contingent? Reading Luhmann against Luhmann. *Theory, Culture & Society*, 18(1): 49–58.

Guttman, A. (1992). Chariot races, tournaments and the civilising process. In E. Dunning and C. Rojek (eds), *Sport and leisure in the civilising process.* Toronto: University of Toronto Press.

Habermas, J. (1970). On systematically distorted communication. *Inquiry*, 13: 205–218.

Habermas, J. (1971). *Knowledge and human interest* (trans. J. Shapiro). Boston, MA: Beacon Press.

Habermas, J. (1979). *Communication and the evolution of society.* Boston, MA: Beacon Press.

Habermas, J. (1982). A reply to my critics. In J. Thompson & D. Held (eds), *Habermas: Critical debates* (pp. 219–283). London: Macmillan.

Habermas, J. (1984). *The theory of communicative action: Reason and the rationalisation of society.* Cambridge: Polity Press.

Habermas, J. (1987). *The theory of communicative action: Lifeworld and system: A critique of functionalist reason.* Cambridge: Polity Press.

Habermas, J. (1990). *Moral consciousness and communicative action.* Cambridge, MA: MIT Press.

Habermas, J. & Luhmann, N. (1971). *Theorie der Gesellschaft oder Sozialtechnologie.* Frankfurt: Suhrkamp.

Hacking, I. (2004). Between Michael Foucault and Erving Goffman: Between discourse in the abstract and face-to-face interaction. *Economy and Society*, 33(3): 277–302.

Hagen, R. (2000). Rational solidarity and functional differentiation. *Acta Sociologica*, 43/1: 27–42.

Hager, P. & Hodkinson, P. (2009). Moving beyond the metaphor of transfer of learning. *British Educational Research Journal*, 35(4): 619–638.

Halas, J. & Hanson, L.L. (2001). Pathologizing Billy: Enabling and constraining the body of the condemned. *Sociology of Sport Journal*, 18: 115–126.

Hansman, C.A. (2001). Context-based adult learning. *New Directions for Adult and Continuing Education*, 89: 43–51.

Hargreaves, A. (1998). The emotional practice of teaching. *Teaching and Teacher Education*, 14(8): 835–854.

Hargreaves, A. (2000). Mixed emotions: Teachers' perceptions of their interactions with students. *Teaching and Teacher Education*, 16: 811–826.

Hargreaves, J. (2005). The emotions of teaching and educational change. In A. Hargreaves (ed.), *The International handbook of educational change: Extending educational change* (pp. 278–295). Netherlands: Springer.

Hatchen, D. (2001). *Sociology in action.* Thousand Oaks, CA: Fine Oaks Press.

Heikkala, J. (1993). Discipline and excel: Techniques of the self and body and the logic of competing. *Sociology of Sport Journal*, 10: 397–412.

Hekman, S.L. (ed.) (1996). *Feminist interpretations of Michel Foucault*. University Park: Pennsylvania State University Press.

Hill, R.J. (2008). Troubling adult learning in the present time. *New Directions for Adult and Continuing Education*, 118: 83–91.

Hochschild, A. (2000 [1983]). *The managed heart: Commercialization of human feeling*. Berkeley: University of California Press.

Hochschild, A. (1997). *The time bind: When work becomes home and home becomes work*. New York: Metropolitan-Holt.

Hochschild, A. (2003). *The commercialization of intimate life: Notes from home and work*. Berkeley: University of California Press.

Hochschild, A. & Machung, A. (2003 [1989]). *The second shift: Working parents and the revolution at home*. London: Penguin.

Hodkinson, P., Biesta, G. & James, D. (2008). Understanding learning culturally: Overcoming the dualism between social and individual views of learning. *Vocations and Learning*, 1: 27–47.

Hodkinson, P. & Hodkinson, H. (2003). Individuals, communities of practice and the policy context: Schoolteachers' learning in their workplace. *Studies in Continuing Education*, 25(1): 3–21.

Hodkinson, P. & Hodkinson, H. (2004a). A constructive critique of communities of practice: moving beyond Lave and Wenger. Seminar paper presented at Intergrating Work and Learning – Contemporary Issues, Australian Centre for Organisational, Voactional and Adult Learning, University of Technology, Sydney, 11 May.

Hodkinson, P. & Hodkinson, H. (2004b). The significance of individuals' dispositions in workplace learning: A case study of two teachers. *Journal of Education and Work*, 17(2): 167–182.

Holt, N.L. & Dunn, J.G.H. (2004). Toward a grounded theory of the psychosocial competencies and environmental conditions associated with soccer success. *Journal of Applied Sport Psychology*, 16: 199–219.

Holt, N.L., Black, D.E., Tamminen, K.A., Fox, K.R. & Mandigo, J.L. (2008). Levels of social complexity and dimensions of peer experiences in youth sport. *Journal of Sport & Exercise Psychology*, 30: 411–431.

Housman, A.E. (1937). *M. Manilii Astronomicon: Liber Primus* (2nd edn). London: Apud Grant Richards Press.

Hunter, L. (2004). Bourdieu and the social space of the PE class: Reproduction of doxa through practice. *Sport, Education and Society*, 9(2): 175–192.

Huston, T.L. (1983). Power. In H.H. Kelley, E. Berscheid, A. Christensen, J.H. Harvey, T. Huston, G. Levinger, E. McClintock, I.A. Peplau & D.R. Peterson (eds), *Close Relationships* (pp. 169–219). New York: Freeman.

Iellatchitch, A., Mayrhofer, W. & Meyer, M. (2003). Career fields: A small step towards a grand career theory? *International Journal of Human Resource Management*, 15(4): 256–271.

Inglis, D. & Howson, A. (2002). Sociology's sense of self: A response to Crossley and Shilling. *The Sociological Review*, 50(1): 136–139.

Isenbarger, L. & Zembylas, M. (2006). The emotional labour of caring in teaching. *Teaching and Teacher Education*, 22: 120–134.

Jacobsen, W. (1996). Learning, culture and learning culture. *Adult Education Quarterly*, 47(1): 15–28.

Jarvie, G. (1990). Towards an applied sociology of sport. *Scottish Journal of Physical Education*, 18: 11–12.

Jarvie, G. & Maguire, J. (1994). *Sport and leisure in social thought*. London: Routledge.

Jarvis, P. (2004). *Adult education and lifelong learning: Theory and* practice (3rd edn). London: Routledge.

Jenkins, R. (1992). *Key sociologists: Pierre Bourdieu*. London: Routledge.

Jenkins, R. (2002) *Pierre Bourdieu* (rev. edn). London: Routledge.

Johns, D. (1998). Fasting and feasting: Paradoxes of the sport ethic. *Sociology of Sport Journal*, 15: 41–63.

Johns, D.P. & Johns, J. (2000). Surveillance, subjectivism and technologies of power: An analysis of the discursive practice of high-performance sport. *International Review for the Sociology of Sport*, 35: 219–234.

Jones, P. (2005). *Introducing social theory*. Cambridge: Polity Press.

Jones, R.L. (2000). Toward a sociology of coaching. In R.L. Jones & K.M. Armour (eds), *The sociology of sport: Theory and practice* (pp. 33–43). London: Addison-Wesley Longman.

Jones, R.L. (2006a). Dilemmas, maintaining 'face' and paranoia: An average coaching life. *Qualitative Inquiry*, 12(5): 1012–1021.

Jones, R.L. (2006b). How can educational concepts inform sports coaching? In R.L. Jones (ed.), *The sports coach as educator: Re-conceptualising sports coaching* (pp. 3–13). London: Routledge.

Jones, R.L. (2007). Coaching redefined: An everyday pedagogical endeavour. *Sport, Education and Society*, 12(2): 159–174.

Jones, R.L. (2009a). Coaching as caring ('The smiling gallery'): Accessing hidden knowledge. *Physical Education and Sport Pedagogy*, 14(4): 377–390.

Jones, R.L. (2009b). Reconceptualising sports coaching: A role for social theory. Paper presented to the 14th Annual Congress of the European College of Sport Sciences (ECSS), Oslo, 24–27 June.

Jones, R.L., Armour, K.M. & Potrac, P. (2002). Understanding the coaching process: A framework for social analysis. *Quest*, 54(1): 34–48.

Jones, R.L., Armour, K.M. & Potrac, P. (2003). Constructing expert knowledge: A case study of a top-level professional soccer coach. *Sport, Education and Society*, 8(2): 213–229.

Jones, R.L., Armour, K.M. & Potrac, P. (2004). *Sports coaching cultures: From practice to theory*. London: Routledge.

Jones, R.L., Glintmeyer, N. & McKenzie, A. (2005). Slim bodies, eating disorders and the coach–athlete relationship: A tale of identity creation and disruption. *International Review for the Sociology of Sport*, 40(3): 377–391.

Jones, R.L., Harris, R. & Miles, A. (2009). Mentoring in sports coaching: A review of the literature. *Physical Education and Sport Pedagogy*, 14(3): 267–284.

Jones, R.L., Kingston, K. & Stewart, C. (in press). Machiavelli in a morality play: Negotiating expectations in football's complex social culture. In D. Gilbourne & M. Andersen (eds), *Critical essays in sport psychology*. London: Human Kinetics.

Jones, R.L., Morgan, K. & Harris, K. (in press). Developing coaching pedagogy: Seeking a better integration of theory and practice. *Sport, Education and Society*.

Jones, R.L. & Standage, M. (2006). First among equals: Shared leadership in the coaching context. In R.L. Jones (ed.), *The sports coach as educator: Re-conceptualising sports coaching* (pp. 65–76). London: Routledge.

Jones, R.L. & Wallace, M. (2005). Another bad day at the training ground: Coping with ambiguity in the coaching context. *Sport, Education and Society*, 10(1): 119–134.

Jones, R.L. & Wallace, M. (2006). The coach as 'orchestrator': More realistically managing the complex coaching context. In R.L. Jones (ed.), *The sports coach as educator. Re-conceptualising sports coaching*. London: Routledge.

Jowett, S. (2005). On enhancing and repairing the coach–athlete relationship. In S. Jowett & M. Jones (eds), *The psychology of coaching* (pp. 14–26). Leicester: British Psychological Society.

Jowett, S. & Cockerill, I. (2003). Olympic medallists' perspective of the athlete–coach relationship. *Psychology of Sport and Exercise*, 4: 313–331.

Jowett, S., Paull, G. & Pensgaard, A. (2005). Coach–athlete relationship. In J. Taylor & G. Wilson (eds), *Applying sport psychology: Four perspectives* (pp. 153–170). Champaign, IL: Human Kinetics.

Jowett, S. & Timson-Katchis, M. (2005). Social networks in sport: Parental influence on the coach–athlete relationship. *The Sport Psychologist*, 19: 267–287.

Kelchtermans, G. (2005). Teachers' emotions in educational reforms: Self understanding, vulnerable commitment and micro-political literacy. *Teaching and Teacher Education*, 21: 995–1006.

Kelchtermans, G. & Ballet, K. (2002a). Micro-political literacy: Reconstructing a neglected dimension in teacher development. *International Journal of Educational Research*, 37: 755–767.

Kelchtermans, G. & Ballet, K. (2002b). The micro-politics of teacher induction: A narrative–biographical study on teacher socialisation. *Teacher and Teacher Education*, 18(1): 105–120.

Kelchtermans, G. & Vandenberghe, R. (1998). Internal use of external control and support for quality improvement: The response to a national policy by primary schools. Paper presented to the Annual Meeting of the American Educational Research Association, San Diego (ERIC-Document ED425/EA 029271).

Kelley, H. (1986). Personal relationships: Their nature and significance. In R. Gilmoure & S. Duck (eds), *The emergent field of personal relationships* (pp. 3–19). Mahweh, NJ: Lawrence Erlbaum.

Kemper, T. (1978). *A social interactional theory of emotions*. New York: Wiley.

Kerka, S. (1998). *New perspectives on mentoring* (ERIC Digest No. 194). Columbus, OH: ERIC Clearing House on Adult, Career, and Vocational Education.

Kilgore, D. (2001). Critical and postmodern perspectives on adult learning. In S. Merriam (ed.), *The New Update on Adult Learning Theory* (pp. 53–61). San Fransisco, CA: Jossey-Bass.

Kilgore, D. (2004). Toward a postmodern pedagogy. *New Directions for Adult and Continuing Education*, 102: 45–53.

Kim, K.-M. (2004). Can Bourdieu's critical theory liberate us from the symbolic violence? *Cultural Studies–Critical Methodologies*, 4(3): 362–376.

Kirk, D. (1992). Physical education, discourse and ideology: Bringing the hidden curriculum into view. *Quest*, 44: 35–56.

Kirk, D. & Tinning, R. (eds) (1990). *Physical education curriculum and culture: Critical issues in the contemporary crisis*. London: Falmer Press.

Kneer, G. & Nassehi, A. (1993). *Niklas Luhmann's theorie sozialer systeme. Eine einführung*. München: Wilhelm Fink Verlag.

Knodt, E.M. (1995). Foreword. In N. Luhmann, *Social systems* (pp. ix–xxxvi). Stanford, CA: Stanford University Press.

Krause, D. (1996). *Luhmann-Lexikon. Eine Einführung in das Gesamtwerk von Niklas Luhmann*. Stuttgart: Ferdinand Enke Verlag.

Kvale, S. (ed.) (1992). *Psychology and postmodernism*. Thousand Oaks, CA: Sage.

Lacoste, M. (1991). Les communications de travail comme interactions [Work communications as interactions]. In R. Amalberti, M. De Montmollin & J. Theureau (eds), *Modeles en analyse du travail* (pp. 191–229). Liège: Mardaga.

Lave, J. (1988). *Cognition in practice*. Cambridge: Cambridge University Press.

Lave, J. & Wenger, E. (1991). *Situated learning: Legitimate peripheral participation*. Cambridge: Cambridge University Press.

Lave, J. & Wenger, E. (1996). Practice, person, social world. In H. Daniels (ed.), *An introduction to Vygotsky* (pp. 143–150). London: Routledge.

LaVoi, N. (2004). Dimensions of closeness and conflict in the coach–athlete relationship. Paper presented to the meeting of the Association for the Advancement of Applied Sport Psychology, Minneapolis, September.

Lawson, H.A. (1993). Dominant discourses, problem setting, and teacher education pedagogies: A critique. *Journal of Teaching in Physical Education*, 10 (1): 1–20.

Layder, D. (1996). *Understanding social theory*. London: Sage.

Layder, D. (2006). *Understanding social theory* (2nd edn). London: Sage.

LeCompte, M. & Preissle, J. (1993). *Ethnography and quality design in educational research*. San Diego, CA: Academic Press.

Lee, D. (2000). The society of society: The grand finale of Niklas Luhmann. *Sociological Theory*, 18(2): 320–332.

Leik, R. & Leik, S. (1977). Transition to interpersonal commitment. In R. Hamblin and J. Kunkel (eds), *Behavioral theory in sociology: Essays in honour of George C. Homas* (pp. 299–323). New Brunswick, NJ: Transaction.

Lemert, C. (1997). *Social things: An introduction to the sociological life*. Lanham, MD.: Rowan & Littlefield.

Lemyre, F. (2008). Reflection and communities of practice to facilitate learning experience of coaching a karate club and school sports program. Unpublished Ph.D. dissertation, University of Ottawa.

Lemyre, F., Trudel, P. & Durand-Bush, N. (2007). The learning experience of youth sport coaches. *The Sport Psychologist*, 21: 191–209.

Lewis, D.J. & Weigert, A. (1985). Trust as a social reality. *Social Forces*, 63(4): 967–985.

Light, R. (2004). Coaches' experiences of games sense: Opportunities and challenges. *Physical Education and Sport Pedagogy*, 9: 115–132.

Light, R. (2006). Situated learning in an Australian surf club. *Sport, Education and Society*, 11(2): 155–172.

Light, R. (2008a). 'Complex' learning theory in physical education: An examination of its epistemology and assumptions about how we learn. *Journal of Teaching in Physical Education*, 27(1): 21–37.

Light, R. (2008b). Learning masculinities in a Japanese high school rugby club. *Sport, Education and Society*, 13(2): 163–179.

Luhmann. N. (1979). *Trust and power*. London: Wiley.

Luhmann, N. (1984). *Soziale systeme. Grundriss einer allgemeinen theorie*. Frankfurt am Main: Suhrkamp.

Luhmann, N. (1993). *Soziologische aufklärung 5. Konstruktivistiche perspektiven*. Opladen: Vestdeucher Verlag.

Luhmann, N. (1995). *Social systems*. Stanford, CA: Stanford University Press.

Luhmann, N. (1997). *Die Gesellschaft der Gesellschaft*. Frankfurt am Main: Suhrkamp.

Lynch, K. (2007). Love labour as a distinct and non-commodifiable form of care labour. *Sociological Review*, 55(3): 550–570.

Lyttle, J. (2001). The effectiveness of humour in persuasion: The case of business ethics training. *Journal of General Psychology*, 128: 206–217.

McCarthy, E.D. (1996). *Knowledge as culture: The new sociology of knowledge*. London: Routledge.

McDonagh, E. (1982). Social exchange and moral development: Dimensions of self, self-image and identity. *Human Relations*, 8: 659–674.

Macdonald, D., Kirk, D., Metzler, M., Nilges, L.M., Schempp, P. & Wright, J. (2002). It's all very well in theory: Theoretical perspectives and their applications in contemporary pedagogical research. *Quest*, 54: 133–156.

Macdonald, D. & Tinning, R. (1995). Physical education teacher education and the trend to prolatarianization: A case study. *Journal of Teaching in Physical Education*, 15: 98–115.

McDonald, G.G. (1981). Structural exchange and marital interaction. *Journal of Marriage and the Family*, 43: 825–839.

Mack, D.E. & Gammage, K.L. (1998). Attention to group factors: Coach considerations to building an effective team. *Avante*, 4(3): 118–129.

McKay, J., Gore, J.M. & Kirk, D. (1990). Beyond the limits of technocratic physical education. *Quest*, 42(1): 52–76.

McMann, S. (2007). *Anthony Giddens: A biography*. Open University. Retrieved from: http://www.open2.net/society/politics_law/giddens.html.

McNamee, M. (1998). Contractualism and methodological individualism and communitarianism: Situating understandings of moral trust in the context of sport and social theory. *Sport, Education and Society*, 3(2): 161–179.

Madison, D.S. (1999). Performing theory/embodied writing. *Text and Performance Quarterly*, 19: 107–124.

Manning, P. (1992). *Erving Goffman and modern sociology*. Stanford, CA: Stanford University Press.

Markula, P. & Martin, M. (2007). Ethical coaching: Gaining respect in the field. In J. Denison (ed.), *Coaching knowledges: Understanding the dynamics of sport performance* (pp. 51–82). Oxford: A.C. Black.

Markula, P. & Pringle, R. (2006). *Foucault, sport and exercise: Power, knowledge and transforming the self*. London: Routledge.

Marsh, I., Keating, M., Eyre, A., Campbell, R. & McKenzie, J. (1996). *Making sense of society*. London: Longman.

Martinek, T. (1983). Creating Golem and Galatea effects in physical education instruction: A social psychological perspective. In T. Templin & J. Olson (eds), *Teaching physical education* (pp. 199–215). Champaign, IL: Human Kinetics.

Marx, K. (1983). *The portable Karl Marx* (trans. E. Kamenka). New York: Penguin.

May, T. (2005). Foucault now? *Foucault Studies*, 3: 65–76.

May, T. & Powell, J. (2008). *Situating social theory* (2nd edn). Maidenhead: McGraw-Hill Education.

Mead, G.H. (1934). *Mind, self and society: From a standpoint of a social behavourist*. Chicago, IL: University of Chicago Press.

Meisenhelder, T. (1997). Pierre Bourdieu and the call for reflexive sociology. *Current perspectives in social theory*, 17: 159–183.

Merriam, S.B. & Caffarella, R.S. (1999). *Learning in adulthood* (2nd edn). San Francisco, CA: Jossey-Bass.

Meyer, J.H.F. & Land, R. (2003). Threshold concepts and troublesome knowledge (1): Linkages to ways of thinking and practicing within the disciplines. In C. Rust (ed.), *Improving students' learning: Ten years on* (pp. 412–424). Oxford: OCSLD.

Miller, P.S. & Kerr, G. (2002). The athletic, academic, and social experiences of intercollegiate student-athletes. *Journal of Sport Behavior*, 25: 346–367.

Moore, R. (2004). Cultural capital: Objectivity probability and cultural arbitrary. *British Journal of Sociology of Education*, 25(4): 445–456.

Morgan, T.K. & Giacobbi, G.R. (2006). Toward two grounded theories of the talent development and social support process of highly successful collegiate athletes. *The Sport Psychologist*, 20: 295–313.

Morrison, K. (2009). Jürgen Habermas. In J. Palmer (ed.), *Fifty modern thinkers on education: From Piaget to the present* (pp. 215–224). London: Routledge.

Mouzelis, N. (1992). Social and system integration: Habermas' view. *British Journal of Sociology*, 43: 267–288.

Muir, K.B. & Seitz, T. (2004). Machismo, misogyny, and homophobia in a male athletic subculture: A participant-observation study of deviant rituals in collegiate rugby. *Deviant Behavior*, 25: 303–327.

Nash, R. (1990). Bourdieu on education and cultural reproduction. *British Journal of Sociology of Education*, 11(4): 431–447.

Nelson, L.J. & Cushion, C.J. (2006). Reflection in coach education: The case of the National Governing Body coaching certificate. *The Sport Psychologist*, 20: 174–183.

Nelson, L.J., Cushion, C.J. & Potrac, P. (2006). Formal, nonformal and informal coach learning: A holistic conceptualisation. *International Journal of Sports Science and Coaching*, 1(3): 247–259.

Nias, J. (1996). Thinking about feeling: The emotions in teaching. *Cambridge Journal of Education*, 26: 293–306.

Nichani, M. & Hung, D. (2002). Can a community of practice exist on-line? *Educational Technology*, 42: 49–54.

Nieto, S. (2000). *Affirming diversity: The sociopolitical context of multi-cultural education.* New York: Longman.

Norman, L. (2008). The UK coaching system is failing women coaches. *International Journal of Sport Sciences and Coaching*, 3(4): 447–464.

Nyberg, D. (1981). *Power over power.* London: Cornell University Press.

O'Brien, J.A. & Kollock, P. (1991). Social exchange theory as a conceptual framework for teaching the sociological perspective. *Teaching Sociology*, 19: 140–153.

Orlikowski, W. (1992). The duality of technology: Rethinking the concept of technology in organizations. *Organization Science*, 3(3): 398–427.

Orlikowski, W. & Robey, D. (1991). Information technology and structuring organizations. *Information Systems Research*, 2(2): 143–169.

Østerberg, D. (1988). *Metasociology: An inquiry into the origins and validity of social thought.* Oslo: Norwegian University Press.

O'Sullivan, M. (2005). Research quality in physical education and sport pedagogy. Inaugural lecture presented to the British Educational Research Association (BERA) PE-SIG, University of Glamorgan, 14 September.

Outhwaite, W. (2009). *Habermas* (2nd edn). Cambridge: Polity Press.

Palinscar, A.S., Magnusson, S.J., Marano, N., Ford, D. & Brown, N. (1998). Designing a community of practice: Principles and practices of the GisML community. *Teaching and Teacher Education*, 14: 5–19.

Parker, A. (1996). Chasing the big-time: Football apprenticeship in the 1990's. Unpublished Ph.D. thesis, Warwick University.

Parsons, T. (1951). *The social system.* London: Routledge.

Perkins, D. (1999). The many faces of constructivism. *Educational Leadership*, 57(3): 6–11.

Pike, E.C.J. & Maguire, J.A. (2003). Injury in women's sport: Classifying key elements of 'risk encounters'. *Sociology of Sport Journal*, 20: 232–251.

Pineau, E.L. (1994). Teaching is performance: Reconceptualising a problematic metaphor. *American Educational Research Journal*, 31(1): 3–25.

Poczwardowski, A., Barott, J. & Peregoy, J. (2002). The athlete and the coach: Their relationship and its meaning: Methodological concerns and the research process. *International Journal of Sport Psychology*, 33: 98–115.

Poczwardowski, A., Henschen, K. & Barott, J. (2002). The athlete and the coach: Their relationship and its meaning: Results from an interpretive study. *International Journal of Sport Psychology*, 33: 116–140.

Potrac, P. (2001). A comparative study of elite football coaches in England and Norway. Unpublished Ph.D. dissertation, Brunel University.

Potrac, P. (2004). Coaches' power. In R.L. Jones, K. Armour & P. Potrac (eds), *Sports coaching cultures: From practice to theory*. London: Routledge.

Potrac, P. & Jones, R.L. (1999). The invisible ingredient in coaching knowledge: A case for recognising and researching the social component. *Sociology of Sport Online*, 2(1). Retrieved from: http://physed.otago.ac.nz/sosol/home.htm.

Potrac, P. & Jones, R.L. (2009a). Micro-political workings in semi-professional football coaching. *Sociology of Sport Journal*, 26: 557–577.

Potrac, P. & Jones, R.L (2009b). Power, conflict and cooperation: Toward a micropolitics of coaching. *Quest*, 61: 223–236.

Potrac, P., Jones, R.L. & Armour, K.M. (2002). 'It's all about getting respect': The coaching behaviours of an expert English soccer coach. *Sport, Education and Society*, 7(2): 183–202.

Potrac, P., Jones, R.L., Brewer, C., Armour, K. & Hoff, J. (2000). Towards an holistic understanding of the coaching process. *Quest*, 52: 186–199.

Potrac, P., Jones, R.L. & Cushion, C. (2006). Power, conflict, and cooperation: Exploring the micro-politics of coaching. Paper presented to the Association for the Advancement of Applied Sport Psychology Conference, Miami, 27–30 September.

Potrac, P., Jones, R.L. & Cushion, C.J. (2007). Understanding power and the coach's role in professional English soccer: A preliminary investigation of coach behaviour. *Soccer and Society*, 8(1): 33–49.

Powers, C.H. (2004). *Making sense of social theory: A practical introduction*. New York: Rowan & Littlefield.

Prado, C.G. (1995). *Starting with Foucault: An introduction to genealogy*. Oxford: Westview Press.

Pringle, R. (2007). Social theory for coaches: A Foucauldian reading of one athlete's poor performance – A commentary. *International Journal of Sports Science & Coaching*, 2: 385–393.

Purdy, L., Jones, R.L. & Cassidy, T. (2009). Negotiation and capital: Athletes' use of power in an elite men's rowing program. *Sport, Education and Society*, 14(3): 321–338.

Purdy, L., Potrac, P. & Jones, R.L. (2008). Power, consent and resistance: An autoethnography of competitive rowing. *Sport, Education and Society*, 13(3): 319–336.

Raffel, S. (1998). Revisiting role theory: Roles and the problem of the self. *Sociological Research Online*, 4(2). Retrieved from: http://www.socresonline.org.uk/4/2/raffel.html.

Reade, I., Rodgers, W. & Hall, N. (2008). Knowledge transfer: How do high performance coaches access the knowledge of sport scientists? *International Journal of Sports Science and Coaching*, 3(3): 319–334.

Rees, T. & Hardy, L. (2000). An investigation of the social support experiences of high-level sport performers. *The Sport Psychologist*, 14: 327–347.

Reese-Schäfer, W. (2001). *Niklas Luhmann zur einführung*. Hamburg: Junius Verlag GmbH.

Reinboth, M., Duda, J.L. & Ntoumanis, N. (2004). Dimensions of coach behaviour, need satisfaction, and psychological and physical welfare of young athletes. *Motivation and Emotion*, 28: 297–243.

Ritzer, G. (1996). *Sociological theory*. Singapore: McGraw-Hill.

Roderick, M. (2006). *The work of professional football: A labour of love?* London: Routledge.

Rogers, A. (2002). *Teaching adults* (3rd edn). Buckingham: Open University Press.

Romero, E.J. (2005). The effect of humour on work effort and mental state. *International Journal of Work Organisation and Emotion*, 1: 137–149.

Romero, E.J. & Pescosolido, A. (2008). Humour and group effectiveness. *Human Relations*, 61: 395–418.

Ronglan, L.T. (2000). Gjennom sesongen. En sosiologisk studie av det norske kvinnelandslaget i håndball på og utenfor banen [During the season: A sociological analysis of the female Norwegian national handball team on and off the court]. Unpublished Ph.D. thesis, Norwegian School of Sport Sciences, Oslo.

Ronglan, L.T. (2007). Building and communicating collective efficacy: A season-long in-depth study of an elite sport team. *The Sport Psychologist*, 21(1): 78–93.

Ronglan, L.T. (2010). Grasping complexity in social interaction: Communication systems in an elite sport team. In U. Wagner, R. Storm & J. Hoberman (eds), *Observing sport: Modern system theoretical approaches*. Schorndorf: Hofmann Verlag.

Rosenau, P.M. (1992). *Postmodernism and the social sciences: Insights, inroads, and intrusions*. Princeton, NJ: Princeton University Press.

Rovegno, I. (2006). Situated perspectives on learning. In D. Kirk, D. Macdonald & M. O'Sullivan (eds), *Handbook of research in physical education* (pp. 262–274). London: Sage.

Sabatelli, R.M. (1999). Marital commitment and family life transitions: A social exchange perspective on the construction and deconstruction of intimate relationships. In W.H. Jones and J.M. Adams (eds), *Handbook of Interpersonal Commitment and Relationship Stability* (pp. 181–192). New York: Plenum Press.

Sabatelli, R.M. & Shehan, C. (1993). Exchange and resource theories. In P. Boss, W. Doherty, R. LaRossa, W. Schuum and S. Steinmetz (eds), *Sourcebook of family theories and methods: A contextual approach* (pp. 385–411). New York: Plenum Press.

Sacks, O. (1995). *An anthropologist on Mars*. Toronto: Alfred A. Knopf.

Sage, G.H. (1989). Becoming a high school coach: From playing sport to coaching. *Research Quarterly for Exercise & Sport*, 60(1): 81–92.

St Clair, R. (2004). Teaching with the enemy: Critical adult education in the academy. *New Directions for Adult and Continuing Education*, 102: 35–43.

Salmela, J.H. & Moraes, L.C. (2003). Developing expertise, the role of coaching, families, and cultural contexts. In J.L. Starkes & K. Anders Ericsson (eds), *Expert performance in sports: Advances in research in sport expertise* (pp. 275–294). Champaign, IL: Human Kinetics.

Sánchez, J.M., Borrás, P.J., Leite, N., Battaglia, O. & Lorenzo, A. (2009). The coach–athlete relationship in basketball: An analysis of antecedents, components and outcomes. *Revista de Psicología del Deporte*, 18: 349–352.

Sanders, T. (2004). Controllable laughter: Managing sex work through humour. *Sociology*, 38: 273–291.

Saury, J. & Durand, M. (1998). Practical knowledge in expert coaches: On-site study of coaching in sailing. *Research Quarterly for Exercise and Sport*, 69(3): 254–266.

Scanzoni, J. (1979). Social exchange and behavioral interdependence. In R.L. Burgess & T.L. Huston (eds), *Social exchange in developing relationships* (pp. 61–98). New York: Academic Press.

Schegloff, E. (1988). Goffman and the analysis of conversation. In P. Drew & T. Wooton (eds), *Erving Goffman: Exploring the interaction order* (pp. 9–135). Cambridge: Polity Press.

Schempp, P. & Graber, K.C. (1992). Teacher socialisation from a dialectical perspective: Pre-training through induction. *Journal of Teaching in Physical Education*, 11: 329–348.

Schempp, P.G., Webster, C., McCullick, B.A., Busch, C. & Sannen Mason, I. (2007). How the best get better: An analysis of the self-monitoring strategies used by expert golf instructors. *Sport, Education and Society*, 12(2): 175–192.

Schubert, J.D. (2002). Defending multiculturalism: From hegemony to symbolic violence. *American Behavioral Scientist*, 45(7): 1088–1102.

Schunk, D.H. (2009) *Learning theories: An educational perspective* (5th (International) edn). Englewood Cliffs, NJ: Prentice-Hall.

Seifried, C. (2008). Examining punishment and discipline: Defending the use of punishment by coaches. *Quest*, 60: 370–386.

Sevänen, E. (2001). Art as an autopoietic sub-system of modern society: A critical analysis of the concepts of art and autopoietic systems in Luhmann's late production. *Theory, Culture and Society*, 18(1): 75–103.

Sfard, A. (1998). On two metaphors for learning and the dangers of choosing just one. *Educational Researcher*, 27: 4–13.

Shannon, B. (1989). Metaphors for language and communication. *Revue Internationale de Systemique*, 3(1): 43–59.

Shaw, B. (1981). *Educational practice and sociology: An Introduction*. Oxford: Wiley/Blackwell.

Shilling, C. (1997). *The body and social theory*. London: Sage.

Shogan, D. (1999). *The making of high-performance athletes: Discipline, diversity, and ethics*. Toronto: University of Toronto Press.

Simmel, G. (1978 [1900]). *The philosophy of money*. London: Routledge & Kegan Paul.

Simpson, R. (2007). Emotional labour and identity work of men in caring roles. In P. Lewis & R. Simpson (eds), *Gendering emotions in organizations* (pp. 57–74). Basingstoke: Palgrave Macmillan.

Simpson, T.L. (2002). Dare I oppose constructivist theory? *The Educational Forum*, 66: 347–354.

Sisjord, M.K. & Kristiansen, E. (2009). Elite women wrestler's muscles: Physical strength and a social burden. *International Review for the Sociology of Sport*, 44(2–3): 231–246.

Skille, E.Å. (2007). The meaning of social context: Experiences of and educational outcomes of participation in two different sport contexts. *Sport, Education and Society*, 12(4): 367–382.

Sloan, T. (1999). The colonization of the lifeworld and the destruction of meaning. *Radical Sociology*, 2(1). Retrieved from: http://www.radpsynet.org/journal/vol1-2/Sloan.html.

Smith, G. (2006). *Erving Goffman*. Routledge: London.

Smith, R.E. & Smoll, F.L. (1996). *Way to go, coach! A scientifically-proven approach to coaching effectiveness*. Potrola Valley, CA: Warde.

Snyder, M. & Kiviniemi, M. (2001). Getting what they came for: How power influences the dynamics and outcomes of interpersonal interaction. In A. Lee-Chai & J. Bargh (eds), *The use and abuse of power: Multiple perspectives on the causes of corruption* (pp. 133–155). Philadelphia, PA: Taylor and Francis.

Sparkes, A.C. (1993). Challenging technical rationality in physical eductaion teacher education: The potential of the life history approach. *Physical Education Review*, 16(2): 107–121.

Spencer-Brown, G. (1969). *Laws of form*. New York: Dutton.

Stets, J. (2003). Emotions and sentiments. In J. DeLamater (ed.), *Handbook of social-pyschology* (pp. 309–335). New York: Academic Plenum.

Stets, J. & Turner, J. (2007). *The handbook of the sociology of emotions*. New York: Springer.

Stichweh, R. (1990). Sport – Ausdifferenzierung, funktion, code. *Sportwissenschaft*, 20(4): 273–289.

Stichweh, R. (2000). Systems theory as an alternative to action theory. The rise of 'communication' as a theoretical option. *Acta Sociologica*, 43: 5–13.

Stones, R. (1998a). Conclusion: Tolerance, plurality and creative synthesis in sociological thought. In R. Stones (ed.), *Key sociological thinkers* (pp. 291–305). London: Macmillan.

Stones, R. (1998b). Introduction. In R. Stones (ed.), *Key sociological thinkers* (pp. 1–18). London: Macmillan.

Strean, W.B. (1995). Youth sport context: Coaches' perceptions and implications for intervention. *Journal of Applied Sport Psychology*, 7: 23–37.

Stroot, S.A. & Ko, B. (2006). Teacher socialization and induction. In D. Kirk, D. Macdonald & M. O'Sullivan (eds), *Handbook of research in physical* education (pp. 425–448). Berkeley, CA: Sage.

Swartz, D. (1997). *Culture and power: The sociology of Pierre Bourdieu*. Chicago, IL: University of Chicago Press.

Tagg, B. (2008). 'Imagine, a man playing netball!' Masculinities and sport in New Zealand. *International Review for the Sociology of Sport*, 43(4): 409–430.

Tangen, J.O. (1997). *Samfunnets idrett. En sosiologisk analyse av idrett som sosialt system, dets evolusjon og funksjon fra arkaisk til moderne tid* [*The sport of the society: A sociological analysis of sport as a social system, its evolution and function from archaic to modern times*]. Oslo: University of Oslo.

Tangen, J.O. (2000). Sport: a social system? A sociological attempt to define sport. *SysteMexico*, special edition: 'The autopoietic turn: Luhmann's re-conceptualisation of the social': 72–92

Tangen, J.O. (2004). Embedded expectations, embodied knowledge and the movements that connect: A system theoretical attempt to explain the use and non-use of sport facilities. *International Review for the Sociology of Sport*, 39(1): 7–25.

Tawney, R.H. (1931). *Equality*. London: Allen & Unwin.

Taylor, B. & Garret, D. (2010). The professionalisation of sports coaching: Definitions, challenges and critique. In J. Lyle & C.J. Cushion (eds), *Sports coaching professionalisation and practice* (pp. 99–117). London: Elsevier.

Taylor, M. (2006). *Rationality and the ideology of disconnection*. Cambridge: Cambridge University Press.

Theodosius, C. (2008). *Emotional labour in health care: The unmanaged heart of nursing*. London: Routledge.

Thibaut, J.W. & Kelley, H.H. (1959). *The social psychology of groups*. New York: John Wiley & Sons.

Thompson, N. (2003). *Theory and practice in human services*. Maidenhead: Open University Press.

Thorpe, H. (2006). Beyond 'decorative sociology': Contextualising female surf, skate, and snow boarding. *Sociology of Sport Journal*, 23: 205–228.

Tierney, W.G. (2001). The autonomy of knowledge and the decline of the subject: Postmodernism and the reformation of the university. *Higher Education*, 41(4): 353–372.

Tilly, C. (1978). *From mobilization to revolution*. London: Addison-Wesley.

Tinning, R. (1997). Performance and participation discourses in human movement: Toward a socially critical physical education. In J.M. Fernandez-Balboa (ed.), *Critical postmodernism in human movement, physical education, and sport* (pp. 99–120). Albany: State University of New York.

Toffler, A. (1990). *Powershift: Knowledge, wealth, and violence at the edge of the 21st Century*. New York: Bantam.

Tomlinson, A. (2004). Pierre Bourdieu and the sociological study of sport: Habitus, capital and field. In R. Guilianotti (ed.), *Sport and modern social theorists* (pp. 161–172). Basingstoke: Palgrave Macmillan.

Touraine, A. (1981). *The voice and the eye: An analysis of social movements*. Cambridge: Cambridge University Press.

Trudel, P. & Gilbert, W. (2006). Coaching and coach education. In D. Kirk, D. Macdonald & M. O'Sullivan (eds), *Handbook of research in physical education* (pp. 516–539). London: Sage.

Tulloch, J. & Lupton, D. (2003). *Risk and everyday life*. London: Sage.

Turner, B.S. (2000). Preface. In B.S. Turner (ed.), *The Blackwell companion to social theory* (2nd edn) (pp. xiii–xviii). Oxford: Blackwell.

Turner, J. (2002). *Face to face: Toward a theory of interpersonal behaviour*. Stanford, CA: Stanford University Press.

Turner, J. & Stets, J. (2005). *The sociology of emotions*. Cambridge: Cambridge University Press.

Usher, R., Bryant, I. & Johnston, R. (1997). *Adult education and the postmodern challenge*. New York: Routledge.

Wacquant, L. (1989). Toward a reflexive sociology, a workshop with Pierre Bourdieu. *Sociological Theory*, 7: 26–63.

Wacquant, L. (1992). The social logic of boxing in black Chicago: Towards a sociology of pugilism. *Sociology of Sport Journal*, 9: 221–254.

Wacquant, L. (1995). Pugs at work: Bodily capital and bodily labour among professional boxers. *Body and Society*, 1(1): 65–89.

Wacquant, L. (1998). Pierre Bourdieu. In R. Stones (ed.), *Key sociological thinkers* (pp. 215–229). London: Macmillan Press.

Wacquant, L. (2005). Nothing beyond its reach (sociologists on society). *The Chronicle of Higher Education (The Chronicle Review)*, 51(49): B14.

Waddock, S.A. (1999). Paradigm shift: Toward a community–university–community community of practice. *International Journal of Organizational Analysis*, 7: 244–302.

Wagner, U., Storm, R. & Hoberman, J. (eds) (2010). *Observing sport: Modern system theoretical approaches*. Schorndorf: Hofmann Verlag.

Weber, M. (1946). Class, status, party. In H.H. Gerth and C. Wright Mills (eds), *From Max Weber: Essays in Sociology* (pp. 180–195). New York: Oxford University Press.

Wenger, E. (1998). *Communities of practice: Learning, meaning, and identity*. Cambridge: Cambridge University Press.

Wenger, E., McDermott, R. & Snyder, W. (2002). *Cultivating communities of practice: A guide to managing knowledge*. Boston, MA: Harvard University Press.

Wenger, E. & Snyder, W. (2000). Communities of practice: The organisational frontier. *Harvard Business Review*, January–February: 139–145.

Wertch, J., del Rio, P. & Alvarez, A. (1995). History, action and mediation. In J. Wertch, P. del Rio & A. Alvarez (eds), *Sociocultural studies of the mind* (pp. 37–55). Cambridge: Cambridge University Press.

Westwood, S. (2002). *Power and the social*. London: Routledge.

Wheaton, B. (2000). 'Just do it': Consumption, commitment, and identity in the windsurfing subculture. *Sociology of Sport Journal*, 17: 254–274.

Widdershoven, G.A.M. (1994). Identity and development: A narrative perspective. In H.A. Bouma, T.L.G. Graafsma, H.D. Stevant & D.J. DeLevita (eds), *Identity and development* (pp. 103–117). Thousand Oaks, CA: Sage.

Williams, S. (2008). Arlie Russell Hochschild. In R. Stones (ed.), *Key sociological thinkers* (2nd edn) (pp. 355–367). Basingstoke: Palgrave Macmillan.

Willis, P. (1977). *Learning to labour*. Farnborough: Saxon House.

Wilson, A.L. (1993). The promise of situated cognition. In S. Merriam (ed.), *An update on adult learning theory: New directions for adult and continuing education*, 57: 71–79.

Wilson, M., Cushion, C.J. & Stephens, D. (2006). 'Put me in coach . . . I'm better than you think!' Coaches' perceptions of their expectations in youth sport. *International Journal of Sport Science & Coaching*, 1(2): 149–162.

Wouters, C. (1989a). Response to Hochschild's reply. *Theory, Culture and Society*, 6: 447–450.

Wouters, C. (1989b). The sociology of emotions and flight attendants. *Theory, Culture and Society*, 6: 95–123.

Wouters, C. (1991). On status competition and emotion management. *Journal of Social History*, 24(4): 669–717.

Wright, T., Trudel, P. & Culver, D. (2007). Learning how to coach: The different learning situations reported by youth ice hockey coaches. *Physical Education and Sport Pedagogy*, 12(2): 127–144.

Wright Mills, C. (1956). *White collar: The American middle classes*. Oxford: Oxford University Press.

Wright Mills, C. (1959). *The sociological imagination*. Oxford: Oxford University Press.

Zeichner, K. & Tabaachnick, B. (1981). Are the effects of university teacher education 'washed out' by school experience? *Journal of Teacher Education*, 32: 7–11.

Zembylas, M. (2005). *Teaching with emotion: A postmodern enactment*. Greenwhich, CT: Information Age.

Zinn, J.O. (2008). Heading into the unknown: Everyday strategies for managing risk and uncertainty. *Health, Risk & Society*, 10(5): 439–450.

Index

Lightning Source UK Ltd.
Milton Keynes UK
UKOW030225150313

207676UK00004B/28/P